CONFRATERNITIES AND SODALITIES IN IRELAND

Colm Lennon, *Editor*

Confraternities and Sodalities in Ireland

Charity, Devotion and Sociability

the columba press

First published in 2012 by
the columba press
55A Spruce Avenue, Stillorgan Industrial Park,
Blackrock, Co. Dublin

Cover by Bill Bolger
Origination by The Columba Press
Printed by SPRINT-print

ISBN 978 1 85607 792 7

Front cover: Banagher–Cloghan, County Offaly sodality excursion, Dún Laoghaire railway station, July 1937. (R. H. Moore Collection, Offaly County Library.)

Contents

List of Illustrations

List of Contributors

CORMAC BEGADON holds a doctorate from NUI Maynooth. His research interests include Catholic spiritual literature, ecclesiastical architecture and clerical education.

LOUISE FULLER was Research Fellow on the NUIM-based research project, 'Religion and social identity in Ireland: the role of the confraternities and parish associations, 1775–1965', funded by the IRCHSS. She is author of *Irish Catholicism since 1950: the undoing of a culture* (Dublin, 2002).

LISA GODSON holds a doctorate from the Royal College of Art, London, where she lectured in critical and historical studies. She is lecturer in the National College of Art and Design, Dublin, in the history of design and material culture, and fellow at the graduate school of creative arts and media.

CAROLE HOLOHAN holds a doctorate from University College Dublin. She has published on the changing position of young people in Irish society in the 1960s.

ROBIN KAVANAGH teaches and researches in the areas of printing and reading in nineteenth-century Ireland and digital humanities. She was also Research Fellow on the NUIM research project on confraternities and parish associations.

DÁIRE KEOGH is President of St Patrick's College, Drumcondra, where he was Senior Lecturer in the Department of History. He has published extensively on the history of religion and education in Ireland.

COLM LENNON retired recently as Associate Professor of History at NUI Maynooth. He was Principal Investigator on the research project on confraternities and parish associations.

MARTIN MAGUIRE is Lecturer in History at the Dundalk Institute of Technology. Among his many research interests upon which he has published is the Irish Protestant experience.

MÁIRE NÍ CHEARBHAILL has a doctorate from NUI Maynooth on the history of the Society of St Vincent de Paul in Dublin, and completed a research fellowship at Maynooth on the history of the Mercy Congregation in education.

NICHOLAS TERPSTRA is Professor of History at the University of Toronto. He has published extensively on early modern urban society, charitable institutions and confraternities.

Preface

The essays in this collection arose out of a conference in September 2007 at NUI Maynooth on the theme 'Honouring God and community: confraternities and sodalities in modern Ireland'. It was held under the auspices of a project on the history of parish confraternities and associations in modern Ireland, which was funded by the Irish Research Council for the Humanities and Social Sciences and hosted in the Department of History at the university between 2005 and 2008. The project aimed at documenting and studying the contribution of parish confraternities and associations to the religious and social history of modern Ireland. At the conference a panel of established scholars and younger researchers presented a series of studies based on the topics being investigated by the project. Besides the speakers whose papers contribute to this volume, Dr Jennifer Kelly and Dr Jacinta Prunty made presentations, while Dr Lisa Godson kindly offered her paper afterwards. The sessions sparked lively and animated discussion on the research findings of the project and stimulated innovative suggestions for further investigation.

The first phase of the project in 2005–2006 had entailed an extensive programme of visits to libraries and archives of dioceses and religious institutions throughout Ireland, carried out by Dr Louise Fuller, as Research Fellow, under the direction of the editor, as Principal Investigator. The purpose was to locate as many records of confraternities and sodalities from the late eighteenth century onwards as possible, and to document and collect materials. This enterprise resulted in the amassing of a substantial volume of information, as well as physical records and memorabilia, and revealed the richness of the sources for the conduct of the research on the phenomenon. Dr Fuller's essay in this collection contains an account of some of her experiences on this research trail.

In 2007 and 2008 Dr Fuller's successor as Research Fellow, Dr Robin Kavanagh, undertook the task of organising the

voluminous research material with a view to listing systemati-
cally and cataloguing all the records. An extensive bibliography
of all the confraternal records was prepared, listing primary
and secondary sources, and incorporating references to
commemorative publications, devotional works, printed rules
for the affiliation and conduct of confraternities and sodalities,
periodical literature containing relevant articles, photographs
and literary sources including memoirs of parish associational
life. An important collection of memorabilia of confraternity
activity, donated by members of the public as well as religious
orders and associations, including membership certificates
and booklets, medals, scapulars and banners, formed the basis
of an exhibition which was mounted in conjunction with the
conference in September 2007. Much of this material was
transferred to the Russell Library in Maynooth College which
has kindly agreed to care for it, thus providing an invaluable
resource for future researchers. A number of interviews
conducted by the project researchers with former members of
confraternities and parish sodalities have been recorded and
form a useful collection of oral recollections of confraternal and
associational life in the parishes.

A website for the project, www.irishconfraternities.ie, was
developed as a tool for the dissemination and use of the findings
in future research. It provides access to the data on over 100
confraternities and sodalities through a variety of search
avenues, including confraternity, branch, location, diocese,
parish, membership, activities, sources and archival material. It
also contains a listing of over 1,000 Irish parishes, linked to the
search engine of the website. As well as making available the
details of each recorded confraternity and sodality, the database
provides access to documentary evidence in digitised form,
including extracts from minute-books, rules of association,
membership lists, newspaper articles and account books,
photographs of confraternity activities, and oral testimonies of
members of sodalities. The online database also makes available
the bibliography of sources for the history of confraternities in
modern Ireland.

The conference marked an important stage in the analysis
of the findings of the research team. Among the questions

addressed were the history of confraternities in Ireland before and after the Reformation, the devotional life fostered by the confraternities and sodalities, the role of the confraternities in the Catholic revival in Ireland after the penal laws and their pervasiveness in an era of Catholic cultural efflorescence, the relationship between the diocesan and regular associations, the dynamic between laity and clergy within the religious organisations, the social, educational and charitable outreach of confraternities, and the pattern of their decline in the mid-twentieth century. These and other aspects of the subject are reflected in the content of the essays presented here. Many other topics remain for investigation, the international context for which research is very suggestively presented in the afterword by Professor Nicholas Terpstra of the University of Toronto whose work in the area of confraternity studies has been a source of inspiration for scholars everywhere.

The editor wishes to express his indebtedness to the Irish Research Council for the Humanities and Social Sciences for funding the project and for the assistance of its personnel throughout the period of the research. The project application was greatly assisted by Professor R. V. Comerford and Dr Kevin Williams, both of whom were consistently supportive. NUI Maynooth, and particularly the Department of History, under the headship of Professor Comerford, provided a most congenial environment for the conducting of research, and I thank all of my colleagues for their collegiality. The Librarian, Dr Cathal McCauley, and staff of the Library in Maynooth were extremely helpful, especially Ms Penny Woods, Librarian, Russell Library, Maynooth College. The association of the project with the work of An Foras Feasa at NUIM under the directorship of Professor Margaret Kelleher has been of immense value. Through An Foras, the project availed of the vision and creativity of Dr John Keating, who devised the database, and of Mr Danny Fallon who brought that vision into reality.

During the course of the research, courteous co-operation was forthcoming from archivists and librarians in a variety of institutions, including the archives of Catholic dioceses and religious orders, as well as those of other religious denominations, and I wish to acknowledge their advice and assistance with immense gratitude. Limerick City Museum kindly lent a collection of confraternity banners on the occasion of the exhibition and conference in September 2007. The researchers are very grateful to the confraternity members who made available through interviews their recollections and reminiscences of participation.

As in any confraternity or sodality, co-working for common goals fosters sociability and fraternity, and it has been my great pleasure to lead the team of highly talented researchers which brought this project and publication to fruition. I would like to acknowledge the work of Dr Louise Fuller who carried out most of the groundwork in the archives and record offices in various parts of Ireland, and thus laid the foundations for the subsequent research and analysis. Dr Robin Kavanagh imposed order on the huge numbers of files amassed during the initial phase, organised the conference in 2007 most efficiently and, with her inimitable vitality and energy, worked on the website and uploaded a vast store of data. I was also fortunate to acquire the skilled assistance of Alex Dowdall and Ciaran McDonnell through the Summer Programme of Undergraduate Research at NUIM.

Finally, the contribution of Dr Máire Ní Chearbhaill has been enormous. She lent her scholarly expertise in the construction of a pilot database at an early phase of the project and she has also adduced her formidable editing skills in copy-editing the essays for publication. For her advice and cheerful optimism at all stages of the process, I am very grateful.

Colm Lennon

1

Confraternities in Ireland: a long view

Colm Lennon

Religious associations of lay men and women have flourished in Ireland since the middle ages. Variously called fraternities, confraternities or archconfraternities, religious guilds, sodalities or simply societies, these bodies have brought together devotees for reasons of spirituality as well as sociability. They have not been confined to the Roman Catholic church, or even the Christian denominations, but have also featured among the Jewish and Muslim communities in Ireland. Their objectives have differed widely over time and place, varying from the purely devotional and self-sanctifying through the charitable and educational to the recreational, or combinations thereof, but membership of all has been premised on affiliation to a religious faith. Wherever they existed, the lay religious societies have fostered through their rituals a distinctive confessional identity and sense of brotherhood and sisterhood among the initiates. In their relations with the wider world, the values of the prevailing social, political and cultural establishments have been embraced or eschewed. At times, the religious fraternities have performed an acculturating role in Ireland in respect, say, of the ethos of the late medieval colony, the reforms of the Catholic renewal after Trent, or the Roman and continental pieties of the ultramontane church. At others, the associations have become foci of resistance or obliquity to religious, political and cultural changes, as embodied in the Reformation, the ascendant Protestant nation, church disestablishment or secular modernity, for example. Their very longevity over six centuries and more, down to the late twentieth century, is due no doubt to the adaptability of

these groups of created kin to major upheavals since the early modern period.[1]

It may be objected that, in examining lay religious associations in Ireland over such duration, conceptual categories are stretched beyond their limits. To apply the nomenclature of confraternity and sodality to late medieval religious fraternities, for instance, could be misleading, if forms and functions are found not to be remotely comparable. Moreover, institutional discontinuity between eras – late medieval, early modern and contemporary – may be more pronounced than continuity. Yet, in view of the long span of survival of lay religious fraternity in Ireland, an attempt at chronological sweep may be justified, at the very least to challenge the restrictiveness of periodic boundaries of medieval and modern. As a framework for the analysis, international confraternity studies provide valuable methodological and conceptual models. Transitions and continuities over time and space have been the stock in trade of scholars working in the field for the past thirty years, and the broadening of their understanding of fraternalism to take account of its multi-valency in many social contexts has been particularly rewarding.[2] Thus contextualised, a possibility emerges of fruitful comparison between religious fraternities of various times and manifestations in Ireland, especially in terms of their rootedness in changing social and cultural milieux.

---

[1] Although there is no comprehensive study of Irish confraternities and sodalities, their presence and significance has been noted by scholars who have surveyed the social history of religion in Ireland. See, for example, for the medieval period, Adrian Empey, 'The layperson in the parish: the medieval inheritance, 1169–1536' in Raymond Gillespie and W.G. Neely (eds), *The laity and the Church of Ireland, 1000–2000: all sorts and conditions* (Dublin, 2002), pp 36–41 and, for the modern, Patrick Corish, *The Irish Catholic experience: a historical survey* (Dublin, 1985), chapters 6 and 7; for the transitional phase at the beginning of the Reformation, see Colm Lennon, 'The survival of the confraternities in post-Reformation Dublin' in *Confraternitas*, vi (1995), pp 5–12.

[2] For a recent conspectus of confraternity studies, see C.F. Black, 'The development of confraternity studies over the past thirty years' in Nicholas Terpstra (ed.), *The politics of ritual kinship: confraternities and social order in early modern Italy* (Cambridge, 2000), pp 9–29; Nicholas Terpstra, 'De-institutionalising confraternity studies: fraternalism and social capital in cross-cultural contexts' in C.F. Black and Pamela Gravestock (eds), *Early modern confraternities in Europe and the Americas: international and interdisciplinary perspectives* (Aldershot, 2006), pp 264–83 and see idem, essay in this volume.

In attempting therefore to divine a pattern in the history of survival, revival and decline of the Irish confraternities, this essay addresses the themes of their organisation and culture, as well as their engagement with the ecclesiastical and secular worlds. Against the backdrop of religious and political change since the late middle ages in Ireland, the dynamics of relations between laypeople and clergy in the confraternities, older religious institutions and the confessionalising state, and newer societies and centralising government in church and nation are worthy of investigation. A consideration of late medieval religious fraternities in Anglo- and Gaelic Ireland as reflections of their spiritual and cultural ethos precedes a discussion of how these bodies adapted to civil and religious reforms in the sixteenth and seventeenth centuries to survive among both Catholics and Protestants. A brief examination follows of how new sodalities under Counter-Reformation auspices with their hierarchical and clerical emphasis subsisted alongside older fraternities in the early modern period for a time, and proved to be more durable in their revived forms in the eighteenth century in providing a platform for a Catholic restoration in the post-penal era. The golden age of Irish confraternities and sodalities in the later nineteenth and early twentieth centuries bears scrutiny in terms of the balance between clerical and lay contributions, and also between active apostolates of charity and education and passive spirituality of devotions and self-improvement. Mention may be made of the role of Church of Ireland parish societies in strengthening Anglican identity in the aftermath of disestablishment from 1870. From the mid-twentieth century, profound social changes called into question traditional forms of pious organisation and the confraternities faced the ultimate challenge to their tenacity and self-confidence. It is hoped that this survey of confraternal activity over a *longue durée* will provide a useful framework for the essays within the volume.

****

Dozens of parish fraternities were founded in eastern and southern Ireland in the areas under English cultural influence between the late fourteenth and the early sixteenth centuries.[3] Their primary purpose was to provide spiritual assurance for the brothers and sisters through masses celebrated by fraternity chaplains at designated altars in parish or monastic churches. Members' funerals and burials were solemnly conducted, and their souls were to be prayed for in perpetuity. The devotional regime of soul masses and other pious rituals, including veneration of patron saints, was complemented by sociable practices, and in some cases the extension of charity and education to parishioners.[4] Many of the fraternities were established as corporations by royal patent which provided for their administration by lay officials who appointed the chaplains and managed the assets. Donations and bequests flowed from the patronage of aristocratic and gentry benefactors, mercantile families and people of humbler station in the community, providing an income which went towards the enhancement of the fraternity chapel and the stipends of the chaplains. The latter officiated at the fraternal altar, assisted in the parish liturgies and sometimes provided charitable functions in the parish at large. In some parishes the fraternity chaplains were selected by the parishioners, and not just the brothers and sisters. In Dunshaughlin, County Meath, for example, the priests were selected by the proctors of the parish church and the 'greater part of the good men of the parish',[5] while at Callan, County Kilkenny, patronage was in the hands of the sovereign of the town and his brethren.[6]

This close intertwining of fraternity, parochial and civic interests was particularly evident in some of the larger towns and cities of medieval Ireland. A blurring of boundaries between

---

[3] See Colm Lennon, 'The confraternities and cultural duality in Ireland, 1450–1550' in Black and Gravestock (eds), *Early modern confraternities*, pp 35–6.

[4] For trends in the development of late medieval confraternities from a comparative perspective, see, for example, V.R. Bainbridge, *Gilds in the medieval countryside: social and religious change in Cambridgeshire, c.1350–1558* (Woodbridge, 1996) and Ken Farnhill, *Guilds and the parish community in late medieval east Anglia, c.1470–1550* (York, 2001).

[5] Colm Lennon, 'The parish fraternities of County Meath in the late middle ages' in *Ríocht na Midhe*, xix (2008), p. 93; *Statute rolls, Edward IV*, i, pp 455–61.

[6] N.B. White (ed.), *Irish monastic and episcopal deeds, 1200–1600* (Dublin, 1936), p. 204.

fraternal and parochial personnel and property occurred in many places, to the extent that the parish has been referred to as 'the confraternity writ large'.[7] Many lay people who were masters or wardens of confraternities served also in parish offices such as churchwarden, applying their experience to the tasks of parochial governance. In several Dublin parishes, the parish estate of lands and houses, incorporating fraternity property, was managed by lay people and chaplains. The latter enjoyed individual and corporate patronage: several were enfeoffed as trustees of property by pious donors, and, while most were selected by the lay associates, some were nominated by the city mayor, as in the case of the chaplains of the fraternities in St Mary's parish, Drogheda.[8] The religious associations were embedded in a nexus of corporate bodies that included the craft and trade guilds, encompassing parish and civity. Like their religious counterparts, the guilds were under the dedication of saints, had devotional locales in urban churches and chapels, appointed chaplains and operated a charitable regime for disadvantaged members. But, although they also recreated kinship, in some cases for those whose familial origins lay nearer or farther afield, they were more exclusive than the fraternities, which bridged social boundaries by incorporating members from a range of professions and backgrounds. Ritual kinship was practised at city level, as in the case of St George's guild, which was the fraternity of the Dublin municipality, the master- and wardenships being held by the outgoing mayor and bailiffs of the borough.[9] Ritual and pageantry on feast-days such as those of St George or Corpus Christi came to symbolise civic achievement and unity in towns and cities such as Kilkenny and Dublin, in the forging of which the guilds and confraternities had played an integral part.[10]

---

[7] Empey, 'The layperson in the parish' in Gillespie and Neely (eds), *The laity and the Church of Ireland, 1000–2000*, pp 26, 36–41.

[8] Lennon, 'Parish fraternities of County Meath', p. 93.

[9] See Colm Lennon, 'Fraternity and community in early modern Dublin' in Robert Armstrong and Tadhg Ó hAnnracháin (eds), *Community in early modern Ireland* (Dublin, 2006), pp 167–78.

[10] Alan Fletcher, *Drama, performance and polity in pre-Cromwellian Ireland* (Cork, 2000), chapters 3 and 4.

To underline the reciprocating nature of the fraternal system and the society of late medieval Anglo-Ireland, the collegiality of the elites may be adduced. The deployment of the military brotherhood of St George Martyr, incorporating leading notables in the defence of the English Pale in the late fifteenth century, attests the role of association in the wider sphere of colonial politics. Among the nobility of the Englishry, there was a vogue for the foundation of colleges of clergy, at once assuring spiritual benefits and familial prestige. The Fitzgeralds of Kildare were associated with the most impressive of these bodies, the college of the Blessed Virgin at Maynooth, County Kildare, which incorporated thirteen clerical personnel.[11] In Howth, County Dublin, under the patronage of the St Lawrence family, a college of clergy was associated with the parish church of St Mary.[12] The Plunketts of County Meath established their collegiate institution at Killeen which housed a fraternity for the parishioners that was served by a community of clerics.[13] The Flemings, barons of Slane, provided for a college and residence for clergy.[14] As key mediators everywhere in the conveying of real property from the secular to the religious sphere, fraternity and collegiate chaplains facilitated close relations between lay elites and church that may have pre-empted later state efforts at reform.[15] At a senior level, the clergy as a corporate body prided themselves on their guardianship of the true principles upon which Anglo-Irish church reform had been established in Ireland. Institutions such as the cathedral chapter of St Patrick's and the canonry of Christ Church cathedral in Dublin were agencies through which they maintained their collective character,

---

[11] Mary Ann Lyons, 'The foundation of the Geraldine college of the Blessed Virgin Mary, Maynooth, 1518' in *Journal of the County Kildare Archaeological Society*, xviii (1994–95), pp 134–50.

[12] F.E. Ball, *Howth and its owners* (Dublin, 1917), pp 40–7.

[13] Anthony Cogan, *The diocese of Meath, ancient and modern*, 3 vols (Dublin, 1862), i, pp 354–6; Olive Curran, *History of the diocese of Meath*, 3 vols (Mullingar, 1995), iii, pp 1061–2.

[14] See T.J. Westropp, 'Slane in Bregia, County Meath: its friary and hermitage' in *Journal of the Royal Society of Antiquaries*, xxxi (1901), pp 424–9.

[15] L.P. Murray, 'The ancient chantries of County Louth' in *Journal of the County Louth Archaeological Society*, ix (1939), pp 181–208.

both institutions being supported by lay fraternities. At a time of heightened sensitivity to the potential loss of an Anglophone influence in eastern and southern Ireland, the bonding force provided by the religious corporations and fraternities helped to bolster communal cohesiveness.[16]

Conventional parish fraternities did not gain much of a foothold outside of the English zone in the late middle ages, due possibly to the large size of the mostly rural parishes and the superfluity of artificial kinship in a society of extended Gaelic clan lineages.[17] While the religious orders of the Pale and Englishry attracted some lay associations, it was the friars mendicant upon whom the confraternal impulses of Gaelic men and women were centred, with Third Orders secular and regular enjoying a huge vogue on the eve of the Reformation.[18] The Third Order of St Francis spread rapidly throughout the western and northern dioceses of the country, linked closely to the Franciscan Observant movement. The growth of communities of regular tertiaries of men and women who opted to live conventually attests to the gradual clericalisation of the minorite Third Order in Ireland, with forty-seven houses being founded in Ireland between 1440 and 1540. Yet, in spite of the trend towards the subsidiarity of the Third Order to the friars of the First, the regular tertiaries asserted their independence in 1457 when one of their own brothers was appointed visitor of all of the houses instead of a mendicant friar.[19] Though organised in a very different way to the parish fraternities of the Anglo-Irish areas, these tertiary associations did penetrate the areas of the English-Gaelic interface, as in the case of the hinterland of Limerick city and Slane in the west of Meath. The extent to which this efflorescence of fraternalism provided the seeds of new Counter-Reformation sodalities in Gaelic Ireland is

---

[16] On the corporateness of the senior clergy, see James Murray, *Enforcing the English reformation in Ireland: clerical resistance and political conflict in the diocese of Dublin, 1534–1590* (Cambridge, 2009).

[17] Lennon, 'Confraternities and cultural duality in Ireland', pp 36–8, 42–4.

[18] Colman Ó Clabaigh, *The Franciscans in Ireland* (Dublin, 2002), pp 80–105.

[19] Ibid., p. 103; see also Aubrey Gwynn and R.N. Hadcock, *Medieval religious houses in Ireland* (Dublin, 1988 edition), pp 263–81.

problematic, though the triumph of the First Order may have subsumed most or all of the vestiges of medieval lay Franciscan piety.[20]

The Protestant Reformation posed a grave challenge to the continuing existence of the religious associations in Anglo- and Gaelic Ireland. Although there was no official dissolution of the fraternities and chantries as occurred in mid-Tudor England, traditional devotions and liturgies were proscribed by the Irish act of uniformity of 1560, while many places of confraternal worship became inaccessible to devotees either through the confiscation of monastic chapels, or the appropriation of parish churches for Anglican services. Moreover, the reformed creed did not countenance the efficacy of good works and intercessory prayer based on belief in Purgatory, which was at the heart of confraternal belief. In these circumstances, the future for the older fraternities in early modern Ireland looked decidedly bleak, but many managed to survive in the changed climate until well into the seventeenth century, sometimes by pleading their charters of incorporation, and sometimes through obfuscatory means.[21] Chaplains continued to be appointed, though sometimes under the guise of 'singing men'. Roman Catholic testators found alternative means of ensuring the health of their souls, now that the route of donation to the parish fraternities was effectively blocked, by using circumspect and opaque formulae in their wills to disguise the nature of their bequests to priests to celebrate mass for their souls.[22] Provision for almshouses and small hospitals was almost certainly a front for fraternity-style institutions to house priests, as well as to dispense charity. Such bequests continued the practice of commemorative soul masses, though perhaps now separated from older parochial institutions. The surviving bodies paved the way for the mission of the Counter-Reformation clergy, not least by preserving fraternity lands and property in the hands of

---

[20] Brendan Bradshaw, 'English Reformation and identity formation in Ireland and Wales' in Brendan Bradshaw and Peter Roberts (eds), *British consciousness and identity: the making of Britain, 1533–1707* (Cambridge, 1998), pp 43–111.

[21] Lennon, 'Survival of the confraternities', pp 5–12.

[22] Clodagh Tait, '"As legacie upon my soul": the wills of the Irish Catholic community, *c*.1550–*c*.1660' in Armstrong and Ó hAnnracháin (eds), *Community in early modern Ireland*, pp 179–98.

Catholic proprietors for the support of seminary priests, as was decreed in a papal directive of 1569.[23]

Outside the sphere of religious activity, the fraternalism of the surviving associations contributed to the resistance to change elicited by the state-building policies of the Tudor and early Stuart monarchs. In the process of centralising the institutions of the state (as well as the church), the rulers now preferred to assert their authority through gubernatorial councils and prerogative courts, looking askance on the corporate privileges of guilds and confraternities. The surviving medieval corporations, including the fraternities and guilds, rallied to the conservation of traditional liberties and privileges. Some of the more prominent religious associations, such as St Anne's and St George's in Dublin, became shadow bodies to the town corporations, with their interchangeable personnel and outlets for business connections and sociability. The bonds of artificial kinship were strong enough to ensure a cooperative relationship between Protestants and Catholics within the civic nexus. Even though the surviving religious fraternities provided a façade for recusant activity, Protestant families such as the Usshers continued their association, particularly with St Anne's fraternity in Dublin.[24] By acting in unison to manipulate the succession to civic office in times of difficulty down to the 1640s, the patricians of the main boroughs, incorporating Protestants and Catholics, secured the conservation of cherished chartered liberties. There was also close co-operation between the Catholic and Protestant aldermen in respect of governmental threats to the monopolies of the merchant guilds and the customers of the ports.

Thus, far from breaking ranks for individual benefit, the old Protestant families were supportive of the corporatist principles underpinning the municipalities.[25] Moreover, the legacy of

---

[23] Colm Lennon, *The lords of Dublin in the age of Reformation* (Dublin, 1989), pp 148–9.

[24] Idem, 'The chantries in the Irish Reformation: the case of St Anne's guild, Dublin, 1550–1630' in R. V. Comerford, Mary Cullen, J. R. Hill and Colm Lennon (eds), *Religion, conflict and coexistence in Ireland: essays in honour of Monsignor Patrick J. Corish* (Dublin, 1989), pp 6–25.

[25] Colm Lennon, 'The shaping of a lay community in the Church of Ireland, 1558–1640' in Gillespie and Neely (eds), *The laity and the Church of Ireland, 1000–2000*, pp 49–69.

fraternalism was carried on among Church of Ireland parishioners throughout the early modern period, albeit transmuted
into confessionally appropriate forms. Within the Anglican
parishes, the tradition of lay office-holding continued, now
within the more formalised vestry system. Charitable ventures
centred on the parish became more organised and profession-
alised. When it came to sustaining some of the older institutions
and hospitals, Protestants from established civic families were
particularly supportive. Perhaps the most remarkable survival
was the resumption of St Anne's fraternity in the parish of St
Audoen in Dublin under Protestant leadership, though with
Catholic participation, from the 1650s onwards. For thirty years,
this body continued to meet on the feast of St Anne to adjudicate
on requests for alms and succour from distressed citizens. Many
of these petitioners stated that they were members of old civic
families including Luttrell, Plunkett and Sedgrave, who had
suffered deprivation and destitution due to political turmoil,
and referred to relatives who had been leading figures in the
previous generation or two. In all cases, the petitioners were
satisfied on the grounds of their being known, though 'shame-
faced poor', and thus belonging to the communion of saintly
citizenry, both living and the dead, and stretching across the
generations while transcending confessional divisions.
Although officially dissolved as a corporate body along with the
remaining Irish chantries in 1695, St Anne's continued on into
the eighteenth century as a charitable association supporting
the King's Hospital, or Blue Coat School, established for the
education of poor boys by the municipality. It may have
been one of a number of such voluntary associations of the
eighteenth-century towns which traced its roots back to the
religious fraternity of the late middle ages.[26]

While the forms of confraternalism that have been identified
as surviving the political and religious upheavals of the sixteenth and seventeenth centuries may be described as resistant
to authority, there was introduced a new form of sodality that
absorbed and indeed reflected the spiritual reform of the
Counter-Reformation. Whereas in many Catholic countries, the

---

[26] See 'The white book of the guild of St Anne, 1655–87' (Royal Irish Academy,
Dublin, MS 12 0 13).

late medieval associations were transmuted (sometimes with difficulty) into instruments of Tridentine reform and the new philanthropy, the anti-establishment nature of the older fraternities in Ireland rendered them less suitable as agencies of Catholic renewal. New religious orders and societies, as well as the older reviving ones, preferred to import the innovative type of sodality that was becoming very popular on the continent. Although superficially resembling the pre-Reformation associations, this new species of confraternity differed from them significantly in a number of respects. For the missioners of the Counter-Reformation, such as the Jesuits, Franciscans, Capuchins, Dominicans, Carmelites and others, the emphasis was on an interiorised devotional regime that took less account of the sociability of religion or the sacralising of place such as parish or urban neighbourhood. Instead, new confraternity pieties centred on the refinement of personal devotion to Christ and the Virgin Mary, and saints that were representative of the Catholic renewal. A high premium was placed on sacramental observance, particularly the reverential hearing of mass and confession. The confraternities of the Counter-Reformation era were under strict clerical supervision, the appointment of spiritual advisors, for example, being no longer in the gift of laymen and women. Confraternities were tied to the residences of the religious orders and affiliated to their international fellowships. The selectivity applied to membership contrasted with the openness of pre-Reformation brotherhood and sisterhood: sodalities were now segregated according to estates, such as students, merchants and artisans, and even the sexes. A deliberate sense of the exclusivity of the fellowships was cultivated in an effort to instil feelings of special merit among members, and to keep the secular world at bay.[27]

Although the Counter-Reformation sodality movement spread rapidly, especially in the urban areas of southern Ireland, its very success contributed to the growing stresses within the Catholic community in seventeenth-century Ireland.

---

[27] See C. J. Black, *Italian confraternities in the sixteenth century* (Cambridge, 1989); R. Po-Chia Hsia, *The world of Catholic renewal, 1540–1770* (Cambridge, 1998); for Ireland, see Brian Jackson, 'Sectarianism: division and dissent in Irish Catholicism' in Alan Ford and John McCafferty (eds), *The origins of sectarianism in early modern Ireland* (Cambridge, 2005), pp 203–15.

Disputes between secular and regular clergy over rights to confraternal jurisdiction were symptomatic of a larger dichotomy in respect of attitudes to the place of revived Catholicism within the Protestant state. Whereas diocesan churchmen such as Bishop David Rothe of Ossory favoured conciliating the regime in the interests of continuing *de facto* toleration of Catholicism, the regular leadership tended to favour a full political restoration of Catholic worship and property.[28] On the face of it, laymen and women appeared to play a subsidiary role in these clerical broils, being appealed to by both sides in conflicts over sodalities and other matters. The city of Drogheda has been taken as a flashpoint in the bitter conflicts over jurisdiction between the secular and regular clergy, most notably in the early 1620s, and certainly layfolk were caught up in these.[29] While there is no doubt that the new Tridentine associations had a broad appeal, the older model of brotherhood persisted among them in the form of the Drogheda chantry. This was a chartered association, founded in 1438 and dedicated to St Anne, which was associated with a congeries of chapels and altars in St Peter's church, served by up to ten chaplains.[30] Like its namesake body in St Audoen's, Dublin, it survived the early Reformation intact, providing a reserve of Catholic quietist piety and transmitting a large portfolio of over 300 properties to the seventeenth-century trustees. It served not only to patronise the Tridentine clergy, whether diocesan or regular, but also to facilitate peaceful relations between members of the confessions down to the 1640s and perhaps beyond.[31] But the violent

---

[28] For the ecclesiastical backdrop, see Thomas O'Connor, *Irish Jansenists, 1600–70* (Dublin, 2008).

[29] See Jackson, 'Sectarianism', pp 203–15; Brian Mac Cuarta, *Catholic revival in the north of Ireland, 1603–1641* (Dublin, 2007), pp 213–24.

[30] Cf. *Calendar of papal registers: papal letters, 1427–47*, p. 39; James B. Leslie, *Armagh clergy and parishes* (Dundalk, 1911), p. 245; idem, *Supplement to Armagh clergy and parishes* (Dundalk, 1948), pp 87, 89; *Register of Octavian, archbishop of Armagh, 1478–1513*, ed. M.A. Sughi (2 vols, IMC, Dublin, 1999), ii, pp 370–1, 432–3; Henry A. Jefferies, *Priests and prelates of Armagh in the age of reformations, 1518–1558* (Dublin, 1997), p. 24.

[31] *Irish patent rolls of James I*, ed. M.C. Griffith (IMC, Dublin, 1966), pp 404–5; Mac Cuarta, *Catholic revival in the north of Ireland*, p. 213; Patrick Little, 'Discord in Drogheda: a window on Irish church–state relations in the 1640s' in *Historical Research*, lxxv (2002), pp 355–62.

denouement to that decade symbolised the uprooting of the expressive new sodalities and their quietist and circumspect alternative lay brotherhoods.

****

The shock to Roman Catholic culture sustained by the passage of the penal laws of the late seventeenth century affected the confraternities no less than other ecclesiastical structures and institutions. Recent research has tended to revise the view that the Catholic church experienced extensive interruption of its worship during the eighteenth century.[32] While little attention has been devoted specifically to the subject of the sodalities and confraternities in this context, it is agreed that they formed a vital part of the revival of Catholic organisation, particularly in the towns.[33] During the early decades of the century, there was in existence a network of places of worship run by the diocesan and religious clergy.[34] By the 1740s, as Cormac Begadon shows in his essay, the confraternities were re-emerging in Dublin, carrying on the traditional devotions associated with the orders such as the Carmelite scapular, Augustinian cincture and Dominican holy rosary. The remainder of this essay presents a sidelong view of the subsequent period of confraternity history within which the contributors to this volume have set their specialist studies, examining the associative phenomena described either as acculturative of or resistant to prevailing religious and social trends. It is thereby hoped to aerate the individual essays through the discourse of confraternity studies.

Devotional confraternities such as those dedicated to the veneration of the eucharist, the rosary, the Blessed Virgin and

---

[32] See, for example, T.P. Power and Kevin Whelan (eds), *Endurance and emergence: Catholics in Ireland in the eighteenth century* (Dublin, 1999).

[33] Corish, *Irish Catholic experience*, pp 133, 169–70; Dáire Keogh, 'The Catholic church in Ireland in the age of the north Atlantic revolution, 1775–1815' in Brendan Bradshaw and Dáire Keogh (eds), *Christianity in Ireland: revisiting the story* (Dublin, 2002), p. 159.

[34] See, for example, Nuala Burke, 'A hidden church? The structure of Catholic Dublin in the mid-eighteenth century' in *Archivium Hibernicum* [hereafter cited as *Archiv. Hib.*], xxxii (1974), pp 81–92.

the Sacred Heart were popular, championed by religious orders such as the Dominicans and Jesuits as well as by individual bishops and missioners. The impetus in many cases came from the orders' continental headquarters which fostered the international associational structures and made available printed works for regional and local adaptation. The latter trend helped to promote a literary upsurge in Ireland in the later eighteenth century, under the aegis of the flourishing Dublin and provincial print trade, allowing for the production of works of Catholic piety and catechesis, many of them associated with confraternal activity.[35] Educational provision for Irish girls and boys by religious pioneers such as Edmund Ignatius Rice, Nano Nagle and Margaret Aylward in the nineteenth century drew heavily upon European Catholic pedagogical models, elaborated after the Council of Trent. These and other Catholic evangelists made full use of sodalities, with their hymn-singing, libraries of spiritual classics and processions on religious festivals with banners and special uniforms, all drawn from continental exemplars. Thus, the confraternities and sodalities, with their associated catechetical activities, assisted strongly in the acculturation of Catholicism in Ireland within the ultramontane outreach of the Roman church in the late eighteenth and nineteenth centuries.

Besides the resuscitation of Tridentine spirituality among Irish Catholics slowly emerging from the penal period, however, there were strong reforming influences at work among them from civil society, many of which were transmitted through religious associationalism. The coincidence of interests between the state and Roman Catholic authorities at the end of the eighteenth century, as manifested, for example, in the establishment of Maynooth College in 1795, allowed for moderate displays of decorous devotion from the early nineteenth century onwards. Social and moral reform was promoted through the formation of the Holy Name society by the Dominican order for the purpose of curbing profanity and swearing among Catholics. The perennial problem of inappropriate waking of the dead was addressed through the establishment of the Purgatorial (or St Joseph) and the Bona Mors

---

[35] See Cormac Begadon, 'Confraternities and the renewal of Catholic Dublin, c.1750–c.1830', in this volume.

societies for the purpose of comforting the sick and dying, and providing devout funerals and burials. A large number of societies came to flourish with the aim of fostering literacy and a knowledge of Christian teaching, such as St John the Evangelist and the Catholic Book societies. Most significant in this category was the confraternity of Christian Doctrine which experienced phenomenal growth throughout the country in the first half of the nineteenth century. It performed an important function in the catechising of youth throughout the parishes, thus forming knowledgeable congregations for worship and Christian practice. The pedagogical enterprises of Rice, Nagle, Aylward and other Catholic educationalists were underpinned by a zeal for moral reform through the inculcation of literacy and habits of sobriety, as well as religious knowledge.[36]

Much of this reforming thrust was achieved through the dynamic participation of lay men and women who undertook leadership roles in concert with clerical partners. The laity were most prominent in the societies that attended the sick, poor and dying, aiding the clergy in bringing spiritual and temporal succour, reciting the office of the dead before masses and over the corpse at funerals, and running their committees, under ecclesiastical supervision. Indeed the religious authorities had actively recruited well-educated Catholics from respectable backgrounds for the running of the Holy Name and other societies, and especially the confraternity of Christian Doctrine. By the mid-nineteenth century, most parishes in the country had laymen and women members taking large classes of girls and boys after last mass on Sundays to instil the precepts of the catechism. In this respect, the balance struck between lay and clerical participation was in many ways similar to that obtaining in the fraternities of the late middle ages. A growing sense of self-confidence among the Catholic community, as the penal legislation was dismantled through to the 1830s, found expression in their participation in a variety of philanthropic and religious associations, which promised to acculturate them within the secular, reforming milieu of early Victorian Ireland, as well as nurture their Catholic devotion.

---

[36] See Dáire Keogh, 'Evangelising the faithful: Edmund Rice and the reformation of nineteenth-century Irish Catholicism', in this volume.

A definite change occurred from the mid-nineteenth century onwards in the clerical–lay dynamic within the religious associations, comparable to that which occurred in the era of the Counter-Reformation. At the same time, their role was transformed from that of fairly vibrant apostolate to quasi-passive devotionalism. This was in large part due to the assertion of Catholic (and indeed Anglican) resistance to aspects not only of zealous Protestant evangelicalism but also of state administrative, social and cultural reforms. Religious associational life gradually became a locus for defensiveness against perceived sectarian aggression, as well as for clerical assertiveness in the face of secular, or rather non-confessionalised, advances in areas such as education and welfare. In facing down the challenge from the evangelicals in education, the religious teaching orders wrested the leadership in Catholic schooling from the lay catechists of the confraternity of Christian Doctrine, and brought this ascendancy to bear in their antipathy to the state's national school system. In like manner the urgency of countering governmental welfare policies towards the poor and the sick projected the male and female religious orders to the forefront of Catholic philanthropy, subsuming much of the lay effort in this regard. Although some lay women continued to play a part in organised visitation of the deprived, most reverted to the role of devout sodalists, while lay men had an outlet for their social activism in the newly-founded Society of St Vincent de Paul from the 1840s. The late nineteenth- and early twentieth-century sodalities were characterised by strong clerical control with lay subsidiarity in the roles of monitors and prefects of attendance and demeanour.[37] An impression of the growing ascendancy of the letter rather than the spirit of the rules of confraternities is gleaned from the records of expulsions, for example, for poor attendance with ritual deprivation of the benefit of confraternal regalia. The strength of the confraternity bond was most clearly

---

[37] For a survey of this period of late nineteenth- and early twentieth-century confraternity and sodality history, see Colm Lennon and Robin Kavanagh, 'The flowering of the confraternities and sodalities in Ireland, 1860–1960', in this volume.

evident, not so much in the processions and devout rituals, but in the decommissioning of the recalcitrant member's medal.[38]

Two very different examples of lay associationalism with contrasting fates call attention to alternatives to the heavily clericalised confraternities which suffered decay and almost total evisceration in the later part of the twentieth century. The Church of Ireland voluntary associations were born of the same impetus towards Christian doctrine for the young in Sunday schools as prevailed in Catholic parishes in the earlier nineteenth century, but they also were reflective of resistance on the part of Anglicans to the religiously neutral state created in Ireland by disestablishment after 1870. They came to assert the primacy of the parish and the patronage role of the laity, particularly women, therein during the decades of their flourishing. Protective of the faith of their co-religionists, these parochial bodies took on responsibility for poor Protestants and for job-seeking youths, and the round of cultural and sporting events that they organised was designed to encourage socialising within the community and to discourage marriages with Catholics. By failing to be more than bonding associations for the Church of Ireland parochial communities, however, these voluntary associations suffered vitiation in the Catholic nationalist atmosphere of the Irish Free State.[39] By contrast, the members of the Society of St Vincent de Paul succeeded in harnessing aspects of the parish confraternities to provide lay leadership in practical charity. While animated by the devotional ambience of institutional Catholicism, the exclusively male (until the 1960s) brotherhood did not countenance the ostentatious piety of the sodalities, eschewing public acknowledgement. As proactive participants in an international Society, the membership responded to the profound changes in Catholic social activism from the 1950s, successfully bridging the chasm between the old devotion and the new forms of Christian witness.[40]

[38] The theme of the efficacy of sodality medals is treated by Lisa Godson in her essay, 'Display, sacramentalism and devotion: the medals of the archconfraternity of the Holy Family, 1922–1939', in this volume.

[39] See Martin Maguire, 'The Church of Ireland parochial associations: a social and cultural analysis', in this volume.

[40] This theme is covered by Máire Ní Chearbhaill in her essay, 'Charity, church and the Society of St Vincent de Paul', in this volume.

For the bulk of the confraternities and sodalities, however, the attempt to absorb the religious, social and cultural changes of the 1950s and 1960s proved to be infeasible. Already, the problems of adjustment had been crystallised in the fruitless efforts to establish youth sodalities in the Dublin archdiocese. Some progress had been made in respect of the fostering of sociability for young men and women in a loose Christian framework of youth clubs. Tensions emerged within the broad Catholic establishment, however, over the relative privileges of school, parish and religious youth sodalities, and, in particular, over the issue of the mixing of youths of different social classes within the associations.[41] Critical self-awareness was evident in the responses of traditional sodalities to the debates of Vatican II, but the attrition of zeal and initiative meant that opportunities to acculturate the reforms in the liturgy and the lay apostolate were too late to salvage the confraternal infrastructure. The effects of what Louise Fuller describes as 'the Second Reformation' in respect of indulgences, while not completely vitiating the system of applied merit to the souls of the living and the dead, narrowed the vital channels of infusion of spiritual energy, bound up with the theology of purgatory. Liturgical changes such as the provision of evening vigil masses in parish churches caused clashes with sodality meetings, while the burgeoning of the culture of mass entertainment proved to be a huge counter-attraction. When the struggle to maintain the confraternities and sodalities entered its final phase after the mid-1960s, the whole infrastructure proved to be insubstantial, given a lack of clerical enthusiasm, lay empowerment and links to the wider civil community.[42]

****

For all their ubiquity and almost universal membership, then, the confraternities and sodalities in Ireland proved to have had

---

[41] See Carole Holohan, 'John Charles McQuaid and the failure of the youth sodalities, 1956–60', in this volume.

[42] Louise Fuller, 'Confraternities, their decline and the problem of sources: background, analysis and review', in this volume.

remarkably shallow roots. Only residual aspects of these Catholic devotional bodies survived to the end of the twentieth century, through the Limerick archconfraternity, for example, and some bodies of tertiaries attached to religious orders. As a concluding perspective, it may be useful to draw again upon the discourse of confraternity studies to attempt to explain the varying fortunes of religious associations within the enduring Irish religious and cultural experience. Historians in the field have recently adapted the concept of 'social capital', drawn from the work of sociological writers, to elucidate the role of confraternities in society. Most eagerly embraced has been the writing of Robert D. Putnam, a political scientist, who developed the notion of civic virtue being elicited from social capital through its networks of reciprocal social relations, deriving from bodies such as confraternities and other associations. Putnam, in fact, in his *Making democracy work: civic traditions in modern Italy*, adduced the historical as well as contemporary experiences of northern and southern Italian states to explain civic disparities within that country. In identifying types of social capital, sociologists have distinguished between bonding and bridging kinds. For Putnam, bonding social capital relates to groups which are homogenous and introverted in their membership, with a strong sense of exclusive identity, while bridging social capital pertains to inclusive groups which encourage the encompassing of people of different social backgrounds.[43]

Applying this paradigm to the Irish confraternities and sodalities surveyed in this study, we find that, in the case of the late medieval fraternities, brotherhood and sisterhood encompassed sociability and charity within the wider parish and community, and that clergy were integrated with laity. They provided bridging social capital that generated broad identities and reciprocity through artificial kinship. The Church of Ireland vestries in the post-Reformation parishes were the inheritors of much fraternal energy and expertise, which were

---

[43] R.D. Putnam, *Bowling alone: the collapse and revival of American community* (New York, 2000), pp 22–3; for the application of Putnam's ideas in the context of international confraternity studies, see Nicholas Terpstra, 'Confraternities, social capital and civil society: comparisons, contexts and questions', in this volume.

used not just in the ecclesiastical sphere but also in the provision of charity and other social services.[44] Vestries, with their fraternal roots, thus transmitted an important legacy to local administration in Ireland. Superficially, the Church of Ireland parochial associations in the late nineteenth and early twentieth centuries resembled their late medieval counterparts, in that they were run by laypeople and focused on charity and sociability. They were preoccupied, however, with reinforcing an Anglican identity for members and promoting intra-confessional social relations, and thus can be considered to be bonding associations.

The confraternities and sodalities of the Catholic renewal after Trent, often segregated in terms of gender, profession and social order, were more introverted than their pre-Reformation forerunners. They were run by secular and regular clergy, and were concerned with the consolidation of a Catholic identity in the difficult conditions of early modern Ireland. Their revived successors, which took root in a changed devotional and worshipping milieu from the early nineteenth century, reflected the ultramontane trends within the Roman Catholic church, and bonded their members in pursuit of self-sanctification through the performance of a wide variety of spiritual exercises under tight clerical control. For the most part, they failed to survive the profound religious and social changes of the mid-twentieth century. Among the few groups that continued to flourish were those which were outward-looking and nurturing of international outlooks and tendencies, most notably the Society of St Vincent de Paul. With a minimal level of clerical direction and a concentration on charitable action in the community, the brothers and sisters have continued to provide a vital bridge between the state social services and the poor and distressed in society.

---

[44] See Rowena Dudley, 'The Dublin parish, 1660–1730' in Elizabeth Fitzpatrick and Raymond Gillespie (eds), *The parish in medieval and early modern Ireland* (Dublin, 2006), pp 277–96.

2

Confraternities and the renewal of Catholic Dublin, c.1750–c.1830

Cormac Begadon

Between the years 1780 and 1830 the religious culture of Dublin's Catholic community experienced what some have called a 'revival', or as others prefer to term it, an 'evolution'. Whatever it is called, there can be no denying that the transformation was nothing short of spectacular. When John Carpenter (1729–86) was appointed archbishop in 1770 the pastoral infrastructure of the archdiocese was not in a healthy state. Attempts to improve it had traditionally been hampered by the expansion of the Protestant state and the subsequent introduction of penal laws. However, as the eighteenth century drew slowly to a close, the climate was becoming gradually more conducive to Catholic renewal and reform. Archbishop Carpenter helped stimulate this transformation by initiating systematic diocesan visitations. He coupled this strategy with the publication of provincial and synodal constitutions setting out guidelines for clerical practice in 1770. His lead in initiating change was subsequently adopted, and enhanced, in the episcopacies of John Thomas Troy (1739–1823) and Daniel Murray (1768–1852). Some changes, such as the renewal of chapels and erection of schools and seminaries, were physical. Others, such as the reorganisation of the parish system, were spatial transformations. The practices of Catholic piety also underwent radical change. By the 1830s the Catholic infrastructural network included schools, libraries, asylums, orphanages and refuges. A central aspect of this reform and renewal of Catholic religious culture was the establishment of a network of confraternities, which were complemented by the expansion of a Catholic religious print culture.

By the early nineteenth century Catholics in Dublin could satisfy their appetites for private piety with a wealth of Catholic devotional literature. However, public piety was also catered for thanks to the establishment of a growing network of religious confraternities and sodalities. This reception of ideas, albeit by a minority of Catholics, did, however, have a gradual impact on the beliefs and practices of the wider Catholic community. Due, in part, to the marriage of private and public piety, increasing numbers of Catholics were becoming 'religiously engaged', playing visible roles in renewal and reform. Both Catholic publishing and religious confraternities were key factors in the evolution of Catholic culture in Dublin in the period before Catholic Emancipation. Improvements in printing and the waning of the Irish government's desire to enforce penal legislation provided Catholic printers and booksellers with an opportunity to expand and supply the burgeoning Catholic population with religious books. Successive archbishops were directly involved in the promotion of the Catholic trade. The expansion of the Catholic print trade, whilst predating the modernisation of the network of confraternities by some years, was in many ways connected to the Catholic community's desire for increased devotion and piety, and in later years, moral reform.

****

By the 1700s the majority of confraternities in Catholic Europe existed for devotional and benevolent purposes. Many bishops encouraged 'Christo-centric and Eucharistic observations', as opposed to the more traditional devotions to the cult of saints.[1] In Dublin this transformation was marked. Newly established confraternities were no longer named in honour of popular, local saints but were generally devoted to the Blessed Sacrament, Our Lady of the Rosary, St Joseph or the Sacred Heart. These dedications were not unique to Ireland but were common in many Catholic countries. Undoubtedly this had

---

[1] John McManners, *Church and society in eighteenth-century France: the religion of the people and the politics of religion* (2 vols, New York, 1998), ii, p. 186.

much to do with the expansion of religious orders by the late eighteenth century. The Jesuits, for example, promoted devotion to the Sacred Heart and to Jesus and Mary. One of the most popular confraternities in Dublin was the Confraternity of the Blessed Sacrament, which advocated adoration and regular reception of the Eucharist.[2] As well as this shift in devotion away from medieval saints towards the Holy Family, the social make-up of confraternities and sodalities in Dublin by the mid-eighteenth century may have been different from their pre-Reformation predecessors. Earlier societies had stressed fraternity and sociability, with many confraternities having strong links with particular sections of society, and some sharing close ties with the various trades and professions. Often membership fees were quite considerable, sometimes prohibiting the poor from joining. However, with the expansion of the Protestant state from the sixteenth century onwards, Catholics were gradually excluded from the various sections of public and commercial life. Thus, Catholic confraternities found it impossible to exist as they had done in their pre-Reformation state. Consequently, membership of newly formed or reinvented confraternities became more diverse. Membership fees were henceforth only nominal, thus opening up access to a broader social spectrum. Indeed while some promoted the reading of devotional books, confraternities were not exclusively reserved for the literate. An advertisement for the Bona Mors confraternity published in 1793 told readers that 'Such as cannot read [the manual of devotion], may say their beads, begging that they may not be absent from the rest in eternal glory'.[3] Membership of many confraternities, especially those with a more devotional nature, appears to have been dominated by females. By the later decades of the eighteenth century it was hoped that confraternities and sodalities would act as examples of evangelical perfection, reaching into social strata which traditionally lacked

---

[2] The rules for the confraternity of the Blessed Sacrament stated that candidates undertake a general confession, and receive communion at least once a month in the previous year.

[3] *Bona Mors: or the art of dying happily in the congregation of Jesus Christ crucified, and of his condoning mother* (Dublin, 1793), p. 7.

religious knowledge and were poorly integrated into parish-centred devotion.

Records charting the existence of confraternities in Dublin are irregular and it is difficult to illustrate any sort of evolutionary process, even as late as the early nineteenth century. While what can be described as Counter-Reformation devotions, for example, those related to the Blessed Sacrament, were in existence in the early eighteenth century, the real growth in confraternities does not appear to have taken place until much later. Indeed Patrick Corish suggests that this process did not begin to occur until the 1740s at the earliest.[4] Even then membership numbers were still relatively low. It is likely that substantial growth in membership did not begin to occur in Dublin until the 1790s. This should not, however, be used as evidence of the Catholic church's indifference towards confraternities. Rather, the apparent reluctance shown by some senior clergy to promote these groups may have been as a result of the political situation that Catholics had to operate under in the eighteenth century. For example, Archbishop Troy was wary of authorising a procession in honour of Our Lady of the Brown Scapular in Dublin city in 1790, citing growing tensions between Catholics and Protestants as the reason for his caution.[5] However, as the penal laws were gradually repealed confraternities became more common and more prominent.

One of the earliest known confraternities to be formed, or re-formed, in Dublin was the confraternity of the Most Holy Name of Jesus Christ. This group had existed for some years prior to 1747 and was under the spiritual guidance of the Dominicans of Bridge Street chapel. In 1748 a papal brief was issued permitting the Irish bishops to erect the confraternity in their dioceses.[6] A little is known about the confraternity thanks to the correspondence of two Jesuits, Thomas Brennan and Michael Fitzgerald.[7] Brennan,

---

[4] Patrick Corish, *The Catholic community in the seventeenth and eighteenth centuries* (Dublin, 1981), p. 85.

[5] Archbishop Troy to Cardinal Antonelli, 27 Apr. 1790 (Dublin Diocesan Archives, Troy papers, AB2/116/5(13)) [hereafter DDA].

[6] Hugh Fenning, O.P., *The Irish Dominican province, 1698–1797* (Dublin, 1990), p. 213.

[7] Brennan was writing from Dublin to his colleague, Fitzgerald, in Rome. See Hugh Fenning, O.P. (ed.), 'Letters from a Dublin Jesuit in Dublin on the Confraternity of the Holy Name, 1747–1748' in *Archiv. Hib.*, xxix (1970), pp 134–54.

who was writing to Fitzgerald in Rome, recalled some of the more favourable developments taking place within the Catholic community in Dublin, especially regarding the confraternity. In one of his letters Brennan forwarded an advertisement outlining the confraternity's objectives. The advertisement informed readers that it had been established as 'the vice of profane swearing and cursing' had grown 'so general in this kingdom, that it has been often wished some method or other could be agreed to suppress it'.[8] While acknowledging its prevalence, Brennan stressed that this growing malaise was not as a result of clerical inactivity or even indifference but was rather due to the actions of impious lay men and women. The onus, therefore, rested with the laity, whose job it was to help eradicate such irreverent conduct. He told Fitzgerald that 'We see the preachers do their part. They are incessantly declaiming against it, but with more zeal than success. The people listen to them, and yet they swear on without any considerable amendment.'[9] To counteract the abuse he said it was

> thought expedient to erect a sodality under the invocation of the name of Jesus ... it is not meaned that any new obligation of conscience will be imposed on those who engage in this pious enterprise: they are only reminded to perform with more fidelity what they were at all times obliged to do by the laws of God.[10]

Brennan argued that what the confraternity required of its members was in no way radical or overly zealous, for what it proposed was nothing other than adherence to the 'laws of God' regarding the single transgression of swearing.

However, its objectives may be viewed as more socially radical when one examines the types of people whom it hoped to attract as members. Ideally these were to be 'the heads of families, or those who have the charge of others with some authority to punish their faults'.[11] They would have 'influence

---

[8] Thomas Brennan, SJ, to Michael Fitzgerald, SJ, 31 Jan. 1746/47 in Fenning (ed.), 'Letters from a Dublin Jesuit in Dublin on the confraternity of the Holy Name, 1747–1748', p. 141.

[9] Ibid.

[10] Ibid.

[11] Ibid.

and authority over others, and zeal enough to employ it against this vice'.[12] It was 'expected from the members of this sodality that they will prevent swearing and cursing as much as possibly they can in those they live or converse with, tho' they are nowise subject to them, remembering that whoever corrects his brother may gain him to God and "save that mans soul from death"'.[13] Evangelisation and moral reform were central to the members' mission. By 1773, with the confraternity presumably still going strong, its activities were publicised by a spiritual director, Rev. John O'Connor, O.P. O'Connor's *An essay on the rosary and sodality of the Most Holy Name of Jesus* (Dublin, 1773) re-emphasised the sentiments of Fitzgerald and Brennan, stressing that the confraternity's goal was 'to stem the dangerous torrent, and to try every preservative to guard against spreading impiety'.[14] O'Connor reinforced the idea of the confraternity stimulating social and religious restoration, stating that it was members' obligation 'to use every lawful effort to effect a reformation, and to stop the dreadful contagion'.[15] While O'Connor emphasised the centrality of lay Catholics to this 'reformation' of public manners, the onus to stimulate it, he believed, lay firmly in the hands of reforming clergy: 'as this duty more immediately concerns ecclesiastics'.[16]

This interest in moral reform was not unique to the confraternity of the Holy Name, with many other groups sharing a similar bent. One of the best known and important groups was the confraternity of Christian Doctrine. Like many others, it had its roots in the Tridentine reforms of the sixteenth century. It was founded in Italy by a priest, Castellino de Castello for the purpose of educating children and unlettered persons in the basic tenets of the Catholic faith. The first confraternities in Ireland were founded some time in the mid-eighteenth century when autonomously-run Sunday schools began to appear. A more uniform and structured approach had been adopted by

---

12 Ibid.

13 Ibid., p. 142.

14 John O'Connor, O.P., *An essay on the rosary and sodality of the Most Holy Name of Jesus* (Dublin, 1773), p. 2.

15 Ibid.

16 Ibid.

the 1780s, most notably in the dioceses of Kildare and Leighlin and Dublin. A branch had existed in Tullow, County Carlow in the early 1780s, where members were even holding an annual Corpus Christi procession.[17] By 1788 Pius VI had granted members plenary indulgences for their works. In the same year the bishop of Kildare and Leighlin, Dr Daniel Delany, wrote to Archbishop Troy thanking him for forwarding a notice of indulgences. Delany stated that he was 'bold to assert with a holy confidence that they, [the confraternities] cannot fail to be productive, ere long, of the most estimable fruits among our poor people'.[18]

Delany, therefore, was in little doubt about the usefulness of the organisation. During the early years of the nineteenth century branches were set up throughout the archdiocese. In the *Irish Catholic Directory 1821* the objectives of the society were summarised as the following:

> Confraternities of the Christian Doctrine, are instituted in every chapel, where poor children are taught the catechism for a full hour every Sunday after last Mass: the boys are taught in the aisle, and the females in the galleries, and after instruction the little office of the most Holy Sacrament, with other devout prayers are recited. These confraternities are governed by a Rev. clergyman, as guardian, by a president, vice-president and treasurer, who are annually elected. The members subscribe 6½d. per month, or 6s. 6d. a year, which provides catechisms, prayerbooks and devout premiums for the children, and which purchases candles for the evening office, and for attending at processions of the most venerable sacrament.[19]

As the confraternity existed predominantly for catechetical purposes, many, but not all, of its members acted as teachers. While many confraternities had associations with the regular clergy the Christian Doctrine was primarily a parochially-based organisation. Although records do not provide a formal date of

---

[17] Thomas McGrath, *Religious renewal and reform in the pastoral ministry of Bishop James Doyle of Kildare and Leighlin, 1786–1834* (Dublin, 1998), p. 30.

[18] Bishop Delany to Archbishop Troy, 14 Nov. 1788 (DDA, Troy papers, AB1 /116/4(72)).

[19] Patrick Cunningham, 'The Irish Catholic Directory 1821' in *Reportorium Novum*, ii, no. 2 (1960), p. 358.

establishment, Troy's letter to Dr Delany in 1788 attests to their existence in Dublin by that stage. In the report of the royal commission on education in Ireland, compiled in 1820, Archbishop Murray stated that 'in the diocese of Dublin, as long as I have been in the ministry, it [the confraternity of Christian Doctrine] has been very much recommended.'[20] It is known, for example, that a confraternity was erected in St Michan's parish in 1799, records showing that it had seventy members in its first year of existence, all of whom were said to be female.[21] A branch was later established in the city parish of SS Michael and John's in 1818, succeeding Dr Thomas Betagh's poor schools, which had provided similar religious instruction for many years.[22] By the 1820s the confraternity had been established in all of the city parishes.

The confraternity's structure was relatively straightforward. Members were to be drawn from respectable and reasonably well-educated backgrounds. It would seem that prior membership of the confraternity of the Blessed Sacrament was required before admission into the Christian Doctrine, supposedly ensuring the integrity of the candidate.[23] Members attended the various prescribed liturgical services, and some were involved in the catechetical classes which took place on Sundays. Catechism classes took place before or after Sunday mass. Boys and girls were taught separately and classes were divided along the same lines as secular schools, with children being grouped together by age. The rules for the confraternity of St Michan's parish outlined the catechetical programme to be followed:

> 1st class, prayers, including the acts of faith, hope and charity.
> 2nd class, small catechism. 3rd class, abridgement of the general

---

[20] *Report of the royal commission on education in Ireland, 1824* cited in Martin Brenan, *The confraternity of Christian Doctrine in Ireland, A.D. 1775–1835* (Dublin, 1934), p. 9.

[21] Myles Ronan, *An apostle of Catholic Dublin: Father Henry Young* (Dublin, 1944), p. 123. Records for 1800 and 1801 show that membership had decreased to twenty-six and twenty-one, respectively.

[22] *Parish of SS Michael and John* (Dublin, 1954).

[23] Brenan, *The confraternity of Christian Doctrine in Ireland*, p. 16. However, other sources suggest that it was easy to gain membership of the confraternity of Christian Doctrine, stating that all one had to do was register with the parish priest, which was in stark contrast with the strict guidelines laid down for the confraternity of the Blessed Sacrament. See McGrath, *Religious renewal and reform*, p. 130.

catechism. 4th class, general catechism. 5th class, Fleury's historical catechism. But to this last class no one is to be admitted but
such as shall be declared fit by some priest of the chapel.[24]

By 1820 the activities of the confraternity had become so
well known that the royal commission on education in Ireland
examined its work in some detail. The commissioners were
considerably alarmed at its activities, compiling a report outlining their suspicions regarding the confraternity's perceived
influence over Catholic children. They alleged that the members
were 'obliged to ... exercise a vigilant Superintendence over the
moral Conduct of each other ... we believe, [that there are]
but few chapels in Ireland in which religious instruction is not
imparted on Sundays'.[25] It may have been the case that the
commissioners believed that the influence of the confraternity
was thwarting the efforts of influential Protestant evangelicals
in both Ireland and Britain, who amongst other things sought to
bring 'Ireland into line with the economic and political as well
as religious trends taking shape in Britain'.[26] The Westminster
government was becoming increasingly mindful of the importance of supporting the religious establishment in Ireland
against the mounting threat of Catholic politicisation, and
therefore any significant process of pastoral or catechetical
reform was going to be of interest.[27] The apparent success of the
confraternity of Christian Doctrine and those Catholic Sunday
schools without canonical approval was detrimental to the
efforts of the Protestant Sunday schools, which had been
educating Catholic children since the early 1800s.[28]

---

[24] 'Rules for the confraternity of Christian Doctrine, St Michan's parish' cited in
Ronan, *An apostle of Catholic Dublin*, p. 124.

[25] *Report of the royal commission on education in Ireland, 1824* cited in Brenan, *The
confraternity of Christian Doctrine in Ireland*, p. 8.

[26] Irene Whelan, 'The bible gentry: evangelical religion, aristocracy and the new
moral order in the early nineteenth century' in Crawford Gribben and Andrew
Holmes (eds), *Protestant millennialism, evangelicalism and Irish society, 1790–2005*
(Basingstoke, 2006), p. 52.

[27] Ibid., p. 65.

[28] During the first decades of the nineteenth century Catholic children attended
Sunday schools in large numbers. Occasionally Catholics priests applied for
funds from the Sunday School Society to establish their own schools. See Irene
Whelan, *The bible war in Ireland: the Second Reformation and the polarization of
Protestant–Catholic relations, 1800–1840* (Dublin, 2005), p. 109.

The catechetical efforts of the Christian Doctrine confraternity were complemented by the activities of other lay societies involved in catechesis and those concerned with effecting change by eliminating so-called societal vices. For example, indulgences for membership of the Purgatorial Society of SS Michael and John's parish stated that it was founded 'to promote the pious dispositions of the faithful of this city, and to render them more charitable to the poor sick, and more zealous to relieve, by their suffrages, the souls in purgatory'.[29] The exact date of its foundation is unknown, but it certainly existed before 1778, when a chapter was recorded in the Franciscan church of Adam and Eve's.[30] Initially the primary function of the society was to visit the sick, preparing them for the last rites and generally providing spiritual comfort. In the *Irish Catholic Directory 1821* the aims of the society were stated as

> to suffragette the suffering souls in purgatory, [and] are instituted in several chapels, in this metropolis. The pious members recite on stated evenings the office of the dead, attend and give spiritual relief to dying persons, and after the decease fulfil the duty of offering up a solemn office for the happy repose before the corpse is brought to burial.[31]

However, by the 1820s the Purgatorial Society had changed significantly, becoming a much more structured and professional organisation. It enjoyed the approval of Archbishop Troy, who passed on indulgences to the society's members. Members' obligations, however, went beyond simply attending to the sick. A printed copy of the indulgences granted to the society in 1820 stated that they assembled

> in church on the first Monday of each month, in the morning, to assist at the most august sacrifice of the mass, offered for the souls in purgatory, and approach the holy communion, for the same intention; and in the evening of said day, recite in choir, the

---

[29] Indulgences granted to the Purgatorial Society of SS Michael and John's parish, Apr.–June 1820 (DDA, Troy papers, AB3/30/5(28)). This branch of the society was founded in 1820.

[30] The Franciscan Library, Killiney contains a list of the Society's subscribers in 1778 (Franciscan Library, Killiney, C86) [hereafter FLK].

[31] Cunningham, 'The Irish Catholic Directory 1821', p. 359.

office of the dead, for the same purpose. Fittingly, for the greater comfort of those suffering souls, they assist at the solemn office and high mass for the dead, which are celebrated on appointed days in the beginning of the four seasons of the year.[32]

The Purgatorial Society appears to have demanded a great deal more of its members than many other confraternities, some of which met only once a month. However, succour for members came in a number of ways. In 1778 the society's rules had stated 'that, when it shall please God, to call any of said subscribers out of this life, a solemn office with high mass and all the masses of the day, shall be offered for the eternal rest of such subscriber and benefactor'.[33] Thus spiritual assistance and petitioning was assured for the deceased member. This succour, or spiritual fraternity, was a means of achieving the objective of 'collective redemption' proposed by the reformers of the seventeenth century.[34]

In some parishes, lending libraries were established. 'The Society of St John the Evangelist, for promoting the exercise of spiritual and corporal works of mercy, is in North King-street, and has a good library in connection with it.'[35] Myles Ronan suggested that this so-called professionalisation was largely due to the efforts of Dr Michael Blake, parish priest of SS Michael and John's and future bishop of Dromore. He suggested that through Blake's activities the society in SS Michael and John's 'became the parent and the great exemplar of many of those societies' that followed.[36] The society by 1830 had been placed under the patronage of St John the Evangelist. *The Irish Catholic Directory 1821* declared that all chapels in Dublin, both secular and regular, had a chapter.[37] It had expanded from its original establishment in Adam and Eve's when in 1817 a branch had been founded in the parish of SS Michael and John's. Here the society was

---

[32] Ibid.

[33] Dublin Friary Purgatorial Society, list of subscribers, 1778 (FLK, C86).

[34] Po-Chia Hsia, *The world of Catholic renewal*, p. 202.

[35] Samuel Lewis, *Lewis' Dublin: a topographical dictionary of the parishes, towns and villages of Dublin city and county*, ed. Christopher Ryan (Cork, 2001 edition), p. 146.

[36] Ronan, *An apostle of Catholic Dublin*, p. 138.

[37] Here there is a little uncertainty as to when the Purgatorial Society was formally absorbed into the Society of St John the Evangelist.

supported by contributions and subscriptions received at the
vestry-door on Sundays. It is governed by a select committee,
who appoint proper members to administer spiritual comfort
to dying persons by prayer, pious reading, and by giving pecu-
niary relief, if necessary.[38]

This new society was established in 'order to promote the pious
dispositions of the faithful of this city, and to render them
more charitable to the poor sick, and more zealous to relieve,
by their suffrages, the souls in purgatory'.[39] In 1821 another
branch was 'lately established in Dun Leary where forty pious
members meet three times a week to say the office of the dead,
and assemble every evening to recite the rosary and other
devotions' while another branch had been erected in St
Michan's soon after.[40] In the same year a pamphlet was
published outlining the role of the society.[41] Thus, the society
emerged as part of a radical process of social reformation.

This desire to reform public morality was common to many,
if not all, confraternities. One of the areas which the Purgatorial
Society hoped to reform was burials and wakes. The allegedly
'unchristian' activities at wakes and burials had been a source
of concern for reform-minded clergy and laity for some time.
Wakes were conducted without clerical supervision, and were
frequently characterised by acts of drunkenness and violence. The
growing opposition of some clergy has been well-documented.
Seán Connolly commented that 'clerical opposition to the festive
wake, in both the eighteenth and nineteenth centuries, was
caused principally by the disorderly conduct for which these
gatherings provided the occasion', namely drinking, dancing
and sexual licence.[42] Archbishops and senior clergy singled
wakes out as a source of considerable immorality as early as
1730, the diocesan statutes declaring that the clergy should

38 Cunningham, 'The Irish Catholic Directory 1821', p. 359.

39 Indulgences granted to the Purgatorial Society, SS Michael and John's,
Apr.–Jun. 1820 (DDA, Troy papers, AB3/30/5(28)).

40 Cunningham, 'The Irish Catholic Directory 1821', p. 359.

41 The society appears to have existed under various names in this period.

42 Seán Connolly, *Priests and people in pre-famine Ireland, 1780–1845* (2nd ed., Dublin,
2001), p. 162.

make efforts to prevent abuses at wakes by imposing public penances on anyone who engaged in lewd games on such occasions.[43] Instead drinking and dancing at wakes were to be replaced by prayer and sobriety, a transformation which was to be overseen by the society's members. The rules for the society state that

> Every member of this confraternity must be ready and willing to read at the office of the dead at wakes, in order if possible to abolish these unchristian and diabolical practices which are alas! but too common at wakes; and are disgraceful and insulting to our holy religion ... The nine members shall attend accordingly at the house of the deceased, for such time as may be allotted to them, and there read the office of the dead, and some pages from a chapter of a religious book.[44]

The society viewed itself as an indispensable weapon in the endeavours to eradicate what they considered 'lurid events', contrary to the renewed sense of morality prevalent amongst the reforming clergy and many conservatively-minded lay Catholics.

Unlike some groups which had a purely devotional nature, the mission of the aforementioned confraternities combined an apostolic focus with personal sanctification as well as moral supervision. While members of other confraternities were asked to live their lives with a renewed Christian charism, membership of confraternities such as St John the Evangelist and the Christian Doctrine required specific public acts of evangelisation and moral supervision. Members were to be of good standing in society, setting a good example to those in need of 'reformation'. Those who held positions of authority within the society were aware that members' standing was essential to the credibility of their undertaking. Those who did not adhere to the rules or brought the society into disrepute faced penalties. The rules of the Society of St John the Evangelist stated that 'Any member that neglects his duty in this point shall receive a public reprimand in presence of the choir in the next office day. He shall pay a fine of five pence for such neglect

---

[43] Ibid., p. 161.
[44] 'Rules for the Society of St Patrick' cited in Ronan, *An apostle of Catholic Dublin*, p. 141.

unless he can give a very satisfactory apology for his absence'.[45] Members were also forbidden from

> sitting down in a public house in the parish, on a Sunday or pay-day, without leave of the president, under the penalty of 10d., and if any be seen drunk, he must pay 2s. 6d. for the first offence, and 5s. for the second, if he be drunk the third time, he shall be expelled from the society, and his name erased from the books.[46]

Sobriety and a good moral standing were the kernel of the society, and transgressions were to be dealt with seriously. By the time Catholic Emancipation was granted the society's primary focus appears to have shifted somewhat. Initially its goal was to assist and pray with the sick and dying. However, by 1830 this had been abandoned for a form of social reform or control. The society's evolving character reflected an overall change in emphasis in the Catholic community in Dublin in this period: the poor, and more importantly, their behaviour, had now become a major concern.

While the interests of confraternities such as the Christian Doctrine or the Most Holy Name of Jesus were catechetical or moralistic there were a growing number of confraternities established in Dublin which had a distinctly more 'devotional' flavour, groups which sought to foster private devotion and piety through communal fellowship and spiritual reading programmes. Of these groups one of the best known was the sodality of the Sacred Heart of Jesus. Devotion to the Sacred Heart had existed since the seventeenth century, after visionaries began reporting that Jesus had appeared to them, displaying his heart as a source of grace and love.[47] Devotion, however, increased dramatically in the wake of reported visions by Marguerite-Marie Alacoque in France in the 1680s.[48] The Jesuits subsequently assumed much of the responsibility for the promotion of the Sacred Heart as a symbol of divine love for humanity. Evidence suggests that an organised form of

---

[45] Ibid.

[46] Ibid., p. 143.

[47] Raymond Jones, *France and the cult of the Sacred Heart* (London, 2000), p. 2.

[48] Ibid.

devotion had begun to develop from the 1740s in Dublin. In 1756 a pamphlet entitled *A devotion for the pious and devout confraternity of the Sacred Heart of Jesus* (Dublin, 1756) was printed for the executors of the late widow Kelly in St Mary's Lane.[49] *Émigré* clergy played an important role in the propagation of its devotion. In 1766 James Connell, a novice in the Jesuit house at Monte Cavallo, Rome, wrote to his father, William Connell, a printer in Dublin, in the hope of encouraging devotion. Connell wished that his father would 'introduce into the family the devotion to the Sacred Heart of Jesus'.[50] Doing so, he said, would bring 'infinite blessing which it will bring down on you & yrs if it be practised with due care and diligence; this devotion has been confirmed by many miracles, one of which happened here in this house where I am at present'.[51] By the 1790s devotion was becoming much more organised, and in 1797 a formal confraternity was eventually established.[52] In 1809 a branch was formed in the recently established Presentation convent, George's Hill in Dublin by the Parisian educated Jesuit, James Philip Mulcaile.[53] Members were asked to make 'the holy hour on one day each year', which is said to have been the first example of this practice in Ireland.[54] In 1809 the sodality had eighty-two members, the majority of whom were women.[55] By 1816 membership had risen to 385.[56] Convents and schools proved to be indispensable tools in the promotion of religious devotion. For example, in December 1815 Archbishop Murray informed

---

[49] Hugh Fenning, O.P., 'Dublin imprints of Catholic interest: 1740–1759' in *Collectanea Hibernica*, no. 41 (1999), p. 108. The widow Kelly had been married to the well-known Dublin printer, Ignatius Kelly of the Stationer's Arms in St Mary's Lane.

[50] James Connell, Jesuit novitiate of St Andrew, Monte Cavallo, Rome, to William Connell, Sign of the White Cross, Cornmarket, Dublin, 25 Jan. 1766 (Presentation Archives, George's Hill, Dublin, A1).

[51] Ibid.

[52] Roland Burke-Savage, S.J., 'Growth of devotion to the Sacred Heart in Ireland' in *Irish Ecclesiastical Record*, cx (July–Dec.1968), p. 197.

[53] Ibid.

[54] 'Rules for the confraternity of Sacred Heart, George's Hill' cited in Roland Burke-Savage, S.J., *A valiant Dublin woman: the story of George's Hill, 1766–1940* (Dublin, 1940), p. 228.

[55] Ronan, *An apostle of Catholic Dublin*, p. 126.

[56] Burke-Savage, 'Growth of devotion to the Sacred Heart in Ireland', p. 199.

the founder of the Religious Sisters of Charity, Mary Aikenhead, that he had obtained 'the privilege of celebrating in your chapel the feast of the Sacred Heart, with its proper mass'.[57] On the feast of the Sacred Heart the following year he preached that

> It was a singular comfort to the little community to find that our congregation was to have the happy privilege of being selected by our Divine Lord to introduce into Ireland the devotion to his Sacred Heart, and it was hailed as a presage that he would in his infinite condescension, allow its members to spread themselves for the promotion of the interests of that loving heart, in labouring for the salvation of souls, and for the consolation of its special favourites, the poor.[58]

Archbishop Murray's involvement in the development of devotion to the Sacred Heart in the 1810s and 1820s suggests that he recognised the importance of the confraternity acting as a means of 'labouring for the salvation of souls'.

While the sodality of the Sacred Heart flourished nationally, with its popularity lasting throughout much of the twentieth century, most groups were much smaller, and were often attached to a particular church or associated with a specific religious order. One such group was the Bona Mors. As was the case with the Sacred Heart, the Bona Mors had been traditionally promoted by the Jesuits. It had been established in Rome in the mid-seventeenth century by the Jesuit, Vincent Caraffa. The principal goal of the Bona Mors, or the 'good death' as it literally meant, was to prepare its members for a peaceful death by living a well-regulated and holy life. The confraternity was active in Dublin in 1793 when *Bona Mors: or the art of dying happily in the congregation of Jesus Christ crucified, and of his condoning mother* (Dublin, 1793) was published by the Dublin printer, Patrick Wogan.[59] Confraternities were by this stage using Dublin's burgeoning Catholic print trade to promote their own

---

[57] Bishop Murray to Mother Mary Aikenhead, 6 Dec. 1815 (DDA, Troy/Murray papers, AB3/30/2(65)).

[58] Sermon preached by Archbishop Murray on the feast of the Sacred Heart, 20 June 1816 (DDA, Troy papers, AB3/30/2(65)).

[59] See Thomas Wall, *The sign of Doctor Hay's head* (Dublin, 1958) for further reading on Wogan and other Catholic printers in Dublin.

activities in the hope of attracting new members. The 1793 edition contains information as to how prospective candidates might become members. It told those interested that they should give their 'names to the father of the Society of Jesus, who keeps the book of the confraternity: This done they shall offer to Christ our Lord, kneeling before a crucifix, the best affections and resolutions their understandings and hearts can suggest'.[60] If their application was successful the member was to attend confession and receive communion, therefore obtaining a plenary indulgence. Membership entailed a relatively simple form of private and public devotion. Members were required to recite the Our Father three times daily, as well as three Hail Marys, 'in memory of the three hours our Blessed Saviour hung upon the cross'.[61] More importantly, they were obliged to receive the sacraments of penance and eucharist monthly as well attend a monthly assembly.[62] For those members who were 'lawfully hindered attending the solemn devotion' they were 'to recite the prayers at home appointed for publick meetings'.[63]

The Bona Mors appears to have been characteristic of many of the devotional confraternities in the period. While the Society of St John the Evangelist and the Purgatorial Society demanded much from their members, with attendance at regular meetings and devotions obligatory, the more 'devotional' confraternities were somewhat less demanding of their members' time. They usually met only once a month, in many cases in the afternoon of the third Sunday of the month. Most meetings appear to have consisted of devotions and sermon followed by a procession and benediction of the blessed sacrament. Others met on a more regular basis and demanded a greater dedication and devotion. The Holy Family confraternity met once a week for prayers and members were required to receive confession and communion once a month.[64] The confraternity of the Sacred Rosaries of Jesus and the Blessed Virgin gathered in Denmark Street chapel,

---

[60] *Bona Mors: or the art of dying happily*, pp 3–4.

[61] Ibid., p. 5.

[62] Ibid, pp 6–7.

[63] Ibid.

[64] Desmond Keenan, *The Catholic church in nineteenth-century Ireland: a sociological study* (Dublin, 1983), p. 138.

presumably under the supervision of the Dominicans. They assembled on the first and third Sundays of each month, where they recited the rosary to the Blessed Virgin on the first Sunday, and the rosary to Jesus on the third Sunday.[65] As well as this there was a procession of the Blessed Sacrament. Similarly, the confraternity of the Sacred Scapular of Our Blessed Lady of Mount Carmel assembled in the Carmelite chapels in Clarendon Street and French Street on the third Sunday of every month for benediction, and sometimes a procession.[66] This presumably would have been followed by a sermon or exhortation of some sort. Another devotional group was the Evening Office Society, founded by the aforementioned Dr Blake in SS Michael and John's in 1815. This society appears to have been a good deal more active, meeting every evening to recite the evening office and vespers on Sundays.[67] Indeed the zeal and commitment of its members was such that they gathered at 3 a.m. on Easter morning to recite the office of the Blessed Virgin Mary and at 2 a.m. on Christmas morning for the same purpose.[68] For the most part, many of the devotional confraternities may have been more interested in promoting personal piety rather than communal devotion. The expanding Catholic print trade no doubt aided the promotion of private piety through its publication of devotional literature.

The efforts of the Jesuits in promoting confraternities were replicated by other religious orders in Dublin, with all establishing third orders and confraternities to cater for lay Catholics. In effect third orders offered lay people the opportunity to become 'associate members'. Members attended regular meetings and received a modified version of the habit of the particular order. However, there was a wide choice of confraternities from which Catholics could choose. While the Dominicans promoted the confraternities of the Holy Name and the Rosary, the Franciscans supervised the confraternity of the Sacred Cord of

---

[65] Cunningham, 'The Irish Catholic Directory 1821', p. 359.

[66] Ibid.

[67] Ronan, *An apostle of Catholic Dublin*, p. 160. The evening office had been regularly recited in the parish since the 1780s when Dr Betagh used to gather some of the boys from the evening school together to recite vespers.

[68] Keenan, *The Catholic church in nineteenth-century Ireland*, p. 160.

St Francis and the Purgatorial Society. The favourite Carmelite devotion was to the Sacred Scapular of the Blessed Lady of Mount Carmel, while the Augustinians favoured the Sacred Cincture of the Blessed Virgin of Consolation. Evidence suggests that confraternities were very much an urban phenomenon in the archdiocese for much of the eighteenth century, and it was not until the development of the confraternity of Christian Doctrine from the 1780s onwards that they spread to rural areas.

****

Establishing confraternities was desirable to reform-minded Catholics for a number of reasons. Their purpose was summarised perfectly in a pamphlet promoting the Society of St Patrick in 1821:

> Religious confraternities – conducive to the salvation of every member – afford a holy union and society of pious brethren-aid and assist the clergyman in the discharge of his duties by instructing the ignorant, reclaiming the sinner, affording comfort to the sick and distressed, and by relieving the suffering souls in purgatory.[69]

Confraternities played a very practical role in providing pastoral care. The confraternity of Christian Doctrine taught children the basic tenets of their faith in a systematic manner, something which the Catholic church previously had great difficulty in doing. In the eighteenth and early nineteenth centuries it did not possess an extensive educational system. Many of the religious orders were in their infancy and their pastoral and educational outreach was limited. Thus, religious education in the Sunday school format was the most viable option. Confraternities vested responsibility in the hands of 'respectable', reasonably well-educated, Catholics, something which senior clergy desired. However, it might be noted that at this time there was no shortage of clergy in Dublin, particularly

---

[69] *The Society of St Patrick* (Dublin, 1821) cited in Ronan, *An apostle of Catholic Dublin*, p. 140.

in the city, a fact which contradicts the theory that lay catechists were used only because of insufficient clerical numbers.[70] It is more probable that leading clergy and laity realised the expediency of harnessing the support of increasing numbers of Catholic lay men and women. An active Catholic middle class was beginning to play an increasingly prominent role in the promotion of new pastoral initiatives, especially in the establishment and maintenance of indigenous religious orders. As the Catholic church in Ireland was not beneficed it relied almost entirely on the support of the laity to finance its mission. Consequently it had to create a system that could foster financial support, a system in which confraternities and sodalities were a central part. Confraternities exerted considerable influence in addressing vices which were of concern to these religiously engaged Catholics. The Society of St Patrick set out to tackle a problem which was one of the gravest concerns for reforming clergy: wakes. However, progress was slow and success did not come overnight. Nonetheless this gradual progression was sufficient for the period in question as it afforded the Catholic community an opportunity to lay the basic foundations for the more extensive process of evangelisation that would take place in the post-famine era.

A central component of this process was confraternities. Archbishop Troy was obviously aware of the benefits confraternities afforded his programme of pastoral reform. In a letter to Sir Henry Parnell, M.P., he bemoaned the pitiful situation in Rathdrum, a large rural parish in the Wicklow part of the archdiocese. Troy suggested that the parish was 'totally destitute of any moral or religious instruction as far as the Catholics are concerned'.[71] This moral destitution, he argued, was in part due

---

[70] Most city parishes had a minimum of five resident clergy by the 1820s. This figure would not have significantly differed, if it all, in the late eighteenth century. See Dáire Keogh, *The French disease* (Dublin, 1993) for evidence of clerical figures in 1798. Seán Connolly commented that 'the confraternity of Christian Doctrine helped to provide badly needed lay auxiliaries to assist in the provision of regular catechetical instruction.' This may be accurate for rural parishes but it should not have been the case for Dublin city parishes, which possessed sufficient numbers of priests to cater for catechetical demand. See Seán Connolly, *Religion and society in nineteenth-century Ireland* (Dublin, 1994), p. 55.

[71] Archbishop Troy to Sir Henry Parnell, M.P., 1816 (DDA, Troy papers, AB3/30/3(8)).

to the low priest–parishioner ratio but more interestingly as a result of a lack of confraternities to cater for lay Catholics. This was, however, in contrast to the situation in Dublin city, where the climate was more favourable to reform. He suggested that

> No parish can therefore be without some degree of moral & religious instruction; of which there is no want in the capital & other cities where there are many charitable institutions for the religious & moral education of the Catholic orphans & other children of both sexes.[72]

This 'moral & religious instruction' was provided largely by lay men and women working as catechists. These men and women acted not only as teachers but also as mediums of social change, continuing their mission of evangelisation in their everyday lives. Many of them aspired to new models of 'respectability' and as a result were more receptive to increased social conservatism,[73] which so often was characteristic of the social and religious outlook of these groups. Central to the programme of catechesis and reform were religious confraternities and sodalities. They acted as autonomously-run pastoral societies organised by secular and regular clergy, but were not usually governed by a central body. They were typically directed by a committee, made up of respected lay Catholics, under the spiritual guidance of a priest. Confraternities were funded exclusively by membership subscriptions, which were payable monthly, but were sometimes augmented by church collections. In this way many Catholics assumed a very visible role in their community, one which required not only attendance but also a financial commitment. Confraternities were also one of the media which promoted acts of popular religious devotions. Amongst others these included novenas, the stations of the cross, benediction and various other devotions. Historians had tended to locate their expansion in Ireland in the post-famine period. More recent investigations have relocated the development of the phenomenom to the later decades of the eighteenth century. In Dublin confraternities and parishes were

---

[72] Ibid.

[73] Connolly, *Religion and society in nineteenth-century Ireland*, p. 55.

active in promoting popular religious devotion as early as the 1740s, and by the 1780s the 'devotional revolution' was truly under way in the archdiocese.[74]

---

[74] Hugh Fenning, O.P., (ed.), 'The 'Udienze' series in the Roman archives, 1750–1820' in *Archiv. Hib.*, xlix (1995), p. 106.

3

Evangelising the faithful: Edmund Rice and the reformation of nineteenth-century Irish Catholicism

Dáire Keogh

There is a tendency amongst religious congregations to 'remake' their founders in ways that satisfy the values of the age. This reflects the double dynamic at the heart of the canonisation process. It is not sufficient merely to display 'heroic virtue' in one's own lifetime, but the actions of the candidate must satisfy the expectations of the generation which declares them a saint.[1] This paradox is most apparent in the life of Edmund Rice (1762–1844), founder of the Presentation and Christian Brothers, who has been represented variously as the consecrated religious, friend of the poor, married father, ethical businessman and devotee of Celtic spirituality. The challenge is to rescue Rice from the layers of hagiography, and to see him as he saw himself and was perceived by his peers. The result is a portrait of a second Ignatius, a founder in the mould of the Catholic Reformation whose priority was the essential business of salvation.

Amongst the foundation myths of the Irish Christian Brothers none has proved as enduring as the notion that Edmund Rice founded his congregation in Waterford to educate boys for whom no one cared. Yet an examination of the evidence suggests, on the contrary, that Waterford, with a population of 30,000, was well served for schools. An extrapolation of the 1841 census returns indicates that it was the third most literate city in Ireland, behind Dublin and Belfast.[2] Indeed, not only were

---

[1] See Peter Burke, 'How to become a Counter-Reformation Saint' in D. M. Luebke (ed.), *The Counter Reformation* (Oxford, 1999), pp 129–42.
[2] John E. Kent, 'The educational ideals of Edmund Rice, founder of the Presentation and Christian Brothers' (M.Ed. thesis, UCC, 1988), p. 56.

males well provided for educationally, but the foundation of Edmund Rice's great school at Mount Sion, in 1802, made no tangible difference to the educational attainment of the city's males. The implication of this analysis suggests that Rice's schools were not established within an educational vacuum, but sought rather to offer an alternative to the learning available in the city. This established a pattern, and the later expansion of Edmund Rice's congregation reflected the desire of local communities to establish parish schools in place of those which were indifferent, if not hostile, to the principles of Catholic education.[3]

The inspiration for this process is reflected in the immediate impetus for Rice's decision to establish his brotherhood, the publication of a pastoral by Bishop Thomas Hussey of Waterford in 1797.[4] The address is best remembered for the controversy it inflamed amongst loyalists by its tactless references to the penal laws, its description of the Church of Ireland as 'a small sect limited to the country of its origin', and its spirited defence of Catholicism as 'the religion of Irishmen'. Reaction to this provocation preoccupied contemporary commentators, but the core of the address focused upon the education question which had occupied Hussey since his appointment to the diocese in December 1796. The bishop's concern was not the shortage of schooling, but that in the absence of free or affordable Catholic education, parents were sending their children to free Protestant schools, which he believed were engaged in proselytism. He shared these concerns with Edmund Burke, informing his political mentor that in the free schools 'the clergy of the establishment wanted to have no catechism taught but the Protestant one, and seemed inclined to assimilate them into the charter schools'. Hussey noted that his anxiety was shared by the Quakers, whom he described as 'the most regular and industrious sect' in the city.[5]

---

[3] See Dáire Keogh, *Edmund Rice and the first Christian Brothers* (Dublin, 2008), pp 137–63.

[4] Thomas Hussey, *A pastoral letter to the Catholics of the united dioceses of Waterford and Lismore* (Waterford, 1797).

[5] Thomas Hussey to Edmund Burke, 9 May 1797: Earl Fitzwilliam (ed.), *The correspondence of Edmund Burke*, iv, (London, 1844), pp 444–6.

The bishop revisited this theme in his controversial pastoral address, in which he urged his priests to remonstrate with parents who were so negligible to send their children to such schools where their 'religion, faith and morals were likely to be corrupted'. If parents failed to respond, they were to be denounced from the altars and ultimately refused the sacraments. It was not enough, however, to condemn proselytising schools if there was no alternative. Towards that end, the bishop had embarked on an ambitious plan to provide an effective network of parish schools in Waterford. Within two months of his arrival he boasted that he had established a charity school in the principal towns of his diocese.[6] Hussey's intervention was welcomed by the widower, Edmund Rice, who added education to the list of charities he supported within the city. In 1799 he joined a committee established by the dean of the diocese to procure 'schoolhouses for the poor children of both sexes', but at a more profound level, Hussey's initiative prompted his choice of vocation, as a teaching brother within his newly established order.[7] Indeed, this was referred to in Rice's panegyric, when his confessor acknowledged the influence of the 'enlightened and apostolic bishop ... [who had] vindicated the cause of free religious education'.[8] A century later, his biographer spoke of 'the natural kinship between the minds and characters of these two men' which 'helped considerably in bringing to fruition the divinely inspired purpose of Edmund Rice'.[9]

The second great influence upon Edmund Rice's vocation choice was Nano Nagle (1718–84), foundress of the Presentation Sisters. Her fledgling congregation provided a model of apostolic religious life which allowed him combine his religious vocation with a desire for service. Yet apart from the institutional debt, Rice shared her desire to effect a moral reformation in the children he taught, a priority which is lost in the simplistic view that they sought simply to educate the poor. Nagle's

6 Hussey, *A pastoral letter to the Catholics of the united dioceses of Waterford and Lismore*.

7 Thomas Hearn to Thomas Hussey, Sept. 1799, Waterford Diocesan Archive.

8 F. R. Fitzgerald, 1 Oct. 1844, cited in John Shelly, *Edmund Ignatius Rice and the Christian Brothers* (Kilkenny, 1863), p. 42.

9 J. D. Fitzpatrick, *Edmund Rice* (Dublin, 1945), p. 85.

panegyric set this ambition in stark relief when it described the horror she experienced on her return from France in 1746. She was struck, not only by the poverty of the people of the Blackwater Valley, but by their ignorance of religion and their gradual decline into superstition and vice:

> she was afflicted to perceive that these poor creatures were almost strangers ... [to the business of salvation, our duty to God, and the great mysteries of religion]. Under a misconception of their obligations, they substituted error in the place of truth: while they kept up an attachment to certain exterior observances, their fervour was superstitious, their faith was erroneous, their hope was presumptuous, and they had no charity. Licentiousness, while it could bless itself, and tell the beads, could live without remorse, and die without repentance; sacraments and sacrileges went hand in hand, and conscience was at rest upon its own stings.[10]

It was this, 'the ignorance of the lower classes ... their consequent immorality, and the ruin of their souls', which prompted her to establish her first free schools in Cork, and led ultimately to the foundation of the Presentation Sisters in 1775.[11]

Nagle's first biographer, Bishop William Coppinger, interpreted her reaction in terms which echoed the anxiety of his contemporary reformers at the alienation of the lower classes from the institutional church and their more general preoccupation with the task of moral reformation. In the absence of effective schooling, reforming bishops had promoted confraternities since the 1770s, particularly the Confraternity of the Christian Doctrine, in an effort to effect this reformation in the Irish church. In doing so, they reflected the confidence of their European contemporaries in the 'ideology of the schools', which argued that only in childhood instruction could vice be destroyed and virtue established.[12] 'All other public charities are eminently contained in this one', Bishop Coppinger argued:

---

10 William Coppinger, *The life of Miss Nano Nagle, as sketched ... in a funeral sermon preached in Cork on the anniversary of her death* (Cork, 1794), p. 8.

11 Ibid, p. 7.

12 Elizabeth Raply, *The dévotes: women and church in seventeenth-century France* (Montreal, 1990), p. 119.

for as an early Christian education will make men honest, sober, temperate, and regular, it will in a great degree make jails, loans, hospitals, and poor-houses unnecessary.[13]

Nano Nagle, Thomas Hussey and Edmund Rice's 'founding circle' shared this faith in the reforming power of education, the necessity of which was highlighted by threats posed by both the explosion of the population, and the influence of contemporary philosophies of 'a novel and dangerous tendency'.[14]

In continental Europe, too, the early modern period had witnessed the emergence of a distinctly Catholic pedagogy which reflected the Jesuit dictum that 'the well being of christianity and of the whole world depends on the proper education of youth'.[15] In contrast to the spirit of the Protestant Reformation, which emphasised the relationship of the individual with God, it rooted man within an ecclesial context and was directed towards his moral formation and the salvation of his soul. These were the sentiments of Nano Nagle and they were the values which Edmund Rice brought to his fledgling congregation. They were clearly articulated in his correspondence, while both his Rule and teaching *Manual* were unambiguous in their definition of the intention for which the Brothers had come together. In the first instance, it was to sanctify their own souls, but also 'to be instrumental in the salvation of the children for whom Jesus Christ died'.[16]

Rice's ultimate ambition, therefore, was not simply education or the material improvement of his scholars, but rather his desire to see them 'godly'.[17] The two were not mutually exclusive, but in John Charles McQuaid's expression, he worked and suffered to form the image of Jesus Christ on the heart of every

---

[13] Coppinger, *Life of Miss Nano Nagle*, p. 7.

[14] Thomas Hussey, *Pastoral letter*, p. 3.

[15] Pedro de Ribadeneira to Philip II, 14 Feb. 1556, cited in J. W. O'Malley, *The first Jesuits* (Harvard, 1993), p. 209.

[16] F. R. Hickey (ed.), 'The Presentation Rule' in *Christian Brothers Education Record* (1981), p. 161; [M. P. Riordan, T. J. Hearn, J. B. Duggan], *A manual of school government; being a complete analysis of the system of education pursued in the Christian schools. Designed chiefly for the junior members of the Society* (Dublin, 1845), p. 7.

[17] Stephen Curtis, *Waterford Freeman*, 10 Sept. 1845.

boy he encountered.[18] In this sense, the Brothers' mission was essentially one of evangelisation. These priorities were enshrined in the opening chapter of Rice's adaptation of the Presentation Rule, which identified the ends of the institute as 'the instruction of poor boys in the principles of religion and Christian piety'.[19] This evangelical imperative has been ignored by modern commentators, who are inclined to emphasise Rice's humanitarian endeavours, in a post-Conciliar age where the 'business of salvation' has assumed a reduced significance. Rice's priority was equally masked in the traditional historiography which exaggerated the conformity of late eighteenth-century Catholics to the institutional church. However, contrary to the popular notion that Catholicism embraced the Irish of all classes, the poor were often alienated from the institutional church, and practice rates were poor, particularly in the west and north of the country where they were as low as 40 per cent.[20]

Rice's Presentation Rule was inspired by the spirituality of the Catholic Reformation and that same spirit defined the character of the Brothers' schools. At its simplest, the school routine which Edmund Rice had developed by 1810 was an attempt to adapt European Catholic pedagogy to the particular needs of the Irish church. And just as the secular instruction in his schools sought to foster internalised self-discipline, so too, the catechesis was directed towards the formation of a religious disposition and commitment to the Catholic way of life. As John Reynolds, lord mayor of Dublin (1850–52), observed, Rice's maxim, was 'instruct the young in the way they should walk, and … they will not depart from it'.[21]

Each school day began with an elaborate morning offering, which reflected not just the Brothers' Ignatian spirituality, but their desire 'to teach the children to offer themselves up to God from the first use of reason':

---

[18] John Charles McQuaid, Foreword, Fitzpatrick, *Edmund Rice*, p. xii.

[19] Hickey (ed.), 'Presentation Rule', p. 161.

[20] D. W. Miller, 'Mass attendance in 1834' in S. J. Brown and D. W. Miller (eds), *Piety and power in Ireland: essays in honour of Emmet Larkin* (Notre Dame, 2000), pp 158–79.

[21] John Reynolds, *Tablet*, 21 Sept. 1850.

Most Merciful Creator! I offer myself to thee this day, with all my thoughts, words and actions, in union with the merits of my Lord and Saviour Jesus Christ. I firmly resolve, by the assistance of thy grace, to avoid sin above all things this day, especially those sins which I am most in the habit of committing. I humbly ask, through the sacred passion and death of my Divine Redeemer, and through the intercession of his immaculate Virgin Mother, for strength to fulfil this resolution. Receive, O Lord, all my liberty, my memory, my understanding, and my whole will; – thou hast given me all that I have, and all that I am, and I return all to thy divine will, that thou dispose of me. Give me only thy love and thy grace; with these I shall be rich enough, and shall have no more to ask. Our Father, Hail Mary, Creed, Glory be to the Father, &c. *Amen.*[22]

There were set times for prayer throughout the day: at noon the students recited the Angelus, and acts of faith, hope and charity; at three the Salve Regina and the litany of the Blessed Virgin were said, while the entire day was punctuated with the recitation of the Hail Mary on the strike of every hour, in keeping with the tradition of the continental orders.

In Rice's timetable, a half-hour was set aside each day for formal catechesis. This he believed was 'the most salutary part of the system'. It was, he argued, 'the most laborious to teachers; however, if it were ten times what it is … we are amply paid in seeing such a Reformation in the children'.[23] During this period, Brothers taught Christian Doctrine, usually from Butler's catechism but, just as in the secular subjects, this was adapted to the ability of the children and was usually memorised.[24] Moreover, the 'question and answer' style of the catechism was considered most appropriate since it actively engaged the children:

It cannot be too often reiterated, that the manner of catechising should be simple and conversational; that the children should be made to speak as much as possible; and, that, anything like a consecutive discourse should studiously be avoided.[25]

---

[22] Hickey (ed.), 'Presentation Rule', p. 162; *Manual*, p. 17.

[23] Edmund Rice to Thomas Bray, 9 May 1810 (Cashel Diocesan Archive, Bray Papers).

[24] Hickey (ed.), 'Presentation Rule', p. 164.

[25] William L. Gillespie, *The Christian Brothers in England 1825–80* (Bristol, 1975), p. 35; *Manual*, pp 146–69.

Yet while this lesson was isolated for formal instruction, the entire day was run through with a Catholic ethos. Indeed Rice's concern for the whole man gave the system its 'mixed character', where religion and the secular subjects were integrated, and taught side-by-side, in contrast to the 'separate' instruction of the technically non-denominational national schools which the other religious orders had joined. The Brothers' rejection of the state system cost them dearly in terms of finance and episcopal support, but in time, Rice's model was championed by Cardinal Cullen who opposed non-denominational education as 'dangerous to the Catholic faith and well calculated to sow the seeds of indifferentism' in youth.[26]

Even the singing, introduced to the schools as a refining influence, was directed towards the moral formation of the boys. It would, in Br Joseph Hearn's view, 'effect the disposition of the children', a sentiment which echoed those of the English educationalist and moral reformer, Mary Carpenter (1807–77), who observed that 'music may be made an important auxiliary in tranquilising and subduing the wild spirits we have to deal with'.[27] It would also serve to make school more enjoyable, contribute to the beauty of parish liturgies and provide an alternative to the popular ballads which offended bourgeois sensitivities. The reading material, too, was carefully selected. Rather than using the chapbooks which were used in many of the Catholic pay-schools, Rice relied on Irish adaptations of European classics, including Fr William Gahan's *History of the Old and New Testament*, which was an abridged version of Joseph Reeve's translation of *Le bible de Royaumont* (1670). He also used Charles Gobinet's *Instruction of youth in christian piety*, first published in Paris in 1665. These texts, however, became less important following the publication of the Brothers' own readers, beginning in 1839.

---

[26] Paul Cullen on the proposed model school at Drogheda, 17 Aug. 1851, *Catholic Directory* (1852), p. 166; see Joseph Doyle, 'Cardinal Cullen, the Powis Commission and Catholic education' in Dáire Keogh and Albert McDonnell (eds), *Paul Cullen and his world* (Dublin, 2010).

[27] Br Joseph Hearn to Br Austin Horan, 12 Mar. 1858 (Christian Brothers General Archive, Rome, 005/42) [hereafter CBGA]; [Mary Carpenter], *Ragged schools; their principles and mode of operation* (London, 1850), pp 47–50, cited in Mary Hilton, *Women and the shaping of the nation's young; education and public doctrine in Britain, 1750–1850* (London, 2007), p. 190.

A further novelty of their schools was the existence of a lending library in the schools, containing about one hundred and fifty books, which the boys were encouraged to read to their parents at night. In this way, the pupils themselves became evangelists. Pious books were also supplied to apprentices in the town who, in return, were obliged to attend the sacraments once a month. Amongst the first expenses recorded for the North Monastery in Cork, was five guineas spent on a bookcase for the library.[28] By 1822, the lending library at Hanover Street contained 268 volumes, mostly catechisms, hagiography and devotional material, including Rice's favourites, *The spiritual combat* and the *Imitation of Christ*.[29] A decade later the library had expanded to over one thousand books. There was still a preponderance of devotional material, but the scope was considerably broader and contained a significant historical section, including Charles O'Conor, Eugene O'Curry, and Edward Hay. There was controversial material, too, including Burke's *Reflections on the revolution in France* and William Corbett's contentious *History of the Protestant reformation in England and Ireland* (1829), while contemporary controversy was represented in James Warren Doyle (JKL), and the English Tractarians, Henry Edward Manning and Nicholas Wiseman. There were pedagogical materials, too, readers and practical manuals, including Michael Donovan's *Domestic economy* (1830), which contained chapters on brewing, distilling, vital occupations in Dublin's inner city.[30]

The library catalogues reflected the focus upon the sacraments that was an integral part of Rice's system. It was not enough to teach the children christian doctrine, but the Brothers sought to instil in their charges a devotion to the church and its practices. This was no mean task, but if, in Magray's phrase, 'Catholicism had to be taught aggressively to the majority of the population', the Brothers' system was designed to meet that

---

[28] Cork Poor Schools committee, 23 Dec. 1812 (Presentation Brothers General Archive, Cork, minute book, 69A).

[29] List of books purchased for Hanover Street school library, 1821–22 (DDA, 33 /5/1).

[30] List of books purchased for Hanover Street school library, 1832–7 (DDA, 33 /5/5).

challenge.[31] The Presentation Rule laid down that the Brothers should accustom the children to 'think and speak reverently of God and holy things'; they were not to be over-curious in their questioning, but rather to 'captivate their understanding in obedience to faith'.[32] The library was an important auxiliary in this task, and the shelves contained classic Tridentine texts such Antoine Arnaud's treatise, *On frequent communion* (1643) and a Dublin edition of John Gother (*c.* 1650–1704), *Instructions for confession, communion and confirmation* (Dublin, 1825).[33]

The Brothers' schools sought to foster an internalised obedience to the church, and a disposition 'to receive instruction from those whom Christ has appointed to rule' it.[34] Children learned 'to honour and respect their parents and superiors', but the Brothers' emphasis on the special reverence due to priests brought criticism that their system tended to prepare, what one critic described as, 'ready instruments for the priests' domination'.[35] They were also taught to examine their conscience in preparation for confession, and Rice's system provided for the reception of the sacrament of penance by the children four times during the school year.[36] The 1845 *Manual*, for instance, contained a *pro forma* school register which included columns in which the boys' monthly confession and communion were to be recorded.[37] This was at a time when frequent reception of the sacraments was rare and the Easter duty often considered sufficient – a reality lost on contemporary historians and their obsession with rates of practice.

As the century progressed, preparation for first communion and confirmation assumed increasing importance and very often the sacraments marked the end of primary school and the beginning of pupils' working lives.[38] Hanover Street school,

---

31 Mary Peckham Magray, *The transforming power of the nuns: women, religion and cultural change in Ireland, 1750–1900* (Oxford, 1998), p. 3.

32 Hickey (ed.), 'Presentation Rule', p. 162.

33 List of books purchased for Hanover Street school library, 1832–7 (DDA, 33/5/5).

34 Ibid.

35 Ibid.; J. C. Colquhoun, *The system of National Education in Ireland* (Cheltenham, 1838), p. 64.

36 Edmund Rice to Thomas Bray, 9 May 1810 (Cashel Diocesan archive, Bray papers).

37 *Manual*, p. 181.

38 Sarah Curtis, *Educating the faithful; religion, schooling and education in nineteenth-century France* (DeKalb, IL, 2000), p. 92.

Dublin had an average daily attendance of 480, yet the returns for 1837 indicate that 200 of the boys made their first holy communion each year.[39] Yet, while religion appears to dominate the day, the focus was less intense than in many Protestant bible schools where frequently the only reading allowed was from the bible. Significantly, too, Rice's regime did not include the de La Salle and Presentation Sisters' practice of daily mass for the children.

Within the schools, too, the Brothers promoted a variety of confraternities, while the first juvenile total abstinence society founded in Ireland was at the North Monastery, Cork. Fr Theobald Mathew, who consciously cultivated contacts with the Brothers, praised their work and expressed his delight:

> That the Christian Brothers had come forward as living examples of the great lessons of total abstinence which they inculcated. He thanked God that he had their active co-operation and that of their numerous pupils whose example alone in taking the pledge was a vast gain for the cause of temperance.[40]

The identification of the cause of education and temperance found expression in Mathew's numerous visits to the Brothers' schools. In 1843 alone, he made at least nine visits to their schools; in September of that year he delivered a charity sermon for the North Richmond Street school in Gardiner Street church which raised one hundred guineas.[41] The 'Liberator' was expected to attend that service, but declined on account of a 'monster meeting' at Clifden. His apology declared, 'the same hour at which your sermon is to take place ... I expect to be addressing a million of men on the heights of Connemara'.[42] Two years later, when O'Connell visited the North Monastery the hall was decorated with two large satin banners; one read *in hoc signo vinces*, while 'temperance and happiness' was emblazoned on the other.[43]

[39] Hanover Street returns, 1837 (DDA, 33/5/5).

[40] Fr Augustine, *Edmund Ignatius Rice and Fr Mathew* (Dublin, 1944), p. 20.

[41] *Freeman's Journal*, 18 Sept. 1843.

[42] O'Connell school annals, 1843 (CBGA, Rome).

[43] Fr Augustine, *Edmund Ignatius Rice and Fr Mathew* (Dublin, 1944), p. 29.

Paul Townsend has described Fr Mathew's temperance crusade as the 'most extraordinary social movement … in pre-famine Ireland'.[44] Yet the success of what O'Connell called this 'moral and majestic miracle' depended upon the cooperation of like-minded agents of improvement.[45] That the Christian Brothers were vital collaborators in that revolution was reflected in the Capuchin's recollection of the day Edmund Rice took the pledge as the happiest day of his life:

> I was aware that when he and the other members of that illustrious body came forward from their mountain, a second Carmel, to diffuse the blessings of temperance as they had those of education, not only through Ireland, but also in England, the principles of the society were placed on a sure basis, even on a rock which the breaking of the tempest could not shake.[46]

The apostle of temperance's faith in the Brothers was echoed by many of their peers. They were, in John Shelly's words, 'no mere hirelings', but men of the world who had embraced the cause of regeneration and as such exercised an influence in society vastly disproportionate to their small numbers.[47]

Beyond the schools, too, the Brothers were often directly involved in preaching and catechetical activity, although such participation was discouraged by the leadership of the congregation. In the context of the so-called 'Second Reformation', they were particularly effective in opposition to the missionary activities of the plethora of biblical societies which descended on Ireland, beginning in the first quarter of the new century.[48] In the Clare town of Ennistymon, the Brothers' ministry included the promotion of new devotions through catechesis and the introduction of various confraternities to the town. In this regard, Br Austin Grace, a native Irish speaker, was particularly useful and each Sunday he would stand at the rear of the chapel, translating the sermons for those who understood no English.[49]

---

44 Paul A. Townsend, *Fr Mathew, temperance and Irish identity* (Dublin, 2002), p. 1.

45 Cited in Fr Augustine, *Footprints of Father Mathew* (Dublin, 1947), p. 107.

46 Fr Augustine, *Fr Mathew and Edmund Rice*, p. 23.

47 John Shelly, *Edmund Ignatius Rice*, p.132.

48 See Irene Whelan, *The bible war in Ireland: the Second Reformation and the polarization of Protestant–Catholic relations, 1800–1840* (Dublin, 2005).

49 M. C. Normoyle, *A tree is planted; the life and times of Edmund Rice* (Dublin, 1977), p. 181.

The Brothers were particularly effective in the cities, where their big schools had an enrolment the equivalent to ten or twelve smaller schools. In Dublin, at Archbishop Murray's parish in Liffey Street, there were no fewer than thirty-six Protestant free schools attended by upwards of one thousand Catholic children. To counteract these, Rice opened a temporary school in Jervis Street in 1828, which was the precursor to the celebrated O'Connell schools.[50] A similar role, of course, was performed by the teaching sisters in their inner city schools, and there is evidence of practical collaboration between the male and female religious orders. By the 1820s the Brothers had 'perfected' their system of education, but in Dublin the Sisters of Charity faced a daunting task at their new school in Gardiner Street, where the 'children were first subdued before they were taught'.[51] Towards that end, Mary Aikenhead, foundress of the Irish Sisters of Charity, sought assistance from Edmund Rice who sent Br Bernard Duggan, who was principal of the Brothers' branch school in Jervis Street, to offer 'in-service' support to the Sisters. The convent annals record his efforts and present a vivid account of the Brother's frantic activity in the classroom, which was a far cry from the impressions formed from a reading of the Christian Brothers' Manual (1845) which he had written, with its emphasis upon the robotic silence of the master. The convent annalist remarked how Duggan, a small and frail brother, 'had to whistle and shout to secure' silence in the classroom, but that he soon took charge. By the time he withdrew from the school, several months later, the Sisters had secured 'perfect order'.[52]

Almost a century later, in 1923, the Sisters of Charity appealed to the Brothers for assistance once more. This time, Sister Agnes Morrogh-Bernard, foundress of the celebrated Foxford Woollen Mills in County Mayo, requested a community of Brothers to teach the mill workers. In her application she appealed to the historic memory of the Brothers:

---

[50] D. V. Kelleher, 'A timely restorer of faith and hope in Ireland' in P.S. Carroll (ed.), *A man raised up: recollections and reflections on Venerable Edmund Rice* (Dublin, 1994), p. 108.

[51] Peckham Magray, *Transforming power*, p. 97.

[52] Annals of the Congregation, 1828–30, SOC/M, cited in Peckham Magray, *Transforming power*, p. 97; [A member of the Congregation], *The life and works of Mary Aikenhead* (Dublin, 1924), p. 106.

[In 1866, Sister Mary Xavier Hennessy, foundress of Gardiner Street], often told me of all we owed to the Christian Brothers for the admirable service they rendered to our Sisters in 1830 when Mary Aikenhead opened her first school. Our poor Sisters had no control over the children, who had been attending proselytising schools and got strict injunctions from their parents to eat all they could get and take the clothes that were going, but to be sure to give plenty of trouble to the teachers. They did so, not knowing how to distinguish between the Sisters of Charity and Mrs Smiley's [proselytising] crowd, until Br Duggan came to the rescue and brought them to their senses.[53]

The tenor of this Foxford application, however, illustrates the extent to which the intensity of the 'bible wars' had been purged from the popular memory of the period. More specifically, it reveals the way in which triumphant Catholicism chose to ignore the scale of the defections to the 'biblicals', and the very real threat which the crusade had posed to the Catholic church. There are, regrettably, few reliable statistics to illustrate the extent of the conversions. However, on the Farnham estate in County Cavan alone, which John MacHale described as 'the strong citadel of the Reformation', over five hundred were reported to have conformed in the winter of 1826–7.[54] The *Dublin Evening Mail* reported in 1826 that the entire population of many Catholic parishes of the county was about to defect to the Established Church and so great was the threat that Archbishop Curtis and four other bishops descended on Cavan town in mid-December 1826 in an effort to stem the tide of defections.[55]

During the famine (1845–50), too, the threat of conversion was keenly felt. In that context, the Brothers were particularly active in opposition to 'souperism' in the urban ghettos which became the refuge of the hungry poor from the countryside.[56] The decision to establish a foundation at Francis Street, Dublin,

[53] Sr Agnes Murrogh-Bernard to Br P. J. Hennessy, 29 Sept. 1923 (CBGA, 189 /2111).

[54] S. J. Brown, *The national churches of England, Ireland and Scotland, 1801–1846* (Oxford, 2001), p. 123.

[55] *Dublin Evening Mail*, 4 Dec. 1826.

[56] Miriam Moffitt, *Soupers and Jumpers: the Protestant missions in Connemara, 1848–1937* (Dublin, 2008).

in 1846 was a direct response to the intrigues of 'perverters' who 'with meal and money bags ... tempt[ed] the poor to forfeit their glorious birthright in heaven for a mess of pottage'.[57] Similar motives brought the Christian Brothers to Dingle (1848), where, according to Father Philip Dowley CM, the 'demon of heresy' had induced 'hundreds of the ignorant poor' to sell their souls 'to the devil by *outwardly* renouncing the faith of their Fathers'. In Kerry, the Brothers worked not just in the school, but they also accompanied the Vincentian 'missioners' to the remote parts of the county, translating, catechising and seeking out apostates.[58] During the celebrations to mark the centenary of Rice's death, a preacher at Tralee recalled the context of their mission in florid terms:

> The Great Famine had brought the threat and the opportunity for proselytism [to Kerry] ... weaklings went down for the bribe and the faithless failed; the selfish sold their souls for gold and the hungry pawned their bodies for bread hoping to redeem it again when the potatoes grew again. The temptation was terrible and souperism had a local triumph for a while. A breach was made in the lines of the church and the Christian Brothers were rushed to the front. The breach was sealed with their aid and the line has never been broken in Kerry.[59]

In many cases, the poorest of the Irish were to be found not on the island, but in bourgeoning English slums where families crowded into small rooms. Yet, while the institutional history of the Brothers perpetuates the notion that 'loyalty to the Catholic faith was of the highest importance' to the Irish diaspora, many immigrants seemed unconcerned about the faith of their fathers, at a formal level at least.[60] Perhaps unsurprisingly, the alienation from the institutional church, which was prevalent amongst the poor in Ireland, transferred across the water. In

---

[57] *Tablet*, 14 Sept. 1854; *Synge Street Annual, 1946–7* (Dublin, 1947), p. 4.

[58] 'Proselytism in Dingle – measures to counteract it', Undated broadsheet [1849?] (CBGA, 035/0406); Br P. J. Murphy to Tobias Kirby (Irish College Archive, Rome, Kirby Papers/721); Philip Dowley C.M., 30 Nov. 1846, cited in Emmet Larkin, 'The parish mission movement, 1850–1880', in Brendan Bradshaw and Dáire Keogh (eds), *Christianity in Ireland* (Dublin, 2000), p. 197.

[59] Sermon of Mgr Donal Reidy, St John's Tralee, 29 Aug. 1944 (CBGA, 192/2139).

[60] Gillespie, *Christian Brothers in England*, p. 15.

1842, for example, Paul Cullen, was alarmed at the terrible spectre in Liverpool where less than half of the hundred thousand Catholics in the city were hearing mass on Sundays.[61] Social reformers, too, were increasingly aware of the link between slum conditions and immorality, a reality borne out in the experience of one London parish priest who warned that 'the children [were] going to hell by wholesale for the want of Brothers to instruct them'.[62]

The Brothers established a reputation for their evangelisation in these migrant communities. The first foundation in England was made in the industrial centre of Preston, Lancashire. Rice travelled to the city in 1825 and was so impressed by the educational needs there, that in spite of a chronic shortage of manpower and funds, he immediately dispatched a community to England. Two Brothers, Joseph Murphy and Aloysius Kelly, took charge of 150 boys and their daily programme was tailored in response to specific instructions from the local clergy. Edmund Rice outlined their task in a horarium which demonstrates the extent of the Brothers' missionary activity, beyond the confines of the school:

The duties to be performed in Preston ... are as follows viz:

1. Three hours school before noon.
2. Three hours afternoon.
3. Catechism and religious instruction twice a week from 6 to 7 o'clock in the evening for those who do not frequent the school.
4. Catechism and Religious Instruction twice a week from 8 to 9 o'clock for those employed in the factories.
5. Religious instruction morning and afternoon on Sundays.[63]

Further schools were planned for Manchester, but the expectations of the local Catholic Board proved unacceptable, especially

61 Paul Cullen to Tobias Kirby, 25 June 1842 (Irish College Archives, Rome, KIR/1842/ 98).

62 P. J. Murphy to Tobias Kirby, 10 Mar. 1843 (Irish College Archives, Rome, KIR 1843/173); cf Heather Shore, *Artful dodgers: youth and crime in early nineteenth-century London* (London, 1999).

63 E. Rice to Fr Dunn, Preston, 24 June 1825 in M.C. Normoyle (ed.), *A companion to a tree is planted* (Dublin, 1977), pp 116–17.

the request that the Brothers 'visit the sick and prepare them for the sacraments'.[64] Twenty years of experience had taught Rice that such missionary activity was beyond the scope of his congregation. Accordingly the Manchester Committee initiated discussions with the Patrician Brothers who accepted the invitation, but it appears as if the vicar apostolic of the district, Bishop Thomas Smith, chose to invite the Christian Brothers in spite of their reservations. That said, once established there, the Brothers' school contributed towards the evangelisation of the city. And just as their radical system at home had involved the boys in the education of their parents, so, too, in Manchester the students became agents of transformation. After Sunday school, the boys were sent out to the 'lofts in different directions' giving instruction to about two thousand people each week. 'So numerous were the conversions', one Brother boasted, 'that the priests could not attend conveniently to all'.[65] In the same year, 1826, the Brothers took over a Catholic school in Soho, London, where the annalist of the congregation recorded that: 'no boy in the school had made his first communion between the year 1803 and the arrival of the first Brother in 1826'.[66] From there they expanded to Sunderland (1836), Liverpool (1837), Leeds (1843), Salford (1844), Bolton (1844) and Birmingham (1845). Perhaps the most overtly 'Counter-Reformationary' of the schools opened in Br Rice's lifetime, however, was the foundation in Gibraltar. Founded in 1835, the school on the Rock was established for the express purpose of eliminating the Methodists' English language schools which had attracted large numbers of Spanish students.[67] Their success was eulogised by Frederick William Faber (1814–63), himself a convert member of the Oxford Movement. In a sermon entitled: 'The apostolic character of the destiny allotted by providence to the Irish nation', he condemned the 'horrors of proselytism', but noted

[64] Gillespie, *Christian Brothers in England*, p. 20.

[65] Br P. J. Murphy to Tobias Kirby, 10 Mar. 1843, Irish College Archives, Rome, Kirby/173.

[66] Gillespie, *Christian Brothers in England*, pp 21–2; *Christian Brothers Educational Record* (1894), p. 469.

[67] Fitzpatrick, *Edmund Rice*, p. 336.

anecdotal evidence that amongst Irish immigrants, 'those who were educated either by the Christian Brothers or the Presentation Nuns never abandoned their faith'.[68]

Inevitably, given these emphases, Edmund Rice's system was not without its critics. Few challenged his pedagogical method, and the considerable material improvement which the schools brought to Ireland, but critics rounded on their religious ethos and the perpetuation of 'popish superstition'. The traveller, Henry Inglis's observations on Mount Sion were typical of many:

> The most important institution I visited [in Waterford] was a Catholic school at which upwards of 700 children were instructed ... although I am far from questioning the motives of the founder Mr Rice or the young men who thus made a sacrifice of themselves, yet I cannot regard favourably an institution under such tuition.
>
> I know too much of Catholicism in other countries to doubt that intellectual training will be made very secondary to theological instruction ... I would rather not see a system of education extensively pursued in which the inculcation of popish tenets forms so chief a part.[69]

Writing in 1825, another critic condemned the Brothers' schools as 'the most intolerant and mischievous which any individual or society has attempted to mask under the disguise of Christian instruction'.[70] Such criticisms, however, were met with indifference by the Brothers, who rejoiced in the eulogies of their co-religionists. In 1851, for instance, the *Irish Catholic Directory* celebrated the opening of the Brothers' school at Seville Place, Dublin, as 'a great moral temple, where the mind is enlightened – the heart reformed – and each one afforded the happy opportunity to obtain his social and eternal destiny'.[71]

---

[68] F. W. Faber, Charity sermon for O'Connell Schools, 19 Sept. 1852 (CBGA, Rome, O'Connell Schools annals).

[69] H. D. Inglis, *Ireland in 1834: a journey through Ireland, in the spring, summer and autumn of 1834* (2 vols, London, 1834), ii, pp 65–6.

[70] W. Phelan and M. O'Sullivan, *Practical observations on the first report of the Commissioners on Irish Education* (London, 1826), p. 33.

[71] *Irish Catholic Directory* (1851), p. 353.

This evangelisation of the poor by the Christian Brothers and the teaching Sisters played a vital part in the renewal of the Catholic church in the decades following Emancipation. Referring to the extent to which the Brothers had effected a reformation and brought the church into line with the practice and discipline of the Council of Trent, Fr Gregory Lynch, reminded Cardinal Cullen of the transformation of the capital:

> All the pious sodalities, societies and all the teachers in the Sunday schools, and even the ranks of the clergy, were mainly fed from the Hanover Street school. The holy and practical Catholics of the parish, and the regular ones at the confessional during the past twenty years, were all educated in their schools.[72]

Through their teaching, catechesis and the promotion of confraternities, they brought the previously alienated poor within the ranks of the church, and provided the backbone of the emerging Catholic Ireland.

This was how Rice's peers remembered him. Certainly, his contribution to secular instruction had effected what Charles Bianconi referred to as 'a quiet revolution in the south of Ireland'.[73] It was on account of his evangelisation and its fruits, however, that Edmund Rice was principally celebrated by his contemporaries as Ireland's De La Salle, a second Ignatius and the 'herald of a new age of Irishmen'.[74] It is instructive to re-examine him within this context, not simply for what it tells us about himself, but rather for the insights it affords into the general history of Irish Catholicism and the critical challenges facing nineteenth-century religious reformers on the island.

---

[72] Rev. Gregory Lynch to Paul Cullen, 1864, cited in Christian Brothers, *The History of the Institute*, i (Dublin, 1957), p. 34.

[73] Charles Bianconi cited in Samuel Smiles, *Men of invention and industry* (London, 1884), p. 254.

[74] Maurice Lenihan, *Tipperary Vindicator*, 9 Sept. 1844.

4

The flowering of the confraternities and sodalities in Ireland, c.1860–c.1960

Colm Lennon and Robin Kavanagh

For almost a century from the 1860s onwards the religious lives of most Irish Catholics revolved around the confraternities and sodalities. Members of four generations of Irish men, women and children were touched by these parish associations, whether as worshippers under their guild shields at the monthly sodality mass, as processionists attired in confraternity regalia and costumes on solemn or festive occasions, as excursionists boarding trains for the annual sodality outing to the seaside, or as devotees at prayer before shrines or statues in church or at home. The pious associations provided a comprehensive system of spiritual security from youth until old age, and, at the time of death, the obsequies of sodalists were especially solemnised by their brother- and sister-members, who preserved the memory of the deceased in their prayers for the souls in purgatory. For most, membership was initiated through children's sodalities in the schools, and the confraternal attachment was carried on through adolescence and into adulthood, framing most aspects of their social and cultural as well as religious experience. Although the clergy were fully in charge of the establishment and overall regulation of confraternities, many laymen and women were chosen to occupy supervisory positions in their branches as officers and prefects, having responsibility for the maintaining of records and the monitoring of attendance. While membership of a confraternity or sodality may have elicited a compassionate disposition on the part of individuals, most bodies did not require specific forms of charitable action of their members. Instead, societies such as those of St Vincent de Paul or the Ladies Association of Charity, which shared many of the characteristics of the confraternities, provided opportunities for direct lay Catholic action in the provision of welfare for the poor and the sick.[1]

In this essay, the authors attempt to describe the quotidian world of the sodalities and confraternities during their ascendancy by drawing on the wealth of data accumulated during the research project. Because of the very immanence and ubiquity of the phenomenon, the tendency towards self-reflection on the part of members was muted, but the records of individual confraternities kept by association officers from all over the country provide a detailed picture with which to construct an overview.[2] In addition, many of the religious bodies that sponsored confraternities and sodalities produced manuals and guides for the organisation and conduct of their business, as well as periodical literature containing reports of the activities of the associations. Morcover, from the early twentieth century onwards, there was a series of informative jubilee publications to mark the silver, golden and other anniversaries of the foundation of individual branches. In attempting to establish a pattern in the substantial number of foundations, account will be taken of the categories, dedications and dispersal of confraternities and sodalities throughout Ireland, including the more notable and popular bodies. It is instructive too to consider the initiatives on the part of ecclesiastical authorities in setting up a myriad of pious associations, the specific purposes and practices of each, and the rules adopted for their regulation. In this context, the role of the clergy as directors may be addressed, and the dynamic between them and the laity assessed. A central topic to be discussed is the devotional regime that framed the members' religious lives, as they worshipped together and practised special pieties. Also significant is the pattern of extra-ecclesial activity, including the members' role in wider parish functions, their socialising and their civic

---

[1] See the essay by Máire Ní Chearbhaill, 'Charity, church and the Society of St Vincent de Paul', in this volume.

[2] For reminiscences of members of sodalities and confraternities, see http://www.irishconfraternities.ie/oral_histories.php; see also Eamon Duffy, *Faith of our fathers* (Bodmin, 2004), pp 23–4, for a contextualising of Catholic devotions in Ireland in the 1950s.

participation. The issue of changing views of the lay apostolate towards the end of the period under review is raised in the light of evidence of a weakening commitment to the traditional confraternities at the expense of new forms of Catholic action.

****

Dozens of Catholic associations operated during the century or so under review. They provided a rich devotional milieu in which every kind of piety, public and private, was accommodated. Children, young men and women, mothers, those striving for temperance, the sick and dying, workers in various callings, all had their particular spiritual needs catered for in this cornucopia of Catholic associations. Not all of these, however, could qualify as confraternities or sodalities in the strict, canonical sense, that is, as formally erected with ecclesiastical authority and affiliated to an international body with its headquarters in Rome or elsewhere. This survey will focus primarily on these formal institutions, but sometimes the lines are blurred between them and other popular associations which may have sometimes been called sodalities (such as Father Mathew's Total Abstinence Society). As to the difference between the sodalities and confraternities, again the nomenclature tended to be applied imprecisely: it was recognised that a sodality was more private in its devotions by comparison to a confraternity, which had a public face (especially on solemn occasions), that its members were less constrained by formal codes of liturgical or sacral dress, and that the pieties were more general than those of the specific religious orders.[3] Perhaps the most notable representatives of the two types in the Irish setting after 1860 were, on the one hand, the confraternity (later archconfraternity) of the Holy Family, which flourished in Limerick, Dublin, Mullingar, Belfast and many other centres, and, on the other, the sodality of the Sacred Heart which was almost ubiquitous throughout the parishes of the Dublin archdiocese by 1960. In this account, the

---

[3] For a discussion of the differences, http://www.newadvent.org/cathen/14120 a.html (accessed 2 Feb. 2012).

terms will be used interchangeably when the bodies are being referred to generically, but the distinction may be preserved where specific associations are being alluded to.

A prodigious range of dedications characterised the over forty confraternities and sodalities for Catholic men and women in Ireland.[4] This was in part due to the zeal of religious orders to promote their own versions of trends in international piety. Many of these were Christocentric, including the Infant Jesus, the Divine Child, the Holy Name, the Holy Face, the Sacred Thirst and Agony, the Holy Cross and Passion, the Holy Blood and the Sacred Heart. Others which reflected Marian devotion were the Blessed Virgin, Our Lady of Mount Carmel, the Immaculate Conception, Our Lady of Dolours and of Perpetual Succour, the Holy Rosary, the Children of Mary and the Immaculate Heart of Mary.[5] New Testament verities celebrated included the Holy Family,[6] and saintly patrons invoked in dedications of confraternities represented the leading figures in the history of religious congregations: St Francis Xavier (for the Jesuits), Saints Augustine and Monica (for the Augustinians), St Imelda (for the Dominicans) and St Anthony (for the Franciscans and Capuchins).

Besides the category of pious society, newly-founded after 1860, older foundations continued to function down through the period. These included confraternities which had their roots in the Counter-Reformation or more recent Catholic revival, some of them affiliated to religious orders. The diocesan-based confraternities of Christian Doctrine and Blessed Sacrament were perhaps the most significant, but also popular were the Bona Mors (or Happy Death) society under Jesuit patronage, the

---

[4] The website of the IRCHSS project for the study of modern Irish confraternities and sodalities contains a database of all of the pious associations that came to light during the research programme: http://www.irishconfraternities.ie.

[5] For the conveying of the devotional history and rationale of associations on the part of religious orders, see, for example, the following periodicals: *The Illustrated Monitor* (1870–78) (a Jesuit-inspired organ to support the sodality of the Sacred Thirst and Agony); *The Irish Messenger of the Sacred Heart* (Dublin, 1888 –) (official organ of the Apostleship of Prayer, with Jesuit patronage); and *The Irish Rosary* (Dublin, 1897 –) (published by the Dominicans to explain and promote the Holy Rosary sodality).

[6] For an early history and appraisal, see T.A. Murphy, 'The archconfraternity of the Holy Family of Limerick' in *The Irish Monthly*, li (1923), pp 209–16.

Purgatorian society with links to the Redemptorists, and, affiliated to the Dominicans, the confraternity of the Holy Rosary.
Even more closely aligned to the religious orders were the Third
Orders of the Franciscans and Dominicans for male and female
tertiaries who felt called to live out in the secular world the
ideals of the friars and religious sisters. A wide variety of
sodalities and confraternities celebrated special devotions of the
congregations, usually centred on proprietary chapels: the
scapulars of the Carmelites (calced and discalced), the cincture
of the Augustinians and the cord of St Francis were among the
most commonly worn sacred insignia by men and women
members of these sodalities and confraternities. Throughout the
period, local versions of cults and societies could supersede the
national ones, bringing into being adapted forms of major
confraternities, such as the Living Rosary society, the Guard of
Honour of the Most Blessed Sacrament, the Altar society of the
Sacred Heart and the various forms of temperance associations.[7]

From the mid-nineteenth century there was not only an
increase in the number of pious associations of men and women
in Ireland but also a rapid dissemination of confraternal activity
everywhere throughout the island. Down to the 1860s, only
about half a dozen confraternal societies were functioning
regularly in the archdiocese of Dublin and throughout much of
the country. By 1866, however, that number had doubled, at
least in respect of the Dublin parishes, to embrace the brown,
blue and red scapulars, as well as the sodality of the Sacred
Heart, and the confraternities of the Most Precious Blood, the
Immaculate Heart of Mary and St Augustine and St Monica.
Whereas the Christian Doctrine had accounted for two-thirds of
all confraternities functioning in 1851, the picture fifteen years
later was much more richly variegated. By 1881, there were
confraternities in all of the fifty-three parishes surveyed in an
episcopal visitation of the Dublin archdiocese. At least thirty-
five had branches of the sodality of the Sacred Heart, while there
were three branches of the Holy Family confraternity. The
largest parish associations were to be found in the inner city
parishes of St Nicholas's in Francis Street, Meath Street (both

---

[7] For details on some of these associations, see http://www.irishconfraternities
.ie/search.php.

Holy Family branches) and Westland Row (a Sacred Heart branch), and the total membership for the parishes surveyed was 13,400 men and 10,650 women, or an average per association of 252 and 200 in the archdiocese, respectively. The confraternity of the Holy Family under the auspices of the Redemptorist order came to be associated strongly with Limerick, but it had dozens of branches throughout Ireland. By 1875, there were 3,300 male members in that city, and in Dublin there were 4,200 men in four separate branches. In twenty-three cities and towns, including Cork, Belfast and Kilkenny, the confraternity had become rooted, with a total of 34,160 men and 10,500 women. Seven years later, in 1882, there were 100 branches in the thirty dioceses with a total membership of 75,990 members. Given that no branch could be established within three miles of an existing one, this rate of growth at three per diocese on average was impressive.[8]

Eighty years later, in 1960, a diocesan visitation in the city and suburbs of Dublin found that there were associations in all of the parishes, with an average membership of 450 men, 800 women (a reversal of the gender balance of 1861) and 980 youths. The largest memberships were now to be found in the newly-established suburban areas such as Ballyfermot (which had 10,000 sodalists of all ages), Crumlin, Walkinstown and Donnycarney. Three quarters of the mens' and womens' associations were branches of the Sacred Heart sodality, and many more were simply listed generically as sodalities. Across the country, all of the dioceses had a colourful tapestry of Catholic associations, not all of them confraternities and sodalities, but the main bodies which had established their presence in the second half of the nineteenth century or before were still in being. These included the societies of the Sacred Heart, Holy Family, Blessed Sacrament, Christian Doctrine, Holy Cross and Passion, Immaculate Conception, Holy Rosary and Immaculate Heart of Mary. Among the newer forms of traditional sodality were Our Lady of the Sacred Heart, sponsored by the Sacred Heart Missionaries in Cork, the Blessed Virgin, pioneered by the

---

[8] The information in this paragraph is based on Dublin Diocesan Archives [DDA], 'Visitation sheets', 1830–1960; and James Cantwell, 'The confraternity of the Holy Family' in *Irish ecclesiastical record* [IER], iv (1883), pp 627–32.

Holy Faith sisters for children in Dublin, and the St Anthony of Padua archconfraternity, under the direction of the Capuchins. It is significant that many of the new quasi-confraternal bodies were focused on Catholic action in the fields of poor relief, welfare of orphans and single mothers, emigrants, ex-prisoners, and protection of youth.[9]

The initiative in establishing the new confraternities and sodalities in Ireland was taken by the religious orders, but the episcopal authorities were also involved, at least in sanctioning the foundations, and indeed as instigators. A context for these devotions was created by the congregations in the form of a history of the cults in their manuals and periodicals. Many were traceable back to the middle ages, and most were consolidated in the Counter-Reformation. Among the pious pedigrees thus presented were those for the Holy Rosary by the Dominicans, with its origin in 1221 and formal erection in 1475, the brown scapular of Our Lady of Mount Carmel by the Carmelites, which began in the thirteenth century and was formalised in the seventeenth, and the Seven Dolours by the Servites of the Blessed Virgin, originating in 1233 and receiving formal recognition in 1667.[10] Some, such as the Jesuits' sodality of Our Lady and the Christian Doctrine, were shown to be products of the Tridentine renewal of the Roman church,[11] while others arose in more recent times, including the hugely-popular associations of the Holy Family, sponsored by the Redemptorists, the Children of Mary, promoted in Ireland by the Sisters of Charity, and the Sacred Heart, largely a diocesan initiative but with Vincentian supervision locally.[12]

A significant stage in the centralisation of all of the successful associations was their erection into an archconfraternity, meaning that they could affiliate to a wider agglomeration,

---

[9] DDA, 'Visitation sheets', 1830–1960; *Irish Catholic Directory* [ICD] (Dublin, 1860–1960). We are very grateful to Dr Louise Fuller for collating the information, and to Dr Máire Ní Chearbhaill for compiling a database of Dublin confraternities.

[10] See the short synopses of the origins and history of these associations in *IER*, xi, pp 845–58, 937–8; xv, 948; and *Irish Rosary*, vol. ii (1898).

[11] See, for example, *Crusaders of Mary: an outline of the sodality of Our Lady* (Dublin, 1942); *IER*, xviii (1905), pp 466–9; 564; (1906), pp 84–8.

[12] *IER*, lvi (1940), pp 232–8; *Manual of the Sacred Heart confraternity* (Dublin, 1965).

normally with a headquarters in Rome or elsewhere. Through this agency, the process of aggregation or affiliation of new branches of a confraternity or sodality in Ireland was facilitated, with the transmission of the relevant privileges and indulgences to the members. The superior of a religious order who wished to erect a sodality or confraternity in his or her jurisdiction required the written permission of the bishop of the diocese before referring the request for affiliation to the archconfraternity.[13] In the case of bishops themselves taking the initiative, the approval of the religious superior of the relevant association was needed, as in the case of the Holy Rosary sodality under Dominican patronage.[14] More and more, though, by the end of the nineteenth century, episcopal power in respect of the establishment of the network of new branches was being asserted. In 1861, the bishop had been granted the right to appoint the director of a parish sodality when the post became vacant. By 1889, the bishops' power to erect sodalities and confraternities was affirmed by Rome, without the need to seek the permission of the religious orders.[15] In the case of the Christian Doctrine, the parish priest had always occupied the role of promoter under episcopal authority, but the momentum for the founding of the Sacred Heart sodality in the 1870s appeared to lie with Cardinal Paul Cullen in his drive to inspire a devotional renaissance in the Dublin archdiocese.[16] Although technically the Vincentian order, with its Irish headquarters at Phibsborough, retained the power of affiliation from the 1870s, in practice the diocesan clergy promoted the huge surge in the number of branches throughout Ireland from the late nineteenth century.

Once canonical approval had been obtained for the erection of a new branch, a diploma of affiliation of the sodality or confraternity was issued by the archconfraternity. Then a spiritual director was appointed either by the bishop or the

---

[13] For examples of the system of dual authority in the erecting of confraternities, see *IER* xi (1890), p. 848, for the scapular confraternity of Our Lady of Mount Carmel, and ibid., p. 937, for the confraternity of the Seven Dolours.

[14] *Irish Rosary*, vol. i (1897), pp 146–7.

[15] *IER*, xix (1906), pp 84–8.

[16] Ciaran O'Carroll, 'The pastoral politics of Paul Cullen' in Dáire Keogh and James Kelly (eds), *History of the Catholic diocese of Dublin* (Dublin, 2000), pp 301–2.

religious superior, and also a register was opened in which the names of all of the entrants to the association were to be inscribed. The director, who was a member of the sponsoring religious order or a diocesan parish priest or curate, was responsible for the overall spiritual guidance of the branch. He it was who arranged for the appointment of lay officers to manage the day-to-day affairs of the association and who chaired regular meetings of the committee or council of the branch. At the monthly Sunday mass for all sodalists the director officiated, having heard confessions of members by way of preparation, and at evening gatherings he preached a sermon and celebrated benediction of the Blessed Sacrament. Arrangements for the annual retreat or mission were made in consultation with the director, though preachers were normally brought in from outside the parish.[17] Third order associations and scapularist societies of the Dominicans, Franciscans, Carmelites, Augustinians and others were carefully tended in spiritual matters by members of those orders, as were the confraternities closely associated with Redemptorists and Passionists.[18] By contrast, the confraternity of the Christian Doctrine was guided by parish priests, and branches of the sodality of the Sacred Heart were consigned to the spiritual care of curates in most parishes down to the 1960s.[19]

The routine organisation of the branches of sodalities and confraternities was placed in the hands of lay men and women (who generally belonged to separate male and female branches). To the lay officers fell the task of the keeping of records of membership, minutes of committee meetings, accounts of entry fees and subscriptions, and attendance. Normally the officership incorporated a president and vice-president, a secretary and treasurer, and prefects and sub-prefects, as well, in some cases, as promoters, librarians and sacristans. The key personnel in terms of record-keeping were the secretary and the

[17] James A. Cleary, 'Confraternities and how to work them' in *IER*, xxix–xxx (1927).

[18] See minutes of men's and women's branches of the confraternity of the Most Holy Cross and Passion, Mount Argus, 1877–1959 (Mount Argus, Dublin, Passionists' Archive).

[19] See *IER*, xviii (1905), pp 466–9, 564; xix (1906), pp 84–8; DDA, 'Visitation sheets'.

treasurer. The better-regulated bodies had councils of up to a dozen, drawn from among the senior officers, who met regularly to order the business of the sodality or confraternity. For effective organisation of large memberships, many confraternities were divided up into guilds or sections of up to a few dozen members, who would occupy assigned benches or pews in the church. These divisions were usually drawn on the basis of residence in a particular locality or road within the parish, and the members thus arranged were under the patronage of a saint whose name was emblazoned on the banner or shield of the guild attached to their bench. As the confraternities expanded, particularly in Limerick, some efforts were made to organise members by trade or profession, again under a patron saint. Each guild or section was under the supervision of a prefect who was aided by a sub-prefect (or steward). Between them, the prefect and sub-prefect marshalled the guildsmen or women on sodality nights, monitoring attendance at meetings and ceremonies, and also overseeing the collection of the monthly or more regular fees from members. Thus, the day-to-day running of the sodalities was in the hands of a coterie of lay people, mostly selected by the director with the council's advice, but sometimes elected from among the members.[20]

In examining the purpose of confraternity and sodality membership, a distinction may be drawn between those associations which had as their aim the promotion of corporal works of mercy and charity, and those which focused on the self-sanctification of the brothers and sisters. The former category, sometimes called 'pious unions', had simpler rules, no probationary period for new entrants and no elaborate rituals. They also eschewed special costumes and regalia. Included in this group are the Society of St Vincent de Paul, the Society for the Propagation of the Faith, the Apostleship of Prayer, the Christian Doctrine confraternity, the Purgatorial and Bona Mors societies and the confraternity of the Immaculate Heart of Mary for the conversion of sinners. In addition, there were associations which related to the spiritual and physical well-being of a definite class of persons, such as Christian

---

[20] Cleary, 'Confraternities and how to work them', pp 173–87, 261–80.

mothers, Catholic godparents and Catholic young men. More specialised still were book societies for the propagation of Catholic literature (such as the one at Paulstown in County Kilkenny), and of liturgical music (the society of St Cecilia), and the societies for priests, mass-servers and sacristans.[21]

By far the more common type of religious association in modern Ireland was that which aimed at the attainment of piety on the part of the individual through devotional practices in pursuit of the assurance of salvation. For example, the Holy Family confraternity stated as one of its aims: 'to give the faithful powerful means of advancing in the way of salvation', the end of membership of the Children of Mary was 'to lead its members to love God above all things ... thus securing their own salvation', and the sodality of Our Lady aimed at making its members 'good Catholics, sincerely bent on sanctifying themselves, each in his state of life, and zealous ... to save and sanctify their neighbour and to defend the church'.[22] The means for the achievement of these goals were prayer, self-mortification, such as fasting, moderate consumption of alcohol, and participation in the rituals and liturgical and sacramental rites prescribed for the association. For members of societies which promoted the wearing or carrying of religious sacramentals, a special devotional efficacy was attached to the symbols such as the rosary, scapular and cincture. The Rosary confraternity, for example, had as its aim the saving and sanctifying of immortal souls by means of prayer and the sacraments, and as its special object the spreading of the devotion of the rosary 'by which the Blessed Mother of the Redeemer is honoured'.[23] In the case of the Brown Scapular confraternity, brothers and sisters were   consoled by the belief that 'whosoever dies wearing this scapular shall not suffer eternal fire'.[24]

Every sodalist and confraternity member committed himself or herself to a regime of private and public devotion in pursuance of the spiritual ends of the association. In some religious

---

[21] For references to these confraternities and sodalities in Irish dioceses in the period, see *ICD* (1860–1960).

[22] *Crusaders of Mary* (Dublin, 1942), p. 9.

[23] *Irish Rosary*, vol. i (1897), p. 146.

[24] *IER*, xi (1890), p. 845.

associations, there were degrees of commitment specified, the more advanced demanding more intensive activities in terms of church attendance and adoration, and most had a period of probation for applicants, ranging from some months to a couple of years. A daily routine of prayer and meditation was enjoined on all, the particular focus being shaped by the pieties of the individual confraternity. Common to all was the requirement to recite morning and evening prayers, the former including a morning offering and the Our Father, a number of Hail Marys, with other special prayers or pious invocations, such as the Angelus in the case of the Carmelists or the Creed in that of the Sacred Heart.[25] Evening practices included an examination of conscience for sodalists of Our Lady, while the confraternity of the Cincture of St Augustine, among others, required the recitation of the rosary.[26] Spiritual meditation and reading was recommended for Our Lady sodalists, while members of the Apostleship of Prayer were expected to fast frequently in reparation for the general vice of intemperance, and the Carmelists to abstain from meat on Wednesdays as well as Fridays.[27] Daily mass and communion became a desideratum for many of the sodalities' members, including the Sacred Heart devotees, the followers of the Apostleship of Prayer were encouraged to attend mass on the first Friday of the month, and those of second degree of membership of the Most Holy Cross and Passion confraternity were expected to perform weekly the Stations of the Cross, preferably on Fridays.[28] Urged upon all sodalists was the cultivation of personal virtues, the respective dedications and devotional milieux suggesting specific qualities such as temperance (in the case of the Sacred Thirst and Agony of Jesus), humility (in that of the Sacred Heart) and chastity (in

[25] http://www.irishconfraternities.ie/view_confraternity.php?id=28&tab=membership; 11&tab=membership (accessed 4 Oct. 2010).

[26] http://www.irishconfraternities.ie/view_confraternity.php?id=52&tab=membership; /view_confraternity.php?id=3&tab=admin (accessed 4 Oct. 2010).

[27] http://www.irishconfraternities.ie/view_confraternity.php?id=52&tab=membership;/view_confraternity.php?id=22&tab=membership;/view_confraternity.php?id=12&tab=membership (accessed 4 Oct. 2010).

[28] http://www.irishconfraternities.ie/view_confraternity.php?id=11&tab=membership; /view_confraternity.php?id=22&tab=membership; /view_confraternity.php?id=57&tab=membership (accessed 4 Oct. 2010).

that of the Children of Mary). For members of the cincture, cord or scapular societies, the constant wearing of the blessed insignia of the order was necessary for full participation in their spiritual advantages, members of the confraternity of the brown scapular being exhorted moreover to place a light every Saturday before a picture of Our Lady of Mount Carmel in their homes.[29]

The public face of the confraternities was shown when men, women and young people assembled in the parish or abbey church of the institution with their guild shields or banners displayed. Attendance at the weekly, bi-monthly or monthly confraternity meeting was a solemn duty for all members, who were required to wear their sodality medals or insignia. At these meetings, special sodality prayers were said and a sermon given by the director; frequently hymns were sung and benediction of the most Blessed Sacrament intoned. Almost universally, central to confraternal practice was the reception of the sacraments of penance and the eucharist at least once a month on a designated Sunday, the first in the case of the Rosary confraternity, the third for the brown scapularists, and the fourth for those in the Cincture sodality. A major event in the life of each sodality and the wider parish was the convening of the annual retreat or mission, held over a number of evenings. Normally the priests who directed the retreats were members of the orders to which the confraternities were affiliated, such as the Passionists in the case of the Most Holy Cross and Passion, and the Redemptorists in that of the Holy Family, but members of these two orders were popular preachers for retreats of many other sodalities, including the Sacred Heart. The retreat comprised a meeting each evening of its duration, at which the retreatants would be taken through a course of spiritual reparation and amendment, with special attention focused on the reception of the sacraments of penance and the eucharist for the concluding mass.[30] Retreats were regarded as occasions not only for piquing the faith and loyalty of sodalists, but also for recruitment of new members. Feasts of particular solemnity in the sodalities'

---

[29] http://www.irishconfraternities.ie/view_confraternity.php?id=28&tab=membership (accessed 4 Oct. 2010).

[30] See an account of the annual retreat of the Sacred Heart sodality in the parish of Sandymount, Dublin, in 1875 in *Illustrated Monitor*, 9 Oct. 1875.

calendar, such as those of the Blessed Virgin for the Marian associations, occasioned special votive rituals, including processions in full regalia.

Members of the confraternities derived substantial spiritual benefits from their participation in these prescribed religious activities. The indulgences or graces derived from the faithful fulfilment of the appropriate conditions provided a safety net for men and women in their quest for salvation throughout their lives. Plenary indulgences remitted all of the temporal punishment in purgatory due for sins committed, while partial indulgences diminished the span in that place of punishment for numbers of days or years. Indulgences could be applied to the souls of the faithful departed, as well as those of the living. Members of confraternities had an abundance of opportunities to avail of these aids. For example, the sodalists of Our Lady could gain seven years and seven quarantines (forty-day periods) of remission for exercises such as attending weekday mass, examination of conscience at night and visiting the sick, poor or imprisoned.[31] Plenary indulgences were available on the occasion of sodality meetings, the reception of communion on sodality Sundays and at the annual retreat, provided, as in the case of all such benefits, that the sacraments of penance and the eucharist were received within a set period, and various prayers were said, including those for the pope's intentions. A special plenary indulgence was to be gained at the moment of death for sodalists of Our Lady, and confreres of the Christian Doctrine, for instance.[32] The latter also received that benefit on reception into the confraternity, and could accumulate seven years' partial remission on each occasion that instruction in the faith was undertaken. Members of the Rosary sodality were likewise advantaged, especially on particular feasts of the Dominican order, and on Rosary Sunday, when multiple indulgences could be gained from separate visits to designated churches.[33] The use of blessed beads and other sacramentals, such as scapulars,

---

[31] *Crusaders of Mary: an outline of the sodality of Our Lady* (Dublin, 1942), pp 62–5.

[32] J.G. McEnnery, *Rules and regulations of the society of Christian Doctrine* (Tralee, 1855).

[33] See, for example, *Irish Rosary*, vol. i, 1897, supplement: 'Calendar and indulgences for June, 1897'.

cinctures and cords, attracted spiritual credit from their being possessed or worn devoutly. Thus, the devout life of all of the confraternities and societies was underpinned by the carefully-calibrated system of indulgences which was designed to earn the faithful remission of time in purgatory, and smooth their passage into heaven.

Besides the spiritual benefits of membership, the religious associations afforded material advantages to sodalists. Tangible symbols, which promoted a sense of belonging to sodalities and confraternities, were provided for by the system of small but regular monetary contributions, which, moreover, aided the practical management. On joining a sodality or confraternity, a new member paid a subscription which remained fairly constant at about one shilling for most of the period under review. In addition, there was a regular fee per week or per sodality meeting, careful note of which was kept by the association's treasurer. This normally amounted to one penny, or two shillings and six pence per annum for the scapularists of the Carmelites. The funds thus gathered were applied to confraternity expenses, ranging from the purchase of vestments for the clergy to the decoration of the confraternity chapel with flowers on feast-days. More importantly, the treasury allowed the associations to acquire sacral objects such as scapulars, cinctures and medals for dissemination to the members, and for shields and banners for the individual guilds or sections of the confraternities. Celebrants' stipends were also covered by these subscriptions. Sodality and confraternity activity was promoted and reported on in a large range of publications, the dissemination of which provided another source of income for the organising bodies, mostly the religious orders. Notable periodicals included the *Illustrated Monitor* which promoted the Apostleship of Prayer and the confraternity of the Sacred Thirst, the *Catholic Layman*, the *Crusader of Mary* and the *Sacred Heart Messenger*. The acquisition of libraries of Catholic literature was facilitated by the collection of members' subscriptions of six pence per month to the Christian Doctrine confraternity, and the Paulstown Book Society benefited similarly.[34] Diplomas and

---

[34] 'Ledger of the Paulstown Book Society, Kilkenny', 1856–71 (Maynooth College, Russell Library).

certificates of membership were issued, which usually contained iconography appropriate to the confraternity or sodality, and sometimes prayers suited to its devotional regime, with space for inscription of the name of the entrant and date of admission.

Outside the church buildings and yards, the confraternities and sodalities had built up a substantial public presence throughout the country. On religious feast-days, including those of patron saints, members of the associations formed into processions through streets and neighbourhoods. In these religious parades, the sisters and brothers were distinguishable by their liveries and costumes, and they marched behind their banners and shields. The Children of Mary wore blue veils and gloves, for example, and members of the Carmelite fraternities were dressed in their ceremonial scapulars. The festival of Corpus Christi in late spring brought together large concourses in most towns, the processions echoing the late medieval assemblages of all stations and ranks with their opportunities for sociability. Some confraternities organised pilgrimages for members to sacred shrines, including a three-day one by the confreres of St Augustine and St Monica in Drogheda to Knock in 1880, the year after first reports of the apparition there of the Blessed Virgin.[35] Some travelled farther, as in cases of the Franciscan tertiaries' trip to Lourdes in 1939, and the visit of representatives of the Holy Family in Limerick to Rome in 1925.[36] The celebration of jubilee years of associations allowed for the venting of pride of membership, frequently expressed with displays of pomp. These included ceremonies and processions for the golden jubilee of the Sacred Heart sodality in Phibsborough in 1924, and the golden and diamond anniversaries of the Holy Family confraternity in Limerick in 1928 and 1938, which attracted up to 10,000 participants.[37] The confraternity brass band headed a march of between 5,000 and 6,000 confreres of the Holy Family in Mullingar for a Eucharistic celebration in 1928.[38]

[35] Minutes of archconfraternity of the Cincture, St Augustine and St Monica, 1880 (Dublin, Augustinian Archives).

[36] Irish Times, 2 Nov.1925.

[37] Ibid., 30 June 1924; 23 July 1928; 4 July 1938.

[38] Ibid., 12 June 1928; http://www.irishconfraternities.ie/view_images.php?type =manuscripts (accessed 4 Oct. 2010).

Confraternity members turned out in significant numbers to swell the ranks at public funerals and commemorations. The latter included a number associated with the career of Daniel O'Connell, such as the centenary of his birth in 1875, when over 7,500 sodalists from all over Ireland joined the procession with banners displayed, the campaign to erect the O'Connell monument in 1882 at which 5,000 members of several confraternities were present, and the centenary of Catholic emancipation in 1929 in Limerick where the archconfraternity was represented in the 15,000 strong march.[39] Among the funeral corteges in which members participated were those of Cardinal Paul Cullen, a great populariser of the associations, in 1878, Cardinal Edward McCabe in 1885 and Archbishop William Walsh in 1921.[40]

In an age of restricted social outlets for many men and women, confraternity membership offered the companionship and fellowship of the like-minded. Apart from the sociability of the regular meetings, a highlight of the social calendar for brothers and sisters was the annual sodality excursion. This was normally to a place of recreation such as Courtown, visited by 750 women from the Most Holy Cross and Passion at Mount Argus in July 1916, or Gort, to which the Brown Scapularists resorted in the early 1910s.[41] The Holy Family confraternity of Mullingar ventured farther, to Llandudno in north Wales.[42] Sodality rail outings were so popular that Great Southern Railways offered an instalment system for the paying of fares to branch treasurers.[43] In an extension perhaps of the habit of prudent financial planning, one of the many projects promoted by the Limerick branch of the Holy Family confraternity was the opening of a savings bank for members, which continued from 1905 to 1933.[44] Confraternity membership provided opportunities for

[39] Irish Times, 7 Aug. 1875; 24 July 1882, 10 Aug. 1882; 17 June 1929.

[40] Ibid., 28 Oct. 1878; 21 Feb. 1885; 13 Apr. 1921.

[41] Minutes of women's branch of confraternity of the Most Holy Cross and Passion, 1916 (Dublin, Passionist Archives, Mount Argus); http://www.irish-confraternities.ie/images/confraternity/141.jpg (accessed 4 Oct. 2010).

[42] Letter of Mr Micheál Ó Conlain, member of Holy Family confraternity, Mullingar (2 Aug. 2007).

[43] Irish Times, 11 Mar. 1938.

[44] Account book of archconfraternity Savings Account, 1905–33 (Limerick, Redemptorists' Archive).

the pursuit of pastimes. Women who were needleworkers or dressmakers could deploy their skills in the sewing of confraternity banners and the preparation of liveries, and women sodalists were also encouraged to provide home-craft clubs for young single women in cities.[45] The Holy Family confraternity in particular favoured the use of hymn-singing in church, and the cultivation of music and song could carry over into the extra-ecclesial sphere. For example, some confraternities had bands, which performed not just on religious feasts but also participated in the wider cultural milieu. Musical evenings and dramatic performances were also popular with the members of sodalities on their nights out, but dancing continued to be frowned upon until the campaign to elicit youth culture in support of the confraternal movement in the mid-twentieth century. Then also sporting activities came to be encouraged, as, for example, among the Catholic Young Men's Association, linked to the confraternity of the Immaculate Conception. Their hobbies and pastimes included billiards, football and tennis.

The moral authority of the confraternities was brought to bear upon campaigns and debates in the social, cultural and political spheres in Ireland in the earlier twentieth century, usually through the intervention therein of prominent clerical directors. The best known case is that of the Redemptorist, Fr John Creagh, who used his position as director of the Holy Family archconfraternity in Limerick to criticise Jewish families whom he objected to as money-lenders in that city, but he had also railed against the abuses by publicans of their licences for selling alcohol.[46] Much of the impetus of the latter campaign against intemperance was channelled into the abstinence movements of the twentieth century, some of which developed as quasi-sodalities, particularly the Pioneer Total Abstinence Society. In like manner, while confraternities and sodalities became associated with campaigns against indecency in the cinema and literature, there were self-appointed groups of Catholics and other denominations which acted as watchdogs

---

[45] http://www.carmelites.ie/Spirituality/scapular.htm (accessed 22 Mar. 2007).
[46] Des Ryan, 'The Jews, Father Creagh and the mayor's court of conscience' in *Old Limerick Journal*, 38 (2002), pp 49–52; 'Fr John Creagh, CSsR: social reformer, 1870–1947', ibid., 41 (2005), pp 30–2.

of morality in the media and press.[47] Confraternity directors
took part in campaigns against immoral behaviour in dance-
halls and night-clubs, the subject of many pamphlets under the
imprint of the newly-established Catholic Truth Society. In the
post-Vatican II period, it became common for directors of
confraternities to lend their voices to calls for social justice in
respect of, for example, the Travelling community, or itinerants,
as they were termed in the parlance of the time, though intima-
tions of such commitment were evident in, for example, the
Limerick confraternity director's support for the rights of
striking coal-workers at Shannon in 1924.[48] As with many
Catholic groups, the confraternities were also linked to the
anti-communism of the 1930s and 1940s, a campaign for the
release of the Hungarian primate, Cardinal Mindszenty, garner-
ing support in 1949 among confreres and sodalists.[49] In thus
taking a political stance, the confraternity representatives were
replicating the commitment of early periodicals such as *The
Illustrated Monitor* to raising the consciousness of members to international issues. Efforts to harness such sentiments in the 1970s
and 1980s campaigns for constitutional change were hampered
by the decay of the confraternal movement after the Council.

****

By the 1950s, it appeared that the influence of the confraternity
movement in Ireland had reached and perhaps passed its
zenith.[50] Not only did powerful directors contribute to national
debates, but the actions of a combined association under the title
the United Confraternities of the archdiocese of Dublin bespoke
the organised power of the movement. There were musters of
up to 10,000 members of the Limerick archconfraternity on
public occasions, and 50,000 people marched under the United

---

[47] See Eamonn Dunne, 'Action and reaction: Catholic lay organisations in
Dublin in the 1920s and 1930s' in *Archiv. Hib.*, xlviii (1994), pp 109–11.

[48] *Irish Times*, 17 Oct. 1925; 13 Dec. 1969.

[49] Ibid., 2 May 1949.

[50] Maurice Hartigan, 'The religious life of the Catholic laity of Dublin, 1920–40'
in Kelly and Keogh (eds), *Catholic diocese of Dublin*, pp 332–6.

Confraternities banner in Dublin on the feast of the Immaculate Heart of Mary in 1949. Behind these impressive figures, however, there were signs of a falling off in membership, particularly among men. To judge by the surviving confraternity records, attendance at meetings and liturgical celebrations was an issue, with consequent implications for fund-raising, but absenteeism had been a perennial problem. As early as 7 April 1867, there was a call for measures to counter 'the growing tepidity' of members of the confraternity of the Most Holy Cross and Passion at Mount Argus.[51] By the early twentieth century it is clear that the means to combat recalcitrance was a frequent topic of discussion at meetings of officers of that confraternity. Here the role of the prefects was central, in recording attendances and following up the laggards. Often this would merely entail a friendly tap on the arm with an exhortation to do better in the future. When lay pressure failed to pay off, a visit from the priest was sometimes arranged to frighten the straying member into compliance.[52] Persistent offenders were liable to be formally cautioned, and in the ultimate sanction, struck off the register, their names actually being erased and their medals and insignia decommissioned. At diocesan level, the visitation of parishes by the bishop came routinely to contain questions on the numbers and memberships of local sodalities and confraternities. Accordingly, confraternal activity was integrated closely within the imperative to maintain devotional allegiance among the faithful. The evidence suggests that the answers to questions were being provided fairly ritualistically, with little variation from year to year in levels of attendance over the decades down to the 1960s.[53]

In many of the remaining essays in this volume, questions concerning the role of the sodalities and confraternities in the mid-twentieth-century decades are addressed in detail. These include the challenge of appealing to youth in an age of expanding mass communication and changing attitudes towards the status of the laity in the Catholic church. In these analyses, there

---

[51] Minutes of men's branch of confraternity of the Most Holy Cross and Passion, 1867 (Dublin, Passionist Archives, Mount Argus).

[52] Cleary, 'Confraternities and how to work them' in *IER*, xxix (1927), p. 173.

[53] See DDA, 'Visitation sheets'.

is a pervasive theme of the decline of traditional confraternities and sodalities, and an attempt is made therein to explain this trend. For the purposes of concluding this overview, it may be noted that, as an antidote to the older rule-bound societies which encouraged lay passivity, there were new developments stemming from the influence of Catholic sociological thinking in Ireland and elsewhere which provided an outlet for more dynamic lay activity. Besides the reinvigorated Society of St Vincent de Paul and the flourishing Pioneer Total Abstinence Society, other societies offering alternatives to traditional confraternal activity were established. These included the Legion of Mary, founded in 1921, which placed an emphasis on visitation of the needy and the troubled between meetings for prayer and reflection. Catholic philanthropy infused the Guild of St Philip, set up in 1948 to provide care and comfort for former prisoners. Existing associations such the Catholic Young Men's Association and the Association for the Propagation of the Faith (renamed the Pontifical Work for the Propagation of the Faith) appear to have promised more active roles for laypeople within the community, the CYMA as a recreational and charitable outlet for young males, and the PWPF as a channel for missionary zeal among laypeople.

5

The Church of Ireland parochial associations: a social and cultural analysis

Martin Maguire

Confraternities, voluntary groups of the laity organised around the cult of a saint and aimed to accumulate a treasury of redemptive merit for the sake of the soul after death, have deep roots in medieval Christianity but are regarded with suspicion in Protestant cultures.[1] For Irish Protestants, steeped in Reformation theology, redemption, which sprang from the sacrifice of Christ, could not be gained by works. Nonetheless the Protestant churches, especially the Church of Ireland, generated a great variety of lay parish associations in which substantial numbers of the community participated at some stage of their lives. The growth of voluntary parochial associations in the early and mid-nineteenth century reflected the influence of the evangelical movements and their determination to promote a serious religion within the culture of Irish Protestantism. In the longer term the enduring influence of the Second Reformation on Irish Protestantism was in its revitalisation of parish life and the central role that evangelicalism conferred on the laity, features which echo the medieval confraternities. Parochial associations empowered the laity, gave a sense of moral purpose to life and acted to bond the community. The flourishing of these lay organisations was seen as a sign of God's saving grace.

The Church of Ireland parish is the oldest continuing ecclesiastical, political and social structure in Ireland. The Church of Ireland, as the church 'by law established', became the legal inheritor of the medieval Christian church as it was brought

---

[1] Adrian Empey, 'The layperson in the parish: the medieval inheritance, 1169–1536' in Raymond Gillespie and W. G. Neely (eds), *The laity and the Church of Ireland, 1000–2000: all sorts and conditions* (Dublin, 2002), pp 7–48.

under state control in the Tudor reformation. After the Reformation, the Church of Ireland parish had a monopoly of public worship and exclusive freedom to exercise religion. Each parish also served as a civil structure of local government through the work of the parish vestry and came under the control of government officials. Therefore the Church of Ireland parish retained considerable influence and authority in Irish state and society despite being the church of a minority of the Irish people, and also despite being only one amongst many Protestant denominations. The Church of Ireland community of all classes have always shown a tenacious loyalty to the religious and social life of their own local parish.[2]

The proselytising organisations that aimed at the mass conversion of the Irish peasantry is one strand of the 'Second Reformation' that has entered popular imagination through the folklore of 'souperism' and has been subject to sensitive and subtle study.[3] However, it is important to note that the evangelical revival that transformed Irish Protestantism in the 'Second Reformation' had many strands. The evangelical impulse also sought to energise and revitalise the Church of Ireland with an enthusiastic religion. The concept of 'conversion', which later meant the proselytising of Catholics, was initially applied to Protestant renewal through the personal experience of salvation. Conversion was usually spoken of as an intense and emotional awareness of sin and redemption awakened by meditation on the Cross and from reading the Bible.[4] This was also expected to lead to a sense of mission and a commitment to a Christian activism. Many early nineteenth-century observers commented on the growth in Dublin of a prudent and serious tone to what had been previously a gay and somewhat

[2] John Crawford, *The Church of Ireland in Victorian Dublin* (Dublin, 2005), pp 45–85.

[3] Desmond Bowen, *Souperism: myth or reality* (Cork, 1970); idem, *The Protestant crusade in Ireland 1800–70: a study of Protestant–Catholic relations between the Act of Union and Disestablishment* (Dublin, 1978); Irene Whelan, *The bible war in Ireland: the 'Second Reformation' and the polarization of Protestant–Catholic relations, 1800–1840* (Dublin, 2005); Miriam Moffitt, *Soupers and jumpers: the Protestant missions in Connemara 1848–1937* (Dublin, 2008) are amongst the main full-length studies on this subject.

[4] D. W. Bebbington, *Evangelicalism in modern Britain: a history from the 1730s to the 1980s* (London, 1989).

dissipated city.[5] Irish evangelicals were inspired by, and modelled themselves on, British examples of evangelical laymen taking on moral causes.[6] The Clapham Sect, led by Wilberforce, campaigned for the abolition of the slave trade and for world evangelisation. The Church Mission Society, founded by members of the Clapham Sect, set an example of lay evangelicals exercising a powerful influence on public morality.[7] In 1814 an Irish branch of the CMS, the Hibernian Auxiliary to the Church Missionary Society, was founded.[8] The CMS youth branch, the Gleaners' Society, has become a ubiquitous presence in the Church of Ireland parishes. Another of the earliest of these lay missionary organisations was the Association for Discountenancing Vice and Promoting the Practice of the Christian Religion (later APCK), founded in 1792. The APCK sought to improve public morality, encourage the observance of the Sabbath but, conscious of the power of the printed word, to cater especially to the growing literate population by distributing bibles, prayer books and tracts.[9] Other lay-dominated societies that sprang from the evangelical revival included the Hibernian Bible Society, founded in 1806, and the Sunday School Society for Ireland, founded in 1809. The Hibernian Bible Society was an off-shoot of the British and Foreign Bible Society, itself another creation of the Clapham Sect.[10] The Sunday School movement was begun by Robert Raikes (1735–1811) in Gloucester when he opened a Sunday school in 1780 to clear the gangs of undisciplined children off the streets. As respectable society responded the Sunday School became a movement and spread across the Anglican world, with an Irish society being founded in 1810. In 1822 Tom Lefroy, a prominent lay

[5] Crawford, *Church of Ireland in Victorian Dublin*, pp 50–2.

[6] John Patterson, 'Lay spirituality and worship, 1750–1950' in Neely and Gillespie (eds) *Laity in the Church of Ireland*, pp 250–76.

[7] Irene Whelan, 'The bible gentry: evangelical religion, aristocracy and the new moral order in the early nineteenth century' in Crawford Gribben and Andrew E. Holmes (eds) *Protestant millennialism, evangelicalism and Irish society, 1790–2005* (Basingstoke, 2006), pp 52–82.

[8] Alan Acheson, *A history of the Church of Ireland 1691–1996* (Dublin, 1997), p. 120.

[9] Acheson, *History of the Church of Ireland 1691–1996*, pp 121–4; Kenneth Milne, *APCK: the early decades* (Dublin, 1992).

[10] Dudley Levistone Cooney, *Sharing the Word: a history of the Bible Society in Ireland* (Dublin, 2006).

evangelical and member of the Dublin legal establishment (now more famous as a supposed beau of a youthful Jane Austen), was amongst the founders of the Scripture Readers Society, formed to send readers of the bible amongst the Irish peasantry.

Evangelicals echoed the British discourse on Ireland under the Union as a 'pathology of backwardness' in which Ireland was always a 'problem'. For some Irish Protestants the cause of this pathological condition was clear. It was the failure to evangelise the Catholics of Ireland, a failure that the Union would help address. The Act of Union set the political context in which a network of clergymen and Irish gentry families of evangelical convictions, with the inclusion of the business and professional classes of Protestant Dublin, led an expectation of a popular Reformation that would raise Ireland to British levels of political, economic and social development through the mass conversion of the Irish peasantry.[11] This analysis achieved its apogee in the Society for Irish Church Missions to the Roman Catholics, founded by English evangelicals in 1849. Mired in allegations of inducing conversions by offering food in famine-racked Ireland, the ICM gave evangelicals an explicit anti-Catholic and Orange reputation. By then, however, as British opinion began to include the Church of Ireland as part of the Irish problem rather than as the answer to that problem, the cultural relationship of Irish Protestantism with the British state was already being fundamentally undermined. Emancipation, which gave civil equality to Catholics, was followed by the Church Temporalities (Ireland) Act 1833, which began the erosion of the Church of Ireland as a self-governing arm of the state. Disestablishment finally severed the connection with the British state, creating a religiously neutral state in Ireland. Disestablishment strengthened the role of the laity within the Church of Ireland and had the effect of turning the church away from identification with the state and back into the parish community.

Since disestablishment the Church of Ireland has been sustained as an institution by the formal, legal structures of the Synod and the Representative Church Body (RCB), but as a community by a vibrant lay culture of voluntary associations. In

---

11 Whelan, 'Bible gentry, evangelical religion, aristocracy', p. 52.

contrast to the essentially congregational structures of the other Protestant denominations, the Church of Ireland has always retained the parish as the basis of its organisation and it continues to be the bedrock of its cultural and social associations. The Big House has overly dominated discussion on the culture of Protestantism in Ireland. Despite the attempts to invest the Big House with an iconic status, Irish Protestantism remains in fact mainly an urbanised culture of the working and middle classes. For these plain Protestants the parish church, and not the Big House, was at the heart of their sense of community, and it is the informal networks of parochial associations that have expressed, in a day-to-day sense, the experience of being a Protestant of the Church of Ireland and being part of its parish-centred local culture.

The attachment of the Church of Ireland community to the parish can be briefly illustrated by the extent of local resistance to the closure of churches, which forms an interesting contrast with un-mourned Big Houses. The Church of Ireland inherited, after Disestablishment, 1,630 parish churches. As a voluntary organisation it was no longer able to avail of state revenues and was dependent on the resources of its members.[12] Disestablishment has also led to the laity assuming a much greater role in the day-to-day life of the parish. Local congregations maintain the parish fabric largely out of their own resources and this has created a strong sense of identity with the local parish. The Church of Ireland was, however, very much over-churched and under-resourced. The solution arrived at by the RCB was to begin closing parish churches and amalgamating them into unions of parishes. During the course of the 100 years since Disestablishment a series of official commissions run by the RCB has reduced by almost half the number of parish churches through sale or demolition. Closure of parish churches has in all cases faced intense local resistance.[13]

Most Church of Ireland parishes sustained an extraordinary range of social organisations, a mix of evangelical, temperance,

---

[12] R. B. McDowell, *The Church of Ireland, 1869–1969* (London, 1975), p. 79.

[13] Martin Maguire, 'Churches and symbolic power in the Irish landscape' in *Landscapes*, 5, no. 2 (Autumn, 2004), pp 91–113.

social, sporting and recreational. Most of these organisations were branches of a national society, and it is the sheer number of parochial associations that is most striking. In the 1930s St George's, a poor inner city parish in decline, characterised by an ageing and poor congregation, could still maintain sixteen different parish societies.[14] A well-off and growing parish such as Clontarf with a Church of Ireland population of just over two thousand souls supported an even more luxuriant growth of forty associations.[15] As a recent oral history of the modern Protestant community in independent Ireland observes: 'The importance of the parish ... cannot be underestimated.'[16]

There are several questions that arise in considering the rich voluntary and associational culture that characterised the laity of the Church of Ireland parish. First, does the rich growth of lay-led organisations in the Church of Ireland reflect a high level of social capital and an engagement with civil society? None of these associations depended on clerical initiative, all grew out of the laity and all were led by the ordinary women (for the most part) and men of the parish. Membership was open to all Protestants, regardless of denomination. These associations are explored here from the perspective of class (what did they offer to working class Protestants?), a generational perspective (what did they offer to young Protestants?), and a gender perspective (what do they tell us about male and female roles in the Church of Irish parish?) to see what general conclusions might arise on the laity and the associational culture of the Church of Ireland parish.

The earliest voluntary associations in the Church of Ireland were directed at the poor and the working class. The increasingly complex class structure of Ireland in the early nineteenth century and the growth in inequality and poverty led to an increase in the numbers of poor and unemployed Protestants. The civil parish vestries which had responsibility for poor relief, for the most part run by members of the established church, whilst tending to favour the Protestant poor, did offer relief to

---

[14] *St George's Parish Magazine* (Oct. 1933).

[15] *Clontarf Parish Magazine* (Mar. 1943).

[16] Heather K. Crawford, *'Outside the glow': Protestants and Irishness in independent Ireland* (Dublin, 2010), p. 75.

all the poor of the parish, including Catholics.[17] When in 1838, the state took responsibility for poor relief through the poor law system it freed up the Church of Ireland parishes to concentrate on the Protestant poor. This coincided with both the growth of evangelical movements within the church that encouraged a providential interpretation of poverty, discouraging excessive human intervention, but also inspiring some to work amongst the poor. In the Dublin slums, what has been described as a 'battle' was fought between the ICM and Catholic activists for the allegiance of the poor in which the underclass of the poorest areas of the city gained some material benefit from the factional competition.[18]

Not all charitable organisations were concerned with proselytising and for most the problem became one of ensuring that the beneficiaries of Protestant charity were exclusively Protestants. An array of parish associations developed to cater for what we might call niche markets of poverty, such as the aged, respectable Protestant females, widows and orphans of clergymen, destitute Protestant orphans, former Protestant servants unable to work, Protestant unmarried mothers, and others. The records of the Association for the Relief of Distressed Protestants (ARDP) founded in 1834, the longest-lived and most pervasive Protestant association dealing with the poor, show a deep anxiety about the potential of poverty to weaken the commitment of the poor and working class to Protestantism. The penetrating level of inquiry into the life of applicants for relief was not to determine the degree of need but rather the degree of commitment to Protestant fundamentals. For instance, possession of a family Bible was *de rigueur*, while marriage to a non-Protestant instantly barred access to the charitable organisations and its funds. In 1892 George Duniam Williams, secretary of the ARDP, compiled a handbook of Dublin charities in which he listed the many highly specialised charitable voluntary organisations at work, mostly divided

---

[17] Ruth Lavelle and Paul Huggard, 'The parish poor of St Mark's' in David Dickson (ed.), *The gorgeous mask: Dublin 1700–1850* (Dublin, 1987), pp 86–97.

[18] Jacinta Prunty, 'Battle plans and battlegrounds: Protestant mission activity in the Dublin slums, 1840s–1880s' in Gribben and Holmes (eds), *Protestant millennialism*, pp 119–43.

along sectarian lines and denominationally exclusive. Williams urged better organisation to eliminate the vast overlapping of effort. He was also suspicious that the applicants for relief had become adept at shaping their requests to suit the charity applied to, a sort of professionalisation of the trade of begging in which applicants had no qualms about pretending to be Catholic or Protestant as the situation demanded. The result of these many voluntary charities catering for the Protestant poor was sufficient relief to prevent complete impoverishment but not enough to actually improve the lot of the poor. The cost to the applicants was loss of privacy and finding their lives heavily policed. The aim was to maintain a strong Irish Protestant identity amongst the poor and the working class, enforce sobriety, but mostly to ensure that the at-risk members of the Protestant churches were not lost to the competition offered by the Catholic charities. However, the ARDP's mode of investigation did ensure some level of intimacy between the poor and their benefactors. Members and subscribers to the ARDP could nominate candidates for consideration. These nominations required some level of understanding of the personal details of the poor and some sympathy for their wretched circumstances. Although it encouraged a prying attitude and no doubt fed resentment, it did ensure that charitable activists from the middle class had to get their hands dirty.[19]

Dorcas meetings also provide an occasion for the middle class women to engage with the poorer Protestants and most parishes had such a society. Inspired by the story in Acts of the Apostles, 9:36–42, of the charitable Dorcas who made clothes for the poor and responding also to the belief that poorer Protestants were ashamed to attend church on Sunday because of their shabby appearance, the Dorcas societies made clothes for the poor. Dorcas groups were serious but also convivial meetings that combined needlework, prayer and conversation whilst reinforcing the connection between Protestantism and respectability, even in the poorer classes.

---

[19] Martin Maguire, 'The Church of Ireland and the problem of the Protestant working class of Dublin, 1870s–1930s' in Alan Ford, James McGuire and Kenneth Milne (eds), 'As by law established': the Church of Ireland since the Reformation (Dublin, 1995), pp 195–203.

An Irishwoman, Mary Elizabeth Townsend, started the Girls' Friendly Society (GFS) in England as an association for the benefit of working class girls, 'whether at home or in service, or employed in shops or factories'. With the ladies of the parish acting as associates and the girls as members the objective was to maintain a parish organisation that would prevent girls going astray, inculcate purity and provide across the parishes a network of middle class ladies to ensure that girls removed from their homes would not be without a friend and guide. The GFS arrived in Ireland in 1877 and branches of the Society were soon established in almost all Church of Ireland parishes.[20]

By the early twentieth century – by which time the state had begun to assume greater responsibility for the poor – Protestant anxiety had shifted to the young and the fear that it was marriage outside the Anglican community, and not poverty, that was eroding the Protestant population. Each marriage represented not only the immediate loss of an adult but also the future loss of the children of the Protestant partner. This fear was given a sharper edge by the *Ne Temere* decree of 1908. Through the twentieth century anxiety about marriage to Catholics increased, with each census showing not only a declining population but also one that was changing its shape: less rural and more urban, more middle-class, an ageing and celibate population. The 1961 census showed that 60 per cent of males and 40 per cent of females in the Protestant population in the age group 20 to 40 were unmarried. The number of Protestants marrying Catholics grew in number, generally Protestant male to Catholic female. The result was a major effort to create a network of parochial social organisations aimed at the young to convey a sense of Protestant superiority and encourage loyalty to the Protestant community, but principally to discourage social mixing with Catholics.

In 1881 Francis Clark, a clergyman in Portland, Maine founded a young persons' society, Christian Endeavour. By 1889 this organisation had a branch in Belfast and by the century's end had branches all over Ireland, with a claimed 10,000

---

20 D. M. McFarlan, *Lift thy banner: Church of Ireland scenes 1870–1900* (Dundalk, 1990), pp 94–5; Kenneth Milne, 'Disestablishment and the lay response' in Neely and Gillespie (eds), *Laity and the Church of Ireland*, p. 239.

membership.[21] Christian Endeavour aimed to create a serious-minded and biblical Christianity in its members through reading and discussion and to encourage the young to become active in parish work. A junior wing called the Young People's Society and a former members' wing called the Comrades' Society soon followed. This ensured that the sense of fellowship and church solidarity was sustained through life.

The Boys' Brigade under the motto 'Sure and Steadfast' was founded in Glasgow in 1883 as a Protestant and imperialist boys' movement to further 'the advancement of Christ's Kingdom among boys and the promotion of habits of obedience, reverence, discipline, self-respect, and all that tends towards a true Christian manliness'. In Dublin members were taught commercial skills such as bookkeeping and shorthand, and these classes were well attended. The Dublin Boys' Brigade maintained an employment agency for the boys, and employers – many of them former members – were encouraged to ask there first for junior clerks, apprentices or assistants.[22] However, it is worth noting that many Protestant boys resented the exploitation hidden by this supposed favouritism and also the implied threat that socialising beyond the Protestant community would lead to a poor reference and diminished prospects later. The growth of uniformed quasi-military youth organisations that combined imperialism with religious high-mindedness saw the proliferation of scouting organisations based on the Church of Ireland parishes.

Discussion on a mixture of amusement and exhortation formed the staple of most of the associations aimed at youth and young adults such as Christian Endeavour, the Young Men's Christian Association, the Young Women's Christian Association, and the parish church associations. Topics for discussion seem to have been chosen to encourage participation without becoming overly contentious and possibly divisive, that is to say they were primarily to facilitate debate as a leisure activity. Typically, the objectives of the Church of Ireland Men's

---

[21] D. A. Levistone Cooney, *A history of the Christian Endeavour movement in Ireland* (Belfast, 1977).

[22] *St Matthew's Parish Magazine* (Apr. 1899, June 1924); *Clontarf Parish Magazine* (May 1924, June 1925, Jan. 1927).

Society were: to band churchmen together in a common effort to promote the glory of God and to help forward the work of the church; to foster the practice of Christian brotherhood and conduct, and to promote opportunities for social intercourse amongst members and associates; to provide for the systematic commendation of members and associates on change of residence.[23]

It is clear that for most young people the social dimension of these associations was of greater importance than the evangelical. Participation in the lectures, debates and discussions always required considerable persuasion. These were generally the winter programmes. By contrast the summer programmes of day excursions and weekly dances were always hugely popular. Social and sporting clubs with no pretence to any other function than providing recreation, but which were exclusively available to Protestants, were the most successful, and gradually social organisations displaced the more evangelical. Thus, by the 1930s most parishes supported a variety of very popular cricket, tennis or badminton clubs in the suburban parishes or soccer and snooker clubs in the city parishes. Associated with these were dances, whist drives and other social events. The associations for the young were formed to encourage and enable young people to socialise exclusively within the Protestant community and, hopefully, marry within the community.[24] Today it would be true to say that the parish associations in the Church of Ireland are focussed overwhelmingly on the social rather than the holy. The decline of the evangelical influence and the growth of a social function also reflect the growing feminisation of the lay voluntary associations of the Church of Ireland.

Women were debarred from the structures of power and authority within the formal administration of the Church of Ireland. Women had no place on the select vestries that ran the parishes nor on the voting representation at the Synods. They were, in short, of low formal status. In contrast, women discovered an informal agency in the parish associations. In fact, women were vital in parish associations as organisers,

23 *Clontarf Parish Magazine* (Jan. 1910).
24 Martin Maguire, 'Community and the Church of Ireland' in Neely and Gillespie (eds), *Laity and the Church of Ireland*, p. 273.

recruiters, fund-raisers and managers. Without this voluntary activity by women the Church of Ireland as a living community would have died. It was a woman, Margaret Magill, who brought the Christian Endeavour movement to Ireland. Dorcas societies were entirely women-run, and, as has been noted, it was a woman who founded the GFS. The most significant and ubiquitous organisation run for and by women was the Mothers' Union. The Mothers' Union was founded in England in 1872 by Mary Sumner and arrived in Ireland in 1887, when the first MU was founded in Raheny parish. Facilitated by the British empire, it became the most characteristic parochial organisation within the Anglican world. The Mothers' Union sought to 'uphold the sanctity of marriage; to awaken in mothers a sense of their great responsibility in the training of their boys and girls, the future fathers and mothers of the empire; to organise in every place a band of mothers who will unite in prayer and seek by their own example to lead their families in purity and holiness of life'.[25] In time the Mothers' Union has become primarily a way to integrate newcomers into parish life, the initial hostility to divorce as inimical to family life was dropped and single women were encouraged to join. The Zenana Missionary Society combined imperialism with women's activism. Named after the part of the Muslim household reserved for women, the Zenana Mission Society was founded in 1880 to evangelise the women of India through schools and medical missions.

With the decline of the evangelical influence, especially in the period after the First World War and the establishment of an independent Ireland, women began to exert a different influence in the parishes.[26] Whereas men dominated the formal structures as clergy and hierarchy, churchwardens, synodmen and select vestry, it was women who dominated the informal voluntary structures and answered the need for religion to serve a social purpose. The parochial associations played a far bigger part in the lives of women than in the lives of men. Women

---

[25] Maguire, 'Community and the Church of Ireland', p. 295.

[26] Oonagh Walsh, *Anglican women in Dublin: philanthropy, politics and education in the early twentieth century* (Dublin, 2005), pp 206–7.

made these clubs and societies warm and attractive places where the Protestant community, especially the young, could find identity and mutual support. Most of these clubs and societies had either all-women or mostly women committees. These parish associations, rather than the select vestry, were the backbone of the parish community. They catered for every age group, for both sexes, all sorts of special interest and sporting activities, literary discussion circles, and associated them in an extensive network of overlapping membership which reinforced communal identity and solidarity. They institutionalised, in a way that formal church services could not, what it was to be a member of the Church of Ireland community.[27] These organisations were primarily sociable. They relied particularly on the women of the parishes who had the time, energy and money to run them. The select vestry might run the official parish but it was women who ran the social parish. Holiness was less important an objective than socialisation; these lay parish organisations developed not as a way to change a community but as a way to arrest change. Most importantly, they were there to ensure, as far as possible, that the young would not socialise with Catholics. The parish lay networks served to facilitate exclusiveness, catering for the members of the parish and their Protestant friends. As the parish declined as a devotional centre, it retained its importance as a focus of social and cultural life for Protestants.

---

[27] Alan Megahey, *The Irish Protestant churches in the twentieth century* (Basingstoke, 2000), pp 55–64; David Hempton, *Religion and political culture in Britain and Ireland from the Glorious Revolution to the decline of empire* (Cambridge, 1996), p. 140.

6

Display, sacramentalism and devotion: the medals of the archconfraternity of the Holy Family, 1922–39

Lisa Godson

In July 1928 the diamond jubilee of the archconfraternity of the Holy Family of Limerick was celebrated in typically lavish style. The city was decorated with spectacular altars, street shrines, triumphal arches, flags and bunting, and thousands of confraternity members processed through the streets wearing their membership medals and carrying banners and statues. On the second day of the celebrations, the superior general of the Redemptorist Congregation was given the freedom of Limerick city, the lord mayor avowing in his address that 'One feared to think what the consequences would be in the city if the Order and all that it meant ceased to exist, as they were inseparably bound up with each other. The city would be utterly helpless.'[1]

Founded by the Redemptorists in 1868, by the Second World War the archconfraternity of the Holy Family in Limerick (ACHF) was widely described as the largest lay organisation of its kind in the world. In terms of numbers alone it was certainly 'inseparably bound' to Limerick city – the all-male membership of about six thousand in 1920 rising to about eight thousand in 1939. Including a boys' section, it numbered more than 10,000.[2] Most of the members were from Limerick city: the membership figures for September 1926 show that only 230 men out of about

---

[1] *Limerick Leader*, 23 July 1928.

[2] Membership figures are drawn from the archives of the Redemptorist House, Limerick, *Holy Family Chronicles Volume II 1898–1975*, henceforth referred to as *HFC II*. Although the figures are precisely recorded, they are often further qualified by annotations indicating that a certain number of members were completely inactive for various reasons (such as imprisonment, incapacitation or working abroad).

seven thousand were from 'country' parishes.[3] The census for that year records that there were 19,045 men in Limerick city, an indication that more than one third of all adult males were members of the archconfraternity.[4]

The Redemptorist leaders of the archconfraternity in Limerick had both spiritual and social position. Their authority was exercised not only in matters of religion and morality, but also, for example, through their role as mediators between members and other powerful bodies such as the British Army during the Anglo–Irish War (1919–1921), and with local employers during labour disputes. Through the visibility of their members in the streets and the extension of the leaders' authority in many areas of daily life, the archconfraternity was pervasive in Limerick city.

The primary religious activity of the ACHF was a weekly meeting held for different 'divisions', on Mondays, Tuesdays and, from 1926, Wednesday nights. At these, prayers, in particular the rosary, were recited, followed by a sermon and benediction of the Blessed Sacrament. The divisions were further divided into sections, arranged according to the parishes that the section members lived or worked in. Each section had a prefect and sub-prefect who recorded attendance at the weekly meetings and checked whether members attended mass and communion in an attempt to regulate adherence to fundamental Catholic practice. The archconfraternity was headed by a 'Spiritual Director', a Redemptorist priest, who also kept a chronicle recording the activities of the organisation.

In addition to the weekly religious meetings, the ACHF held an annual retreat and special devotions at different times of the liturgical year. It also held social events and excursions, ran a bank for members from 1905 to 1933 and was active in guarding against 'immoral' entertainment. In 1927, the director appointed a committee to go to the first performance of plays at the Lyric Theatre every week and 'if they saw anything objectionable to let him know and he would have it changed'.[5] Another committee in September 1938 was asked to 'to keep a watch on

---

[3] *HFC II*, Sept. 1926.

[4] Census of Population, 1926.

[5] *HFC II*, Dec. 1927.

pictures' in the Savoy Cinema and elsewhere.[6] In this way, the organisation played a fundamental role in the religious, economic, cultural and social life of both its members and Limerick city.

The celebrations for the diamond jubilee and other major occasions were the most spectacular manifestations of the ACHF's ceremonial material culture. Occasions on which the archconfraternity performed ranged from once-off events, such as anniversaries, to regular church feasts such as Corpus Christi. However, elements of publicly-performed ceremony were also an aspect of many of the weekly meetings, in particular the journey of men to and from the church. Entries in the archconfraternity chronicle refer to the bands associated with particular sections 'playing the men' to or home from meetings. These public performances of piety were presented as acts of devotion, and the processions might be read as an articulation of the moral and social power of the organisation.

The material culture of the archconfraternity might be located in a number of areas: the banners and regalia used for the public rituals performed by the organisation, the ornate certificates of membership that were exhibited in domestic interiors, and even the archconfraternity members themselves as displayed corporately in processions and other ritual journeys. This material culture was significant not only in its contribution to the aesthetic effect or devotional inspiration provided by the organisation, but in its role in ritualising and disciplining the members. The disciplinary mechanisms through which the bodies of the members of the archconfraternity and the archconfraternity as a body were produced as ritualised and disciplined were largely effected through ceremonial and material culture, particularly as it pertained to Catholic sacramentalist culture and ritual.[7]

Many of the ACHF artefacts remain in the Redemptorist monastery in Limerick, with many more in the collections of Limerick City Museum. However, the main focus of this essay is on seemingly more mundane objects: the medals of membership

---

[6] *HFC II*, Sept. 1938.

[7] The term 'disciplinary mechanism' is particularly drawn from Michel Foucault, see *Discipline and punish: the birth of the prison* (London, 1977) and *The History of sexuality*, 3 vols (London, 1978,), vol. I.

that worked as private devotional artefacts, sacramental devices and badges of belonging. Informed by methodologies drawn from art history, material culture studies and sociology, an examination of the form and use of these medals suggests an approach not only to the archconfraternity and other pious associations but to Catholic material culture in general in this period.

Sacred material culture is fundamental to the operation of any Catholic organisation, most clearly through the central importance of sacraments in the church. In the 'devotional revolution' of the nineteenth century, alongside the great increase in religious personnel and institutions in Ireland there occurred the introduction of a wide range of religious objects. These were distributed in a number of ways, for example, through 'ecclesiastical warehouses' that sprang up from the 1840s, through religious orders importing statues and prints from abroad, and through parish missions.[8]

Emmet Larkin has described the parochial mission movement as 'the single most important factor in making and consolidating the devotional revolution', and an essential aspect of this was the distribution and instruction in the use of religious objects.[9] As with other orders, the Redemptorists heavily promoted the use of sacramental and devotional artefacts at parish missions and then later through the confraternities, often founded in the wake of the mission. In his study of the Congregation in the nineteenth century, John Sharp states that at missions 'prayer was facilitated by the cultic artefacts of the Church, such as rosaries, scapulars, holy pictures ... and medals, which were blessed in abundance towards the close.'[10]

A Redemptorist confraternity handbook of 1929 carries an appendix outlining the use of particular devotional objects. In a section 'Blessed Crosses, Medals, &c.' it instructs that

---

8 Evidence drawn from advertisements that appeared in the *Irish Catholic Directory*, 1838–1900, and from religious archives, for example, archives of the Sisters of the Holy Faith, Glasnevin, Dublin; archives of the Ursuline Convent, Blackrock, Cork. See also Lisa Godson, 'Catholicism and material culture in Ireland, 1840–1880' in *CIRCA*, 103 (Spring 2003), pp 38–45.

9 Emmet Larkin, 'The parish mission movement, 1850–1880' in Brendan Bradshaw and Dáire Keogh (eds), *Christianity in Ireland: revisiting the story* (Dublin, 2002), pp 195–204, p. 195.

10 John Sharp, *Reapers of the harvest: the Redemptorists in Great Britain and Ireland, 1843–1898* (Dublin, 1989), p. 172.

Any person who carries about with him, or keeps in his room or other fitting part of the house, a cross, crucifix, rosary, beads, image or medal of Jesus Christ, or any Saint canonised or mentioned in the Roman Martyrology, which has been blessed by a duly authorised priest, is entitled to gain the above-mentioned Papal Indulgences. In a Crucifix it is the figure of Our Lord to which the Indulgences are attached; it may be of wood, ivory, &c., but not of lead, or any substance which can easily be melted or broken. Beads made of glass may be indulgenced provided they are strong and solid.[11]

This suggests just some of the important aspects of sacramental objects – their placement either on the person or in an appropriate place in the domestic interior, the necessity of its having been empowered by an appropriate agent, and then the material substance of the object itself. The very specificity ('beads made of glass ... provided they are strong and solid') is typical of regulations regarding devotional objects. In her study of the material culture of Christianity, Colleen McDannell asserts that the detailed rules concerning the use of sacramental objects is an example of the way the authority of the Catholic church is 'constructed and maintained not merely through overt coercion but also the micromanagement of power'.[12] McDannell is referring here to the intercessionary and mediating role of agents of the institutional church, but this 'micromanagement' also suggests the relations between different constituencies of the church. For example, as John Sharp discusses in relation to the Redemptorists' 'privileges' in bestowing particular objects and being empowered to bless others, they could not only transmit spiritual riches, usually indulgences, to others, but 'also had a vested interest in exalting the authority of Rome as the dispenser of all these privileges'.[13]

The important role of sacramentals in the culture of Irish Catholicism from the devotional revolution until the Second Vatican Council (1962–5) suggests that members of the confraternity were already habituated to the sacred use of objects

---

[11] *Manual of Our Lady of Perpetual Succour by a Redemptorist priest* (London, 1929), p. 307.

[12] Colleen McDannell, *Material Christianity: religion and popular culture in America* (New Haven, Yale, 1995), p. 24.

[13] Sharp, *Reapers of the harvest*, p. 96.

before becoming members. The church and its agents such as confraternities made great use of sacramentalist material culture as a way of inculcating a specifically Catholic religious habitus. The first step was when an individual became a member of the archconfraternity and was conferred with a medal of membership. He was then expected to wear this at, to and from all meetings, monthly communion and all public ceremonies connected with the organisation. Like other sacramentals, there were very specific rules governing the meaning and use of the medals.

Figures 2.1 to 2.18 show the range of these medals in the collection of Limerick City Museum. In most of them the pattern is the same: an image of Jesus, Mary, Joseph and the Holy Spirit in the form of a dove on one side (referred to in the museum catalogue as the reverse) and an inscription on the obverse. The majority of medals in the museum refer to the archconfraternity, for example in the form of 'Archconfraternity of the Holy Family Established by Pius IX April 1847' in figures 2.1 and 2.7.

This side was sometimes more elaborate, as where the instruments of the Passion are depicted (figs 2.3 and 2.5) or where the hearts of Jesus, Mary and Joseph are represented (figs 2.9, 2.11, 2.13, 2.15 and 2.17). Most have some form of inscription on the reverse side as well, such as simply 'Jesus Mary Joseph' (fig. 2.2), or the more invocatory 'Holy Family patron and protector of our association we have recourse to you' (fig. 2.14) and 'Holy Family protect us' (fig. 2.18).

The reverse sides of the different medals are similar in both iconography and composition. Variations rest mainly with the inclusion of particular elements such as St Joseph's flowering rod and palm trees. No singular visual source is evident in any one of the medals; instead, they are a conflation of established ways of representing the Holy Family.[14]

These visual conventions are firstly of biblical or New Testament apocryphal narrative scenes based around the account of the Flight into Egypt. The main element included on some of the medals is the presence of a palm tree (figs 2.4, 2.6 and 2.8). This was often shown in Counter-Reformation

---

[14] Visual evidence for this is drawn from the photographic collection of the Warburg Institute, London.

paintings of the *Rest* (or *Repose*) on the *Flight*, its presence drawn from the apocryphal gospel of the pseudo-Matthew that narrates how a palm tree under which the family sheltered bent down its branches so they could gather its fruit. Examples include depictions by Annibale Carracci, *Rest on Flight into Egypt*,[15] and Francois Boucher, *Rest on the Flight into Egypt*.[16]

However, in such depictions Jesus is shown as an infant whereas on the medals he is clearly a child. Despite the presence of the palm trees, which indicate that the scene is the *Repose*, the images of the family on the medals might be based on imagery of the *Return from Egypt* when Jesus was typically represented as a young child, for example, as depicted by Jacob Jordaens in *The Return of the Holy Family from Egypt*.[17] The other popular art historical depiction of Jesus as a child is the *Finding in the Temple* when Jesus was twelve years old.

The imagery of the archconfraternity medals might be a conflation of two of the episodes from the *Flight into Egypt* episode: the *Repose* and the *Return*. However, each medal also includes the Holy Spirit in the form of a dove, which does not appear in typical depictions of either of these scenes. Its inclusion might relate the imagery to the more unusual and hieratic subject of the *Heavenly and Earthly Trinities*, conventionally painted in relation to the *Finding in the Temple*, for example, by Bartolemé Esteban Murillo in *The Heavenly and Earthly Trinities*.[18] In this, Murillo depicts the child Jesus with Joseph and Mary – the 'earthly' trinity, with God the Father – and the Holy Spirit as a dove above the child Jesus, suggestive of the 'heavenly' trinity.

The *Finding in the Temple* relates to the episode when Jesus was left behind in the Temple in Jerusalem, where he was found by his parents in debate with the Jewish scribes (Luke 2:41–51). It usually depicts the return of the Holy Family from the Temple accompanied by God the Father and the Holy Spirit, thus showing the 'earthly' trinity of Jesus, Mary and Joseph and the 'heavenly' trinity of God the Father, Son and Holy Spirit. This

---

[15] Annibale Carracci, *Rest on Flight into Egypt*, c.1600, The Hermitage, St Petersburg.

[16] Francois Boucher, *Rest on the Flight into Egypt*, 1737, The Hermitage, St Petersburg.

[17] Jacob Jordaens, *The Return of the Holy Family from Egypt*, c.1616, Gemaldegalerie, Berlin.

[18] Bartolemé Esteban Murillo in *The Heavenly and Earthly Trinities*, c.1675–82, National Gallery, London.

subject seems to have become established following the popularisation of devotion to the Holy Family by St Teresa of Avila, St Ignatius Loyola and in particular St Francis de Sales, who wrote that the Holy Family was 'a Trinity on earth representing in some sort the most Holy Trinity. Mary, Jesus, and Joseph – Joseph, Jesus, and Mary – a Trinity worthy indeed to be honored and greatly esteemed!'[19] The age of Jesus and the inclusion of the dove on the archconfraternity medals indicate that the imagery of the heavenly and earthly trinities could be a source, but that is not what is actually depicted, as God the Father is not included in any of the scenes.

The design of the archconfraternity medals in Limerick could be described as a collection of signs that signify the Holy Family without conforming to any particular narrative. The identity of individual members is clear, but by taking elements from a number of different narratives of the Holy Family that involve particular props and attributes such as the palm tree and the dove, the group is clearly signified as 'the Holy Family'. In fact, the appearance together of narratively incompatible elements such as Jesus as a young child, the palm tree and the Holy Spirit, make the medals in one sense over-signed, containing as they do a superfluity of significance.

However, the function of the imagery on the medals was not a narrative one but rather one of signification and identification. As such, the depiction of the Holy Family is hieratic and iconic and ultimately devotional. If the classification of the side with the inscription as 'obverse' and the pictorial side as 'reverse' is correct, the design of the medals can be seen to have both a public and private face. When worn publicly, for example for processions, with the obverse displayed outwards, the primary communicative function of the medal was to identify the wearer's social identity as a member of the archconfraternity. The reverse, 'private' side of the medal relates to individual religious experience, and the depiction of the Holy Family reminds the owners of the different aspects of the devotion they have pledged themselves to.

---

19 *The spiritual conferences of St Francis de Sales*, trans. F. Aidan Gasquet, and Henry Benedict Mackey, pp 373–4 cited in Joseph F. Chorpenning, Introduction to *The Holy Family in art and devotion* (Philadelphia, 1998) p. 41, n. 17.

One use of the medals therefore was that they carried depictions. In her essay on devotional medals, the cultural historian, Eli Heldaas Seland, remarks that religious images have at least three basic functions: a normative function in presenting *civitas Dei*, objects of faith that the owner or viewer identifies with; a formative function in shaping a *sensus fidelium* in terms of suggesting a common identity with other believers, and a way of making the sacred present – what she describes as a *'praesentia sacri et genius loci'*.[20] These are undoubtedly important functions but to focus only on the imagery is to ignore the other side of the medal – the inscription that fixed the object's identity as the possession of a member of the archconfraternity of the Holy Family, Limerick.

These medals were presented to members by the director as part of their initiation into the confraternity at a 'consecration' ceremony following a rite set out in detail in the manual.[21] Candidates knelt, holding the medals in their hands and made the Act of Consecration promising to be faithful to the rules of the confraternity. The medals were then blessed with holy water and by particular prayers said over them. In his book *Confraternity work and its problems.* Fr James Cleary, director of the ACHF from 1923 to 1927, advised that this ceremony be carried out with 'as much solemnity as possible' remarking that priests should realise the power of such ceremonies 'to impress the minds of ordinary lay folk'.[22]

As well as the medals being charged with meaning in terms of operating as the material sign of membership, the 'use' (presumably the wearing of them) carried indulgences.[23] Indulgences were also granted for membership of the confraternity, with those attached to the medal designated as 'real' and those related to membership as 'personal' in accordance with canon law.[24] They were 'apostolic' indulgences, described as

---

[20] Eli Heldaas Seland, '19th century devotional medals' in Henning Laugerud and Laura Katrine Skinnebach (eds), *Instruments of devotion: the practices and objects of religious piety from the late middle ages to the 20th century* (Aarhus, 2007), pp 157–72, p. 169.

[21] *Manual of the archconfraternity of the Holy Family*, p. 15.

[22] James A. Cleary, *Confraternity work and its problems* (Dublin, 1932), p. 43.

[23] *Manual of the archconfraternity of the Holy Family*, p. 25.

[24] See W. H. Kent, 'Indulgences' in *Catholic Encyclopedia* (15 vols, New York, 1913), vol. 7, pp 783–8.

Fig. 1   Certificate of confraternity membership from the early twentieth century

Figs 2.1–2.18 Medals of the archconfraternity of the Holy Family, Limerick
(*Courtesy Limerick City Museum*)

Fig. 2.1

Fig. 2.2

Fig. 2.3

Fig. 2.4

Fig. 2.5

Fig. 2.6

Fig. 2.7

Fig. 2.8

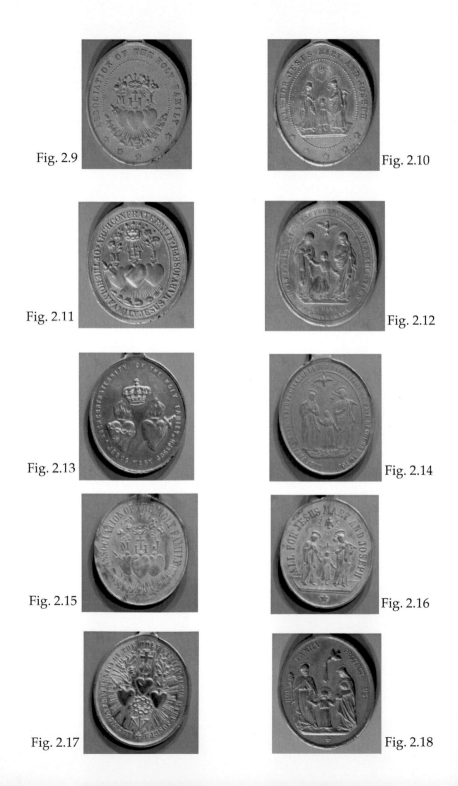

Fig. 2.9

Fig. 2.10

Fig. 2.11

Fig. 2.12

Fig. 2.13

Fig. 2.14

Fig. 2.15

Fig. 2.16

Fig. 2.17

Fig. 2.18

Fig. 3   Chantry chapel, St Audoen's, Dublin
(*Reproduced in* Dublin Penny Journal, *1832*)

Fig. 4   Women's confraternity members walk through
the streets of Dundalk, 1931
(*Courtesy National Library of Ireland*)

Fig. 5   Men's confraternity, Clonard, taking part in
procession, Belfast, 1957
(*Courtesy Redemptorist Congregation*)

Fig. 6   Confraternity group in Lourdes, early 1930s
(*Courtesy Passionist Congregation*)

Fig. 7 Child of Mary medal
(Courtesy Joan Finlay)

For Members of the Sodality of the Blessed Virgin.

Official Sodality Directory. New edition. Price 4d. (Postage 2d.) The **Official Sodality Directory** explains what a Sodality is, its History, Purpose, Rules, Indulgences, etc., and gives full directions for the method of establishing and conducting it.

Sodality Manual. By the late Rev. J. A. Cullen, S.J. Cloth, 1s. 6d. (1s. 7½d. post free). A collection of spiritual exercises and devotions for members of the Sodality of the Blessed Virgin.

The Child of Mary before Jesus Abandoned in the Tabernacle. 31st edition; 200th thousand. Enlarged and improved. Cloth, 1s. 3d.; leather, 2s.; imitation morocco, 2s. 6d.; calf, 3s. (Postage 1½d.). A book of prayers compiled by the late Rev. Francis Daly, S.J., of convenient size, which contains a unique collection of prayers for various devotions, and specially suited to members of the Sodality of the Blessed Virgin.

Madonna. The Official Organ of the Sodality in Ireland. Published monthly. Price 1d. (by post 2d.). Annual subscription 2s. Special terms for quantities. Yearly bound volume, cloth, 1s. 6d.; post free.

24. BOOKS ON THE BLESSED VIRGIN.

Prayers to the Blessed Virgin. Compiled by Rev. William Stephenson, S.J. 5th edition; 50th thousand.

Queen of May. By Rev. P. Gannon, S.J. 5th edition; 45th thousand.

Our Lady. A Novena of meditations on the principal feasts of the Blessed Virgin. By Rev. J. McDonnell, S.J. 8th edition; 70th thousand.

The Rosary. Our Lady's Mystical Garden. From the German of Father Moscher, S.J. By E. Leahy. 3rd edition; 35th thousand.

His Mother's Beads. Meditations on the Fifteen Mysteries of the Rosary. By Mother St. Paul.

The Virgin Mother. A series of Lenten Lectures by Rev. R. Kane, S.J. Parts I., II., III., IV. (four separate books).

The "Hail Mary" and "Hail Holy Queen"; developed according to the Second Method of Prayer of St. Ignatius of Loyola. By Rev. F. X. Schouppe, S.J. (Translated from the French).

Our Lady of Lourdes. By E. Leahy. 17th edition; 180th thousand.

The Miracles of Lourdes. By E. Leahy. 6th edition; 45th thousand.

The Call of Lourdes. By M. J. Giblin.

"IRISH MESSENGER" SERIES

The Sodality of the Blessed Virgin Mary in Ireland

A Short History

By REV. JOHN MacERLEAN, S.J.

THE PRIMA-PRIMARIA MADONNA

OFFICE OF THE "IRISH MESSENGER"
5 GREAT DENMARK STREET, DUBLIN, C. 14

1928

PRICE TWOPENCE

Fig. 8 Cover pages from sodality publication

those which the Pope 'attaches to the crosses, crucifixes, chaplets, rosaries, images, and medals which he blesses, either with his own hand or by those to whom he has delegated this faculty'.[25] Within this context the medals were clearly sacramental objects; their meaning was transformed through the actions of the priest so that they became semi-sacred objects. The rules for apostolic indulgences clearly state that as well as their being blessed, their owner had to perform certain 'works' to obtain the indulgences – in the case of the confraternity, by attending meetings and saying certain prayers:

> It may be observed that, the possession of the cross or medal or other indulgenced object is not the sole or immediate condition for gaining the indulgences attached thereto by the blessing of the Holy Father or his delegate. But the possession enables the recipient to gain the various indulgences on the performance of certain prescribed good works or acts of piety.[26]

By tangibly turning individuals into confraternity members through the conferring of medals, the organisation was marking these men as apart from non-members. It might be suggested that this was the first act in a 'ritualisation' process as defined by Catherine Bell to explain the nature of ritual, and the social personae of those who partake in it.[27] Bell defines ritualisation as a psycho-social concept as 'practices that strategically differentiate themselves from others, privileging themselves as more powerful in the process'.[28] Ritualisation through material culture seems significant in relation to many of the practices of the confraternity, particularly in relation to the formation of particular historical subjectivities – as men, as members of the archconfraternity, as citizens of Limerick, as participants and as spectators in and of the archconfraternity.

The confraternity medals and practices around their conferring, use and display were an effective way of differentiating not only members from non-members, but also sacramental artefacts from everyday objects. As well as setting members

[25] Ibid., pp 788–9.

[26] Ibid., p. 788.

[27] Catherine Bell, 'Discourse and dichotomies: the structure of ritual theory' in *Religion* 17 (Spring, 1987), pp 95–118.

[28] Bell, 'Discourse and dichotomies', p. 96.

apart from non-members, internal distinctions were made through confraternity medals and practices around them. For example, special medals were conferred to mark length of membership with the number of years (25, 40, 50, 60, 70 or 75) denoted mainly by the colour of the ribbon and also of the metal – silver for up to 50 years, and gold thereafter.[29] At the awarding of these medals, again a particular ceremony was performed by the priest.[30] On significant occasions, it seems medals were sent to members who no longer lived in Limerick – the chronicle includes a letter sent from New York in 1938, the seventieth anniversary of the ACHF, 'from one of the seven original members who joined at the foundation', thanking the director for the medal and blessing.[31]

A further visible distinction made between members was that the section prefects wore chains of office, and the orderlies, who acted as stewards at processions and other occasions, wore a ribbon of a particular colour. This use of material culture to denote and reward rank was clearly of concern to the leaders and exemplifies the way power could be managed through material objects. For example, in 1924 the director, Fr James Murray, made the following entry in the chronicle:

> This year, the director abolished the use of chains by the pref and the subp. of the boy's confrat and introduced in their stead, a medal with red ribbon like that of the orderlies, but of lesser width.
>
> The main object was – since familiarity breeds contempt – to prevent want of respect for the office of pref and subp on the part of boys transferred from the boys' to the mens' confrat. If they see boys like themselves wearing chains as pref and subp, they will have no respect for their pref and subp when they enter the men's confrat.[32]

Generally speaking, the medals had little intrinsic value as they were made of almost worthless materials. However, they

---

[29] Limerick City Museum, Inventory number 1998.0573.
[30] Evidence from references in *HFC II*.
[31] *HFC II*, Oct. 1938.
[32] *HFC II* Mar. 1924 – 'pref' and 'subp' almost certainly refer to 'prefect' and 'sub-prefect'.

were commodities in the sense of costing at least some money and, as mass-produced objects, by being interchangeable at the point of manufacture and sale. However, in their ritual usage, the medals, once blessed and conferred on members, were de-commodified in terms of monetary worth: they had no common exchange value. They were then not only singularised as precious possessions of the members but endowed with measurable spiritual capital – a capital specific to the owner.[33] As such, they might be termed inalienable possessions, a term used by the anthropologist Annette B. Weiner in defining objects that in terms of commodity exchange cycles are transcendent and out of circulation and 'which are not easy to give away'.[34] While the objects that Weiner concentrates on are inalienable generally because of their history, the membership medals of the confraternity were inalienable because they were absolutely singular to each member in spiritual terms. In some sense, then, they were part of the members' property in the Lockeian sense of property – to whose thesis that 'every man has a property in his own person created out of the labour of his body and the work of his hands' might be added – in Catholic terms – the state of his soul, as expressed in material form by such tokens as the confraternity medal.[35]

Part of the rules of the confraternity regarding expulsion of members was that when someone was expelled, the medals would cease to carry spiritual favours.[36] Just as the director had the power to attach spiritual favours to the medals, he could also denude them of this power, and by doing so, de-sacralise and re-alienate them. Again, there were very strict rules governing the actual form this expulsion should take and at which point the medals might cease to carry spiritual favours. In the

---

[33] The use of the terminology of singularisation and de-commodification is drawn from Igor Kopytoff, 'The cultural biography of things: commoditization as process' in Arjun Appadurai (ed.), *The social life of things: commodities in cultural perspective* (Cambridge, 1986), pp 64–94.

[34] Anette B. Weiner, *Inalienable possessions: the paradox of keeping-while-giving* (Berkeley, 1972), p. 6.

[35] John Locke, *Two treatises on government*, ed. Peter Laslett (2nd edn, Cambridge, 1963) [originally published 1690], p. 114.

[36] Evidence from references in *HFC II*.

chronicle, the director, Fr James Murray, stated: 'However careless a man may be, if validly received, he enjoys favours, indulgences (code 692) etc. until legitimately expelled.'[37]

The chronicle makes many references to expulsions – sometimes carried out *en masse* as in December 1929 when 300 members were expelled 'as their attendance was disgraceful', and in March 1936 when 100 were expelled.[38] There are no references in the chronicle to these members physically handing their medals back or any regulation stating that this should happen. However, Cleary's work ruled that, when expelled members were readmitted, 'they should not be allowed to wear their medal again for a period of two or three months' although this could be difficult to enforce.[39] In such cases, not only were the medals denuded of power, but the member suffered 'punishment' (Cleary's term) from the lack of this visible marker and the comfort it gave. Even if a medal was returned, its primary meaning was completely altered, as it was no longer a sacramental object with the spiritual capital conferred on it at consecration. In fact, these medals had experienced a spiritual 'death' in relation to the system of sacred objects and in Catholic terms might be said to have gone through a substantial and material change. This applied to other Catholic sacramental objects – for example, the rules governing rosary beads and indulgences as outlined in the Redemptorist *Handbook of the Confraternity of Our Lady of Perpetual Succour* states that with rosary beads indulgences can only be gained if they are 'not used for the purpose of gaining the indulgences by any person excepting the owner' and that 'at his death the blessing is lost'.[40]

Other sacramentalist aspects of the material habitus of the confraternity were a number of blessed objects acquired by the organisation and usually displayed, generally by being hung in the room where the men assembled every week. Again, the fact that they were blessed made them substantially and materially special: the church had particular formulae for blessing a whole range of objects, thus denoting the way objects could be made

---

37 *HFC II*, Mar. 1927.

38 *HFC II*, Dec. 1929, Mar. 1936.

39 Cleary, *Confraternity work*, p. 86.

40 *Handbook of the Confraternity of Our Lady of Perpetual Succour*, p. 306.

sacred. This range included crosses, images, church organs, processional banners, new bells and even telephones and typewriters.[41] Those displayed by the confraternity included a signed photograph of the pope blessed by him for the members.[42] Other blessed objects were given a particular status within the public rituals of the confraternity. At a retreat in 1934 a local sea scouts' band played outside the church at the closing ceremony, the director Fr John J. Murray reportedly expressing his pleasure at their attendance 'coming as they did with the Pope's blessing on their uniforms and on the flag they carried' and 'when the director held it [the flag] up at the door [...] it was really cheered.'[43]

While public sacramentalism was a key aspect of Catholic and so archconfraternity material culture, private devotion was also significant. There are a number of references in the chronicles to the fact that the membership medals were worn by men under their clothing when they were not deliberately on display.[44] This was not an untypical practice for Catholics, particularly after a decree was made in 1911 regarding medal-scapulars, suggesting that 'the medal should be always worn except perhaps when it is laid aside for a few moments [...] so it would not be safe to put it aside at night'.[45] The men may have worn other medals and scapulars as well, perhaps that of Our Lady of Perpetual Succour, as this was a particular devotion of the Redemptorists.

The church promoted medals as a devotional aid, and the wearing of Holy Family medals under clothing is likely to have been seen as such. That the confraternity was concerned with the bodily discipline of members is not in doubt, and that allegiance to it was worn on the body in private suggests the medal as a material reminder of the central devotional focus of the organisation – the Holy Family. Partly a mnemonic device, it was also an impulse to prayer. While the chronicle as a record of

---

[41] The 'Notes and Queries' section of the *Irish Ecclesiastical Record* (published from 1864) contains fascinating material on this.

[42] *HFC II*, Nov. 1928.

[43] *HFC II*, Apr 1934. The papal blessing was given at the Catholic Boy Scouts of Ireland pilgrimage to Rome in March 1934.

[44] Evidence from *HFC II*.

[45] *Irish Ecclesiastical Record*, xxix (1911), p. 325.

public and organisational activity obviously did not record private devotion, the members were expected to recite certain prayers individually at set times every day, and were exhorted to private prayer.[46]

Through the medals, the material culture of the ACHF was not just confined to, or solely activated at, the identifiable and recorded times and spaces of the weekly meetings and public rituals of the organisation, but was continually and physically with the members. This was symptomatic of the organisations' concern with the regulation of individual behaviour in private as well as corporate expressions of piety and public decorum. Through their continual material presence with the members the ritualisation work could be sustained, even when the members were not obviously 'performing'. In a way, this continual presence was an attempt to produce members that were not just actors, but thoroughly and continually part of the organisation.

It has not been possible to uncover how members prayed in private, how the medals might have aided or informed their prayers or even whether or not most of them did actually wear them under their clothing. However, that there were regulations about private prayer and an expectation that the medal should be worn at all times does suggest again that the leaders conceived of the role of material culture as an integral instrument of the religious habitus of the confraternity, according to Bourdieu's definition of habitus as a system of general generative schemes that are both durable (inscribed in the social construction of the self) and transposable (from one field to another).[47]

There is a paradox at the heart of religious material culture. While 'worldliness' and materiality might be represented as dichotomous with spirituality and immateriality, the passion for immateriality 'puts even greater pressure upon the precise symbolic and efficacious potential of whatever material form remains as the expression of spiritual power'.[48] The physical

---

[46] *Manual of the Archconfraternity of the Holy Family.*

[47] Pierre Bourdieu, *The logic of practice* (Cambridge, 1990), pp 54–65.

[48] Daniel Miller (ed.), 'Materiality: an introduction' in *Materiality* (Durham, 2005), pp 1–50, p. 22.

forms and usages of the confraternity medals exemplify this dynamic between materiality and immateriality that is so central to Catholic material culture. The medals show the ways the appearance and use of a religious object must be tightly controlled and circumscribed to better express the ineffable, and how highly prescribed ways of treating and interacting with objects can make them ultimately mutable.

7

John Charles McQuaid and the failure of youth sodalities, 1956–60

Carole Holohan

In 1956, the archbishop of Dublin, John Charles McQuaid, issued a circular to parish priests in his diocese asking them to
take note of a new query on the visitation form. This form was a
type of questionnaire issued to parish priests in advance of the
archbishop's call, and the query he referred to concerned youth
sodalities. McQuaid expressed how this aspect of their pastoral
duty had been causing him concern of late:

> The ignorance revealed in the continuation and technical
> schools, the negligence of our young emigrants in practising the
> faith, the lapses in sexual morality in some areas, the appear-
> ance of youth gangs (a feature which, however, must not be
> exaggerated) and most particularly, the entire absence of any
> instruction for tens of thousands who go to Sunday mass – are
> all factors which oblige me to take special notice of the facilities
> afforded youth by the clergy.[1]

The answers to his query were given for the most part orally to
the archbishop's secretary, Fr Christopher Mangan, who called
on the parishes prior to McQuaid's visit and compiled a report to
brief the archbishop of the situation. While the role of the parish
sodality was to ensure that people attended the sacraments,
McQuaid viewed the conference or talk given by the spiritual
director as a possible tool with which to comprehensively deal

---

[1] The brackets inserted are the archbishop's own. McQuaid desired that a circular letter be sent to all parish priests in the Dublin diocese on 12 March 1956
(Dublin Diocesan Archives [hereafter DDA] McQuaid Papers, AB8/b/XXVIII).

with young people, providing as it did an opportunity for a priest to directly instruct large numbers on a parish basis.[2]

Traditionally members of a sodality were of about the same 'age, sex, occupation and condition in life', resulting in separate sodalities composed of women, students or working men. This helped the director adapt his instructions to the needs of the sodalists. Hymns were sung and announcements of church events were made at monthly or weekly sodality meetings. This was followed by a short conference on subjects touching the spiritual progress of the members.[3] While sodalities had once engaged in apostolic work, ranging from teaching catechism to organising social clubs, by the late 1950s their range of activities had diminished. Nevertheless, they continued to exist in all parishes in the Dublin diocese, and were composed of men's, women's and children's sections. Sodality membership required attendance at a monthly devotional meeting and at both mass and communion on one Sunday of the month.[4]

This essay examines attempts by McQuaid to create a system of youth sodalities for those aged between fourteen and eighteen years in his diocese. The report compiled by Mangan reveals the many problems associated with forming youth sodalities in terms of organisation, attendance and class division. The paper will place these problems within a wider context, with reference to changes within the social category of youth and developments within the sphere of youth welfare work. While its focus was specifically on youth, Mangan's report provides an insight into parish sodalities in the diocese of Dublin more generally.

---

[2] Handwritten memorandum with the heading, 'Pastoral activities', 1959; handwritten memorandum with the heading 'Youth sodality section', 31 Dec. 1959 (DDA, McQuaid Papers, AB8/b/XXVIII).

[3] T. I. Mulcahy, *The sodality manual, official manual for the sodality of Our Lady in Ireland* (Dublin, 1934).

[4] Alexander J. Humphreys provided this description of what sodality membership entailed for an artisan family living in a Dublin parish in the period 1949–51; Alexander J. Humphreys S.J., *New Dubliners* (London, 1966), p. 106.

I

McQuaid's query reflected the increased importance attached to the social category of youth and the development of an international debate on teenagers in the 1950s. This is particularly evident from his reference to 'youth gangs' and 'lapses in sexual morality'. Nineteenth-century conceptions of adolescence as a period of turmoil and vulnerability, defined around the biological changes of puberty, resurfaced in articles on teenagers, as their position in society transformed. The period after the Second World War saw the economic enfranchisement of working class youth in many Western countries due to increased demand for unskilled and semi-skilled labour. This led to the expansion of the commercial youth market which provoked a resurgence of adult concerns. The market facilitated the development of new youth subcultures, which were seen as detrimental to young people themselves and to the future of society as a whole. Commercialised youth subculture quickly became associated with rising crime levels and juvenile delinquency, as well as sexual permissiveness. Youth became both a victim of the market and a danger to society. Middle class youths were largely excluded from these concerns due to their longer years of schooling and more secure career structure, and it was their working class counterparts who provoked controversy and concern.[5]

Despite the absence of an immediate post-war economic boom, Ireland was not immune from these developments. The year 1956 saw so-called 'riots' in Irish cinemas as teenagers danced in the aisles at screenings of *Rock around the clock*, while the archbishop's reference to continuation and technical schools implies that his concerns were with regard to working rather than middle class youths.[6] The attempt to establish youth sodalities could be considered as McQuaid's first foray into youth welfare work. He had displayed a consistent interest in

---

[5] Bill Osgerby, *Youth in Britain since 1945* (Oxford, 1998), pp 26–7; Kenneth Roberts, *Youth and leisure* (London, 1983), p. 21.

[6] Disturbances in cinemas were reported in Dublin, Drogheda and Sligo; Kevin Rockett, *Irish film censorship: a cultural journey from silent cinema to internet pornography* (Dublin, 2004), pp 146–9; *Irish Times*, 1 Sept., 16 Nov., 17 Nov. 1956.

the spiritual formation of young people throughout his career and, presiding as he did over a highly clericalist system, he maintained that work in this area should take place at parish level.

Mangan's 1956 report estimated that the Catholic youth population of the 'city' and 'rural' parishes surveyed was 31,500.[7] Parish priests were to be encouraged to create for these youths a youth sodality. McQuaid's chief concern was that a significant proportion of this group were not receiving any religious instruction. In 1950 it was estimated that only 45 per cent of Dublin children went beyond primary school, into a technical, continuation or secondary school.[8] Having left national school, religious instruction therefore ceased to be obligatory for a large number of teenagers. While most parishes had women's, men's and children's sodalities, those who comprised the category of youth could easily fall between two stools, perhaps feeling too old or too young to comfortably participate in the respective meetings. It was important that something be provided for those who had left the children's sodality (which was organised through the national school), as this period of traditional absence from the sodality – 'the sodality gap'– was likely to coincide with the time when issues of morality, particularly those relating to sexual relationships, were to the fore of young people's minds – or as McQuaid once described these years, the time when 'a boy or girl thinks of getting married!'[9]

Details of the activities of a girls' youth sodality already in existence in the parish of St Mary's pro-cathedral, in Dublin's inner city, are provided in Mangan's report. This sodality was organised into ten guilds, with each guild coming from a particular street or group of streets. The sodality meeting consisted of 'the life of a saint (which was run as a serial); the rosary; [and] instruction of doctrine and benediction'.[10] Fr Stephen Clancy

---

[7] 'Summary of statistics relating to youth sodalities in city', 1958–61 (DDA, McQuaid Papers, AB8/b/XXVIII).

[8] Humphreys, New Dubliners, pp 62–3.

[9] The exclamation point is the archbishop's own; Memorandum entitled 'Youth sodalities', 1959 (DDA, McQuaid Papers, AB8/b/XXVIII).

[10] See parish of St Mary's pro-cathedral in Fr Christopher Mangan's report. It was entitled 'Youth sodalities' and was divided into two sections representing city and rural parishes. Hereafter the report will be cited as 'Youth sodalities', 1956 (DDA, McQuaid Papers, AB8/b/XXVIII).

described how the Legion of Mary 'help[ed] out' by providing prefects for each of the guilds. While Catholic Action groups like the Legion were already active in providing facilities for youth, McQuaid was anxious that the parish priest would have direct contact with young people. This was most likely a reflection of his belief that the priest was the appropriate person to guide those who were thinking of 'getting married!' Speaking at a meeting of chaplains of the Catholic Boy Scouts of Ireland in 1959, McQuaid addressed this issue as he discussed 'how to instruct boys in things sexual'. 'You need a scheme' asserted the archbishop, 'you need a language. You need courage and delicacy … in my belief, every single boy ought to be prevented by clear instruction … [from] stumbling into worry, ignorant knowledge and faults.'[11]

When visiting the parishes, Mangan encouraged the formation of separate male and female youth sodalities for those aged between fourteen and eighteen years. He described the special instruction that teenagers needed to the parish priest of Narraghmore, Fr Joseph Young:

> I told him that your grace wished these children to get special instruction for themselves (to bring home to them in a way they could grasp the fundamentals of the faith which they had learned in school – the incarnation, redemption, grace, mass and the sacraments and to link this knowledge up with practices of piety, such as the rosary [and] using a prayer-book at mass … then special talks on marriage, sex, vocation in the general sense, the seventh commandment, [and] their relations to their parents) and that your grace also wishes that these teen-agers should be in touch with the priest at this stage of their lives, have confidence in the priest and approach him to have their problems solved.[12]

---

11 McQuaid's handwritten speech, which was delivered to chaplains of the Catholic Boy Scouts of Ireland at the first national conference of chaplains held in Greystones, Co. Wicklow, 27–30 Oct. 1959, 27 Oct. 1959 (DDA., McQuaid Papers, AB8/b/XXI/16/6).

12 Narraghmore was a rural parish in Co. Kildare; 'Youth sodalities', 1956 (DDA, McQuaid Papers, AB8/b/XXVIII).

II

This exhortation serves to place McQuaid's attempts to establish youth sodalities in the context of changes in the diocese and within the nuclear family. Habits of religious practice, the role of the parish in the community and generational change in 1950s Dublin were identified in Alexander J. Humphreys's sociological study, *New Dubliners* (1966). The research for the study was conducted between 1949 and 1951 and encompassed twenty-nine Dublin families, with one parent in each family representing the 'new Dubliner' – a first generation urbanite or a son or daughter of an immigrant born, raised and living their married life in Dublin. Eleven of the families studied were of the artisan class, which included skilled workers in the trades and what was described as 'the lowest echelon of administrator'. Humphreys described this as the most useful class to study as it contained characteristics of the clerical and employer / managerial class above it, and of the general labourer class below it.

A large part of the study described the life of the Dunn family from the Coombe area of Dublin, detailing their activities as general, prevalent or alternate with regards to other artisan families. Humphreys observed that the 'new Dubliner' had not become secularised, nor had urbanisation produced a significant decline in devotional practice. Family members attended mass and confession every week, and were involved in personal devotions one or two evenings a week. If exception was made of the father, John Dunn's daily attendance at mass and membership of the St Vincent de Paul Society, and of the membership of the Dunn women in various religious organisations other than the sodality, the pattern of the Dunns' religious behaviour could be said to be quite general and uniform for all artisan families. This observation demonstrates that for this upwardly mobile section of the working class, sodality membership was extensive. While the wife and mother, Joan, attended the women's sodality with her daughters, Maureen, aged twenty-four years, and Sheila, aged twenty-three years, the husband and father, John, attended the men's sodality with his sons, Jerry, aged twenty-one years, and Liam, aged sixteen years.[13]

---

13 Humphreys, *New Dubliners*, pp 106, 157.

Humphreys's treatment of changes in the nuclear family, particularly in the relationship between parents and their children, revealed changes which would undoubtedly affect the sodality organisation, given that it saw the mingling of parents and their older children. He referred to a recent 'revolution in leisure provision' as well as noting increases in the disposable income of young workers. These factors contributed to notable generational differences. The following description of working youths by one father could be attributed, wrote Humphreys, to any of the families studied:

> once the girls start working, even if they are only fifteen ... years old, they demand a good deal of independence and in nine cases out of ten they get it ... As a rule, they go wherever they want to go and they go very frequently, sometimes every night in the week. And they are always out to dances and movies. This takes them all over town ... I think the reason why it was so different when I was a boy is that any claim to independence a boy or a girl might make then, they simply could not back up because they were not bringing in the money they are today. And the increase in the number of movies and dances and especially the dance halls has had a lot to do with it too.[14]

The so-called 'revolution in leisure provision' and the existence of these outlets 'all over town' had led to another generational difference. Children's associations were much more likely to reach beyond their own neighbourhood, and intermarriage between neighbours had sharply declined. Humphreys also described how the three Dunn children until about three years previously had handed over their entire weekly earnings to their mother, who in turn gave them back a weekly allowance. This practice had changed, and the children were instead making a weekly contribution to the family funds, the amount of which they determined themselves.[15]

References to increased levels of income, and more impor-tantly disposable income, among younger workers indicated that the absence of an immediate post-war boom did not imply privation for many of Dublin's young urban workers.

---

[14] Ibid., p. 173.
[15] Ibid., pp 101, 131–2.

The report of the government Commission on Youth Unemployment, delivered the same year Humphreys completed his survey, reflected this situation by suggesting that schools provide young people with instruction in thrift:

> With increasing wages and increases in the number of wage earners in families, substantial sums of money are now the weekly income of many families whose members have no training in the spending of money and no experience in the best methods of buying what is good, useful and practical. The fluctuating value of money leads to an attitude of mind that tends to bring savings and thrift into disfavour and accentuates the fear that present money savings will be of little value when needed in the future. The tendency now is to spend and not to save.[16]

III

The increased independence of working youths was undoubtedly a factor in the decline in sodality membership and attendance witnessed in the late 1950s. Mangan was informed by more than one parish priest that the scheduling of the sodality meeting with the day that wages were paid had a detrimental effect on attendance levels amongst young people. That parish priests recognised the difficulty in attracting working youths to the sodality may account for the small number of youth sodalities which had emerged by 1956.

After interviewing priests of both the urban and rural parishes in the diocese, Mangan noted that, while the number of parish sodalities specifically for those aged between fourteen and eighteen were few, many were being catered for in a variety of different ways. Some were in sodalities which were not parish-based, for example sodalities attached to clubs or secondary schools and those organised by nuns, while some children's sodalities catered for those aged up to sixteen years, so they included those attending technical or continuation schools. Furthermore, where numbers were small or where the practice was ongoing, priests suggested to Mangan that

16 *Commission on Youth Unemployment 1951, Report* (Dublin, 1951), pp 19–20.

teenagers be inducted into the men's and women's sodalities, forming a special guild.[17]

McQuaid's circular had referred not just specifically to sodalities but rather to 'the facilities afforded to youth by the clergy'. Mangan's 1956 report revealed that the youth of many parishes were involved in girls' and boys' clubs, some parish-based, others run by local nuns, the Legion of Mary, the Society of St Vincent de Paul and the St John Bosco Society. While clubs focused on the recreational rather than on the spiritual, there was some cross-over as most had a chaplain. In one youth club organised by the St John Bosco Society, sodality membership was obligatory.[18] Similarly in St Joseph's parish, East Wall, football street leagues catering for thirteen- to eighteen-year-olds operated under the banner of the parish's juvenile sodality, with sodality membership being mandatory for those wanting to play. In Crumlin a youth sodality was attached to a marching band. In Ballyfermot there was a similar link between leisure and spiritual activities, and youth clubs and their affiliated youth sodalities attracted large numbers.[19]

Many of those priests who had managed to form youth sodalities without the carrot of leisure provision complained of poor attendance levels. In the parish of Our Lady of Consolation, Donnycarney, Fr James Robinson PP complained that of 603 boys in the fourteen to eighteen age group, 471 were on the roll of a youth sodality but average attendance for the evening meeting was 180, and at Sunday communion it was 220. Fr Myles Ronan, PP of St Michan's parish, Halston Street, similarly complained of his two youth sodalities being small, with only 50 per cent of the fourteen- to eighteen-year age group being members. He referred to the running of the youth sodality as

> hard work on the part of the priest in charge of it, harder work
> than is involved in the running of an adult sodality because the

---

[17] In the parishes of City Quay and St Joseph's, Berkeley Road, for example, young people between the ages of fourteen and eighteen years were already being encouraged to join the men's and women's sodalities in the parish; 'Youth sodalities', 1956 (DDA, McQuaid Papers, AB8/b/XXVIII).

[18] 'Annual general report, Cumann Naomh Eoin Bosco', 1 Nov. 1957 (DDA, McQuaid Papers, AB8/b/XXI/122/2).

[19] 'Youth sodalities', 1956 (DDA, McQuaid Papers, AB8/b/XXVIII).

priest has to be constantly going after the youths who do not attend and then he must make the sodality service attractive and have side lines such as games etc. to draw the youth.[20]

Other parish priests had turned solely to clubs and the purveyance of leisure in terms of providing for teenagers, some expressing to Mangan their need for premises and equipment, and complaining of losing young parishioners to clubs in neighbouring parishes which had better facilities.[21]

McQuaid's desire for parish-based youth sodalities faced numerous obstacles. This was particularly true of the rural parishes where no youth sodalities had emerged naturally. Sodalities were much more prevalent in working class areas which comprised so many of the city parishes, with one parish priest describing rural parishioners as 'not as sodality minded, as city people'.[22] It was noted by Mangan that there had been a 'thriving' club for domestic servants in Sutton, which was run by the Legion of Mary. The club was 'declining' because fewer people in the area had servants than used to be the case. The inclusion of this observation in the report indicates an assumption that devotional practices such as the sodality were considered the preserve of members of the working class. Mangan's assertion that the parishioners of Straffan–Celbridge represented 'a close community' and were 'very good' gives the impression that smaller rural parishes were much less of a concern than their larger urban counterparts. This attitude reflected that of the Commission on Youth Unemployment which McQuaid chaired. Unoccupied youths in urban areas were the main concern of the commission's members as a young person in a city 'with nothing to do and all day to do it' was considered to be in much greater moral danger than his country counterpart. The report noted that:

in rural districts and in country towns the technically unoccupied young person will rarely be without some form of occupation that will, at least, keep him employable. And because of environment and the fact that he is personally known to a substantial

---

[20] Ibid.
[21] Ibid., see St Joseph's parish, Church Road.
[22] Ibid., see parishes of Howth and Narraghmore.

proportion of residents, the probability of his getting into trouble is less than that of the young person idle in a city. The bigger the city, the larger is the number of such young persons and the greater their moral danger.[23]

Mangan found it impractical to suggest a formal youth sodality in most rural parishes due to the relatively small number of young people. Instead it seemed expedient to get youths into the adult sodalities and have them kept back or arrive early for their sodality meeting, a practice that was ongoing in some city parishes.[24] Emigration was also more prevalent a concern in rural areas and therefore a larger youth issue. In the then rural parish of Dundrum, Fr Dominick Ryan PP proposed that the men and women in the adult sodalities be asked to send prospective young emigrants in their families to see the priest before they left, so that the latter could put them in touch with members of the clergy residing in their destination location.[25]

In the city parishes there were also numerous obstacles to the development of parish-based youth sodalities. Firstly, there were sodalities attached to the churches of the religious orders. Maurice Hartigan describes how those sodalities established by the religious orders were in fact the most influential.[26] In the parish of St Andrew's, Westland Row, Fr John MacMahon who organised the boys' youth sodality complained of losing parishioners to the sodalities of the religious churches on Clarendon Street and Whitefriar Street of the Carmelite order. Mangan suggested to McQuaid that he approach the superiors of the religious churches on the parish borders, to ask them to keep the parochial clergy informed about parishioners attending their sodalities. 'This could be done', continued Mangan, 'in the case of all the religious churches in the city'. To which McQuaid replied, 'I agree. The pastoral care is ours.'[27]

---

[23] *Commission on Youth Unemployment, Report*, p. 4.

[24] See the parishes of Malahide, Ballymore Eustace and Athy; 'Youth sodalities', 1956 (DDA, McQuaid Papers, AB8/b/XXVIII).

[25] Ibid., see the parish of Dundrum.

[26] Maurice Hartigan, 'The religious life of the Catholic laity of Dublin, 1920–1940' in James Kelly and Dáire Keogh (eds) *History of the Catholic diocese of Dublin* (Dublin, 2000), pp 331–48.

[27] See the parish of St Andrew's, Westland Row in 'Youth sodalities', 1956 (DDA, McQuaid Papers, AB8/b/XXVIII).

Similarly, sodalities attached to youth centres run by An Comhairle le Leas Óige (CLÓ) hampered parish-based sodalities. CLÓ was formed in 1942 out of concern for the absence of definite social or educational organisation for the many young people in Dublin who had left school. It assisted existing youth clubs by providing instructors, equipment on loan and leadership training. The Catholic Youth Council (CYC), a body that essentially undercut much of the work undertaken by CLÓ, was subsequently formed in 1947.[28] With McQuaid as its president it acted as a federative body for Dublin youth clubs and represented an attempt to provide a Catholic alternative to a secular body, something the archbishop of Dublin had successfully executed in the past.[29] CLÓ set up two training centres in Dublin's city centre, one on Upper Mount Street and another on Great Denmark Street. Members of the Legion of Mary undertook leadership courses with CLÓ and subsequently operated the youth centre on Mount Street, 'Brugh Phádraig', while leaders from the Society of St Vincent de Paul looked after 'Brugh Mhuire' on Great Denmark Street.[30] Both of these centres had their own chaplain. Fr Stephen Clancy of St Mary's parish noted that more youths in his parish were members of the sodalities attached to the 'brughanna' run by CLÓ. Of 390 boys in the parish only forty were in the parish sodality. Similarly Fr John Mac Mahon of St Andrew's parish described the loss of significant numbers of youths to sodalities attached to CLÓ's centres.[31]

While administrative difficulties hampered the development of parish-based youth sodalities the report indicated that youth attendance at any form of sodality was far from exemplary. Attracting working youths was not an easy task. Both Fr Fergus O'Higgins of the city parish of the Holy Family, Aughrim Street, and Canon Michael V. Burke from the parish of the Most

---

[28] Memoranda relating to the Catholic Social Welfare Bureau (DDA, McQuaid Papers, AB8/b/XXI/52).

[29] For an analysis of how McQuaid tried to ensure that Catholic bodies provided welfare services for Catholics, see Lyndsey Earner-Byrne, *Mother and child: maternity and child welfare in Dublin 1922–60* (Manchester, 2007), pp 90–108.

[30] The word 'brugh' refers to a dwelling place; *Comhairle le Leas Óige seachtain na n-óg, souvenir and programme of youth week,* 11–18 June 1944 (DDA, McQuaid Papers, AB8/b/XXVIII).

[31] 'Youth sodalities', 1956 (DDA, McQuaid Papers, AB8/b/XXVIII).

Precious Blood, West Cabra, informed Mangan that Friday
night was an awkward one for the sodality meeting as the older
boys got their wages on that night. Fr Norbert O'Leary, PP of the
parish of St. Nicholas's Without, Francis Street, noted how
working boys tended to regard themselves as men particularly
from aged seventeen, and felt that they would therefore prefer
to be in a men's sodality rather than one specifically for
youths.[32] Similarly in 1959, when the issue of youth sodalities
re-emerged, it was suggested that it was necessary to have
youth sodalities incorporate thirteen-year-olds as in a number
of cases boys and girls left school at that age and in their first
week of work it was felt that 'they may well grow, in their own
estimation, a year'.[33] These observations reveal the independent
nature of working youth given their removal from the authority
of a school, as well as how their decision to use their disposable
income on leisure pursuits was considered to be directly detrimental to sodality attendance levels.

It was also difficult to attract secondary school pupils, the
vast majority of whom could be considered middle class, to the
parish sodality. In the parish of Sacred Heart, Donnybrook,
practically all the children aged fourteen to eighteen years were
attending schools and school sodalities outside the parish. The
parish priest, Fr Timothy B. Condon PP suggested that
McQuaid communicate with the superiors of all the secondary
schools and ask them to supply each parish priest with a list of
names of students from their parish, presumably so that they
might be directly encouraged to attend their parish sodality. In
the parish of Our Lady of the Rosary, Harold's Cross, Fr Kevin
Brady PP informed Mangan that while he was strongly in
favour of having the secondary school boys in a youth sodality,
it was difficult to attract them, mentioning specifically 'the
Terenure College boys'. Mangan responded by saying that
these youths 'would always be in a parish but not always in a
school'.[34]

---

[32] Ibid.

[33] Correspondence to Fr James Ardle MacMahon, 1959 (DDA, McQuaid Papers,
AB8/b/XXVIII).

[34] 'Youth sodalities', 1956 (DDA, McQuaid Papers, AB8/b/XXVIII).

McQuaid had noted that 'boys are the graver problem' and initially youth welfare work focused primarily on male youths. In both the city and rural parishes of the diocese nuns were often given the responsibility for dealing with young females. Some priests, who were making their first forays into youth work, inquired of Mangan if there would be any objection to nuns looking after the girls of this age group. Mangan replied that there would be no problem with this 'as long as the nuns agreed to look after all the girls of this age group'. He noted that they were inclined to allow the 'good' ones to be in their sodalities, refusing admission to those who were 'not so good', and whom Mangan and McQuaid were 'especially anxious' to cater for. In the parish of City Quay, the nuns who ran the schools on Townsend Street operated a Children of Mary sodality, which catered for girls aged from fourteen to twenty-four years. Mangan considered them to be 'selective' in their choice of member.[35] This indicates that some nuns were inclined only to afford membership to those of the working class considered 'respectable' and not to those considered 'rough'. These terms can be used to distinguish a status hierarchy within the working class. Writing for *Hibernia* magazine, Conor O'Neill in his description of the inhabitants of an inner city parish, revealed that these terms were used in an Irish context. He referred to the 'respectables' as being

> engaged in the better employments, relative to the area. They are strongly committed to respectability and to an occupational identity. Great efforts are made by them to keep up appearances, both in dress and in their dwellings. Independence is accorded a high value and charity would only be availed of by them as a very last resort. The roughs are the broken minority … They divide into three categories; casual labourers and those in uninsured employment, the chronically unemployed and the criminals.[36]

To summarise the findings of Mangan's report, there were numerous obstacles to the formation of parish-based youth sodalities. In the rural areas relatively small numbers

---

[35] Ibid., see parishes of Killester–Raheny and City Quay.
[36] Roberts, *Youth and leisure*, pp 10–11; *Hibernia*, 6 Oct. 1972.

combined with emigration worked against the project, while in urban areas, sodalities attached to the religious churches, secondary school sodalities, those run by CLÓ, the disposable income of working youth, and class division all thwarted their potential success. Mangan estimated that of 31,500 Catholic youths in the fifty-six parishes surveyed, approximately 10,000 were not catered for by either a youth sodality or a special guild in an adult sodality.[37] In general most parish priests had seemed enthusiastic about a new initiative for teenagers (although in view of McQuaid's impending visit this perhaps was the most judicious attitude to take). Many had already turned to leisure provision as a way of encouraging youths into the church's fold. At this stage, however, McQuaid was concerned with religious instruction rather than with leisure provision.

Mangan's 1956 report had noted how leisure provision in the form of a marching band, youth clubs and football leagues had contributed to sodality attendance amongst youths in the parishes of Ballyfermot, Crumlin and East Wall. These parishes were predominantly working class and Humphreys described how, what he termed the labouring class, had more contact with the clergy than other classes, including the artisan class. Various types of boys' clubs were concentrated and even flourished within labouring class neighbourhoods in inner city areas around Dorset Street, Killarney Street and the quays. Humphreys recorded disagreement amongst labouring class parents regarding an increase in levels of delinquency, with some arguing that levels had declined in the face of increased occupational opportunities and improved living conditions. Others felt that among people who had not benefited from these improvements, 'decline in parental control over the children, and the growing tendency of parents to find their recreation outside the home and to leave the children more to themselves' had intensified the problem. Despite this disagreement he found that labouring class parents were in general accord about the positive effects clubs had in reducing delinquency.[38]

---

[37] 'Summary of statistics relating to youth sodalities in city', 1958–61(DDA, McQuaid Papers, AB8/b/XXVIII).

[38] Humphreys, *New Dubliners*, pp 203–6.

The issue of delinquency resulted in the increased provision of youth clubs in the late 1950s. In 1957 Monsignor John F. Stokes opened and blessed the new Oliver Plunkett boys' club in Drogheda, noting that:

> His Eminence [Cardinal John D'Alton] would like it to be known that he considered it necessary to provide our young people not only with opportunities for healthy recreation and intellectual self improvement, but also to provide a powerful antidote to juvenile delinquency which even in provincial towns, unfortunately displays an upward trend.[39]

Similarly in 1959, an editorial in *Hibernia* described clubs as part of the solution to the problem of delinquency:

> Modern youth is handicapped by the pressures of those teenage industries which dangle before them all sorts of delights, which they feel they must have for themselves. In 1959 there has been a growing concern at the increase of juvenile crime in Ireland. Doubts have been voiced about the adequacy of the courts' corrective measures. Boys' clubs and other youth organisations have not been receiving assistance, in the form of help and financial assistance, which they are badly in need of.[40]

McQuaid had desired that the sodality be used as a way of communicating with young people and of counteracting their associated problems. By the end of the decade, however, the youth club and the provision of leisure facilities was increasingly viewed as the solution to the youth problem.

IV

Mangan's report appears to have been shelved in 1956 but it resurfaced three years later, after Monsignor Michael Troy of the parish of the Assumption of Our Lady, Ballyfermot, whose own parish in 1956 had thriving youth sodalities and clubs, suggested a scheme involving youth sodalities, this time with a

---

[39] *Irish Catholic Directory*, 1957, p. 654.
[40] *Hibernia*, 'Christmas number', 1959.

view to rescuing what he described as the 'semi-defunct' adult sodalities. He described how

> The sodality spirit is on the wane and one of the reasons for it is that there is a sodality gap between the time when a young person leaves school at 14 and the time that the young person reaches the age of 18 or 19, when he or she would normally join an adult sodality. During these critical four years, the sodality habit is broken and many of these young people become ignorant of the faith and indifferent to it and do not join the adult sodalities.[41]

He proposed that exhortation was clearly not enough, and that action was needed from a central authority. He recommended the establishment of a 'diocesan youth sodality service', with a director, a young priest, who would visit the parishes. He described his own experience with young people and sodalities, explaining how he took sixth class children, those aged eleven and twelve years, into the youth sodalities in order to give them training in going to the sodality meeting from home. He suggested that schools send a list of boys and girls in sixth class to the parish priest to facilitate this.

Having viewed Troy's proposal, Mangan headed to Ballyfermot to interview him. Troy explained that he could 'see no other way of ... putting ... adult sodalities ... permanently on their feet except by starting at the bottom with the children and making them parish minded and sodality minded'. He called for greater devotional training in the school to prevent a situation whereby adolescents didn't have any real devotional practices of their own. In the 'crisis of adolescence', explained Troy, they 'may be confirmed in indifference'.[42]

When writing up a record of this interview for McQuaid, Mangan's support for Troy's scheme was clear. He noted that it would provide priests with much-needed encouragement in parish work. 'A number of them in my age group,' wrote Mangan, 'are agreed that the parish sodality system is doomed to die, and they do not know what to put in its place if anything'. At the top of Mangan's report on his interview with Troy, he

---

[41] 'Notes taken of interview with Father Troy of Ballyfermot and Mangan', 1959 (DDA, McQuaid Papers, AB8/b/XXVIII).
[42] Ibid.

wrote a brief note to McQuaid: 'No reference to clubs, sports etc., because I got afraid of the length. But you know where MCT [Monsignor Canon Troy] would fit them in: adjuncts to the youth sodalities'.[43] Youth clubs were in fact an integral component to Troy's scheme. He desired that sodality prefects be given leadership courses on club work, solidifying a link between the two. He suggested that members of the Catholic Girl Guides and the Catholic Boy Scouts of Ireland, if members of a parish youth sodality, could then act as leaders in the parish youth club. Troy's desire to see a more formal link between the clubs and sodalities reflected his position as both a parish priest and the director of the Catholic Youth Council. He also suggested a drive to get government funding to help provide premises and equipment, noting that 'in view of present talk on youth delinquency we are in a position to bargain'.[44]

Mangan's 1956 report had demonstrated the benefits of using leisure activities as a means of attracting young people to the youth sodality. However, Troy was not encouraged to develop his youth club/sodality scheme. Instead, at the behest of McQuaid, a memo entitled 'Youth sodalities – their necessity' was prepared by one of his secretaries, Fr James Ardle MacMahon. This memo argued that clubs and other organisations did not normally tend to foster a sense of parish consciousness to the extent that a parish youth sodality could.[45] Mangan's 1956 report had, however, already demonstrated the difficulties associated with parish-based youth sodalities. They were hamstrung by many factors, including class division. This issue often emerged in Mangan's report. In the case of the parish of Glasthule he found it practical to suggest a youth sodality with different guilds for the children going to the different secondary schools and for those who were working, in order to overcome the problem of 'social distinction' in the parish. Similarly with regards to the parish of Foxrock–Cabinteely, Mangan reported,

> There is a problem of social distinction in the parish which makes the solution of the teenage problem difficult. Quite a

[43] Ibid.

[44] Canon Michael Troy to Fr Liam Martin, 23 Jan. 1959 (DDA, McQuaid Papers, AB8/b/XXVIII).

[45] 'Youth sodalities – their necessity', 1959 (DDA, McQuaid Papers, AB8/b/XXVIII).

number of the well to do people will not join the sodalities, although they go to their duties on their own.[46]

In 1959, however, clerical responses to MacMahon's memo suggested the possible role of the sodality in breaking class barriers in Dublin. One of the respondents proposed that:

> Not every boy likes to serve mass, or join a football club, or a boxing or a boys' club; only the parish youth sodality – comprehensively organised to include all the youth of the parish, no matter where they work or go to school – can cater for each one. The youth sodality is an invaluable aid to break down that unchristian social consciousness that splits so many organisations in Dublin. Boys and girls who have attended sodality and mass together ... without any distinction of class, will not so easily fall into this very narrow manner of acting.[47]

Another respondent optimistically noted that the youth sodality 'will help to eliminate the tendency for the people of higher social standing not to join sodalities in the parish'.[48]

Not all the responses to MacMahon's memo were so supportive, however. He had suggested that a new survey be distributed, which would inquire of young people the reasons why they didn't attend sodality meetings. That this does not seem to have gone ahead may be attributed to strong opinions expressed about its futility. Fr Shan Ó Cuív of Corpus Christi parish, Drumcondra, having been issued with a draft questionnaire, commented on the pointlessness of the endeavour:

> to my mind, the one reason why children who are nominally members of a sodality do not attend regularly is that they know of no compelling reason why they should attend. In this they are a faithful reflection of their parents' apathy where parochial sodalities are concerned.[49]

In order to demonstrate young people's apathy towards devotional practices like the sodality Ó Cuív provided some

---

[46] Ibid., see parish of Foxrock–Cabinteely.

[47] Correspondence for the attention of Fr James Ardle MacMahon, 1959 (DDA, McQuaid Papers, AB8/b/XXVIII).

[48] Memorandum entitled 'Youth sodalities', 1959 (DDA, McQuaid Papers, AB8/b/XXVIII).

[49] Fr Shan Ó Cuív to Fr Liam Martin, 10 Nov. 1959 (DDA, McQuaid Papers, AB8/b/XXVIII).

reports of the prefects of the girls' branch of the confraternity of the Blessed Sacrament in his parish. The excuses given to prefects for failure to attend included such brief explanations as, 'sick', 'went to a dance' and 'forgot to come'.[50]

Prior to writing his memorandum, 'youth sodalities – their necessity', MacMahon had suggested to McQuaid that in order to induce the children to attend the youth sodality, it might be a good idea to organise outdoor games, or to show films. But the archbishop had informed him that 'this will grow of itself'.[51] When the Catholic Boy Scouts of Ireland was reconstituted in 1928 by the hierarchy, it was made clear that the association was not to take the place of the religious sodalities or confraternities, or in any way be detrimental to their success.[52] McQuaid's reluctance to embrace the idea of using youth clubs as a means of encouraging sodalities suggests that he feared that the former could be detrimental to the latter's survival. However, by the end of 1959 it had become apparent that providing for the leisure time of young people was the most effective way of reaching them, given their reluctance to attend traditional forums. On 31 December 1959 McQuaid wrote a memo, which made notes about linking 'youth sodalities with the youth clubs and associations'.[53] It seems that Troy's idea was attractive to McQuaid but he clearly did not desire that youth work in his diocese be developed by Troy himself. Instead he desired that this role be undertaken by Monsignor Cecil Barrett.

Barrett had a long history of working as McQuaid's right hand man on many social issues and in 1960 he replaced Troy as the chairman of the Catholic Youth Council.[54] Barrett was director of the Catholic Social Welfare Bureau. 'Father Barrett,' wrote McQuaid, 'wants to see for himself the question of the necessity

[50] Ibid.

[51] Memorandum entitled 'Youth sodalities', 1959 (DDA, McQuaid Papers, AB8/b/XXVIII).

[52] Catholic Boy Scouts of Ireland, organisation and rules (Dublin, 1928); Maurice Curtis, 'Catholic Action as an organised campaign in Ireland, 1921–1947' (PhD thesis, University College, Dublin, 2000), pp 382–3.

[53] Handwritten memorandum with the heading 'Youth sodality section', 31 Dec. 1959 (DDA, McQuaid Papers, AB8/b/XXVIII).

[54] John Cooney describes Barrett as the archbishop's chief advisor on adoption and social issues. See John Cooney, John Charles McQuaid, ruler of Catholic Ireland (Dublin, 1999), p. 297; Earner-Byrne, Mother and child, p. 204; McQuaid to Barrett, 21 Dec. 1960 (DDA, McQuaid Papers, AB8/b/XIX/53).

of these sodalities. He will begin by seeing what policy clubs have in regard to youth sodalities.'[55] Barrett conducted a tour of clubs in the diocese but a youth sodality service never emerged. Instead he concentrated his efforts on developing the youth club system. The quick disappearance of a role for the sodality in diocesan youth work indicates that they were not viable.

Barrett initiated youth leadership courses, which reflected international developments in youth welfare work. These leadership courses were to be filled by boys from Dublin's secondary schools. These boys came from the ranks of the Colleges Volunteer Corps, originally the Archbishop's Volunteer Corps, formed as a type of Praetorian Guard for the archbishop at the Patrician Congress in 1961. After the congress McQuaid decided not to disband the corps, and instead aimed to establish in the corps a trained group of young men who would be the leaders in the social works of the parishes of the diocese.[56] Having completed youth leadership courses organised by Barrett, these middle class boys went on to act as leaders in the youth clubs of working class boys and girls in the diocese of Dublin.[57] This idea differed from Troy's in that youth leaders came from a body controlled by the archbishop and whose members were predominantly middle class, rather than organisations like the Girl Guides and the Boy Scouts, which were national bodies.

V

When reflecting upon changes in Irish society in the early 1960s, which provoked something of an identity crisis as church, state and people grappled with traditional and modern notions of themselves, Rev. E. F. O'Doherty, Professor of Logic and Psychology at University College Dublin, noted

> The more a society is subject to change, the more will the self-image change, and with it the real content of the culture. This

---

[55] Handwritten memorandum, 19 Jan. 1960 (DDA, McQuaid Papers, AB8/b/XXVIII).

[56] McQuaid to Fr C. P. Crean, 10 Jan. 1963 (DDA, McQuaid Papers, AB8/b/XXVIII).

[57] Taken from handwritten speech used by McQuaid at a youth leadership congress, 3 Mar. 1963 (DDA, McQuaid Papers, AB8/b/XXVIII).

will be recognised earlier by members of the younger group, whose self-image is still plastic, who are still in [the] process of forming their self-image of the culture. They will find it at variance with the image projected by the older age group; in other words they will find the real image communicated by life at variance with the projected or ideal one communicated by the devices of the society itself.[58]

While Fr Shan Ó Cuív's observation that young people's attitudes to sodalities reflected their parents' apathy indicated that the waning power of the sodality system did not provoke a generational conflict, it was amongst the younger generation that changes in the habits of religious practice were most evident. In 1959 O'Doherty had suggested that organisations like sodalities could possibly provide the group structure and identification that adolescents craved.[59] The problems in getting youths to attend sodalities by the late 1950s demonstrate, however, that it was difficult to centre peer group activity within the confines of traditional church structures. Furthermore, Mangan's 1956 report had revealed the role class difference played in the sodality system. It appeared highly unlikely that a sodality could have the power of bringing members of different social classes together.

In 1959 Mangan expressed his fear that the sodality system was doomed to die and neither he nor his peers knew what to put in its place. In terms of diocesan youth work, McQuaid and his right hand-man, Barrett, focused on youth clubs from 1960 on, often following the example of secular youth bodies. The term sodality does not emerge in the McQuaid papers relating to youth work after 1959, with one exception. In 1971, the archbishop was informed by an organiser of a branch of the Catholic Young Men's Society that his branch had been disintegrating over the past decade, or longer. McQuaid wrote back: 'We must bow to the inevitable. The CYMS even more than confraternities and sodalities, has melted away. And nothing can restore it in our time.'[60]

---

[58] E. F. O'Doherty, 'Society, identity and change' in *Studies*, 52 (Summer 1963), pp 125–35, p.130.

[59] E. F. O'Doherty, 'Spiritual formation of the adolescent' in *Studies*, 48 (Spring 1959), pp 68–77, p. 75.

[60] McQuaid to Mgr R. J. Glennon, 4 Feb. 1971, (DDA, McQuaid Papers, A/8/b/XXI/30).

8

Confraternities, their decline and the problem of sources: background, analysis and review

Louise Fuller

Confraternities in Ireland were already in decline in the 1950s. While the records show that sodalities and confraternities limped on until the 1960s and even the 1970s, the radically new thinking which emerged from the Second Vatican Council, 1962–1965, was to spell the death knell of Irish Catholic devotional life, as it had been experienced since the latter half of the nineteenth century. This essay examines the confraternity phenomenon and its decline against the background of previous investigations of the broader Catholic cultural change taking place in Ireland since the 1950s,[1] and in the context of historical developments in the universal Catholic church it poses some questions about a vibrant feature of Catholic cultural life, which is now the stuff of folk memory and nostalgia.

When approaches were made to clergy who had been active in confraternity groups in the 1950s, reactions to the proposed research were mixed. On the one hand, there was bemusement at the fact that anybody was interested at all in the study of a phenomenon that had well and truly disappeared. On the other hand, a feeling of sadness was expressed by many – a kind of sentimental yearning for a different, simpler faith and devotional life, a way of life that was all-embracing; a similar response was echoed by many to the effect that confraternal activity finished after the Vatican Council. When enquiries were made as to the possible existence of source materials, the response in many cases was that record books were not kept – that the confraternity group met on such and such a day, or evening

---

[1] See Louise Fuller, *Irish Catholicism since 1950: the undoing of a culture* (Dublin, 2002).

and had mass and prayers. In many cases it was simply called the confraternity, which name was used interchangeably with sodality.

From the outset the research was approached in terms of the larger picture of changing religious devotional life in Ireland, as opposed to simply focusing on individual confraternities in particular parishes and religious communities. Diocesan and religious order archives were circularised and the bishops of each diocese were contacted, and for the most part the response was good. As regards parish records of confraternities, the researcher was repeatedly told that they would have been disposed of after Vatican II, an interesting finding in itself. That said, some very valuable records were found, in parish, religious order and diocesan archives.

It could be asked, to what extent do attitudes to the care of the records and memorabilia of the confraternities, reflect the position of the clergy in regard to the passing of the phenomenon? It could also be asked, how did a movement which was so powerful practically disappear overnight? Of course, what really happened was that they, as it were, petered out and this is where the records that are extant speak for themselves. For instance, on many occasions it was found that ledgers and minute books, which were kept meticulously in the 1940s and 1950s, were gradually completed in less detail, more casually or carelessly, and then suddenly the entries stopped, as if the whole process ran out of steam. The fact that confraternities or sodalities were never formally shut down, meant that they limped along with lesser numbers of members, with less commitment and enthusiasm and in many cases, if there were minute books or ledgers, they ended up in members' homes, perhaps in the attic, the garage, or some such place.

For the most part, no provision was made, or contingency plans set in place, to collect, preserve and care for the records – importance, it would appear, was not ascribed to them. In the case of religious orders, where there was a confraternity or a third order, records were often better preserved. Partly, this was because unlike the parish church, religious tended to stay in the same locale for longer years, whereas secular clergy moved around. The same clergyman might be assigned to the third order or confraternity for long periods, as in the case of Fr Bernard Cuffe, who was spiritual director of the Carmelite confraternity in Loughrea, for about thirty years.[2]

How is the decline explained and analysed? To what extent is it just part and parcel of the change in Catholic culture and the lessening influence of religion on the way of life of Irish Catholics, which began slowly from the 1950s, influenced by cinema, increased mobility, more exposure to television, all of which influences accelerated in the 1960s. Changes in the economy, educational change, the influence of the 'new' theology validated by Vatican II, more access to travel, pop culture, access to entertainment – all of these reasons are well-rehearsed and valid. Is there anything more to be said? Was it just part of the wider change in Catholic life and Irish social and cultural life in general: in a word, the impact of modernisation? One explanation is that much of the devotional practice that had characterised the pre-Vatican II Irish church, was de-emphasised, if not totally discouraged in the post-conciliar period. Did manifestations of this kind of devotional life and practice, of which confraternal activity would be a supreme example, prove to be an embarrassment, which clerics preferred to forget ever existed? The church had 'moved on', so to speak. The primary emphasis was on the mass, and paraliturgical activity suffered as a consequence. The spiritual director had been an important feature of confraternity and sodality life. It was hierarchical – there were prefects who kept an eye on people's attendance.[3] If a member was missing, or deemed not to be keeping the rules and fulfilling the requirements, he/she could be cautioned and indeed dismissed from membership.[4]

An examination of the typical devotional material geared to the laity in the 1950s and even up to the 1960s, reflects a

---

[2] Interview with Fr Bernard Cuffe of the Carmelite Friary, Loughrea, Co. Galway.

[3] See section books in which prefects marked members present at confraternity; Archives, Carmelite Friary, Loughrea, Co. Galway; Congregation of the Passion archives, Mount Argus, Dublin; Cathedral, Ennis, Co. Clare.

[4] Cards were issued to members naming their sections and prefect and reminding them of the next meeting. Prefects would present attendance books to spiritual directors who would review attendance and then ask prefects to ascertain reasons for absence and report back to the spiritual director.

patriarchal approach to a compliant laity. Some examples serve
to capture this. A prayer book for men issued by a Redemptorist
priest and published in Dublin in 1957, urged men to

> enter gladly into the Confraternity or Sodality that is established
> where you live. These sodalities and confraternities are so many
> Noah's Arks which will save you, who live in the world, from
> the deluge of sin and temptation that everywhere surrounds
> you ...[5]

Quoting from St Alphonsus and from St Francis de Sales, the
author went on say that, from experiences of missions, 'we
know the utility of these confraternities. As a rule, a man who
does not attend the meetings of a confraternity or sodality
commits more sins than twenty men who attend them ...'[6] In
the corresponding *Prayer book for women* the same advice about
joining the confraternity or sodality is given, with the additional
suggestion that the Children of Mary sodality is recommended
'to enable you to practise more easily those virtues so dear to
Our Lady – humility, charity and chastity'.[7] The same author
went on to caution: 'Be faithful to the rules of the sodality and in
particular to its meetings. Always be (or become) an active
member of that branch of the sodality where you reside.'[8] These
prayer books were published in the 1950s, but in terms of their
ethos they are a reminder of that much quoted phrase: 'the past
is a different country' – they belong to a different era.

What was remarkable about the confraternities was that they
embraced the whole community practically – men, women,
youths and children. The church today is often described as an
ageing church and one dominated by women. Yet men were
strongly represented in the confraternity movement. So again
the question could be posed – what was it that attracted and
focused men's energy then, and why has it, by and large, been
absent from the church since? More general questions could also
be posed – what role did the confraternities fulfil? What has
been the impact, if any, of their loss, and what has filled their

---

[5] Leo O'Halloran, CSsR, *Prayer book for men*, revised ed. (Dublin, 1957), p. 49.
[6] Ibid.
[7] Leo O'Halloran, CSsR, *Prayer book for women* (Dublin, 1957), p. 92.
[8] Ibid.

place? In theory, the aim of confraternities and sodalities was to enhance the spiritual and devotional lives of their members and to confer spiritual benefits on them. Likewise they were designed to encourage among their members the regular reception of the sacraments and in many cases their success was measured by the numbers they brought to the altar rails. Examples of this mentality are evidenced in registers, where sections of confraternities are allocated to certain Sundays of the month to receive communion and in some cases numbers receiving were counted.[9] But the confraternities and sodalities had a wider dimension also – as a social outlet, a way for the clergy to channel youthful energies into religion-related activities and a vehicle for lay people to wield power and influence and exercise leadership in their own locale, at a time when the lay person's role was, in the immortal words of Bishop Ernest Primeau of Manchester, New Hampshire, during the debate on the church at the Second Vatican Council, to 'believe, pray, obey, pay'.[10]

There is plenty of evidence that all of these possibilities existed. For instance, Fr Christopher Lee, writing in the *Furrow* in 1950 and reflecting back on his experience as curate of a parish in west Limerick in the 1930s, wrote:

> The Sunday evening meetings of the confraternity were a grand affair and took on something of the character of a parish social gathering. In the long evenings of the spring and summer the men folk ambled along towards the church after their tea, in time for a second chat before the devotions. The younger men came on their bicycles, as did many of the girls.[11]

Referring to the guilds representing different districts, he pointed out that this gave the members 'a special interest in the good name of their localities, they enjoyed a friendly rivalry in having the best attendance'.[12] From his experience he pointed out that

---

[9] Index books for different divisions of confraternity. See figures for communion for Monday's division for April, May, October in the years 1885, 1886 and 1887. See also figures for Tuesday's division in May and October 1886, Redemptorist archives, Mount St Alphonsus, Limerick.

[10] Xavier Rynne, *The second session: the debates and decrees of Vatican Council II, from 29 September to 4 December 1963* (London, 1963), pp 111–12.

[11] Christopher Lee, 'A rural confraternity' in *The Furrow*, 1, no. 1 (Feb. 1950), p. 26.

[12] Ibid., p. 27.

confraternities 'acted as a leaven of good in the whole parish'.[13]

Fr Paul Madden, a Passionist priest from the Mount Argus community, writing about his own experience of organising the very successful Mount Argus youth sodality, gives advice to prospective spiritual directors not to be put off by troublesome boys – that in his experience they present 'an opportunity that is truly heaven-sent'.[14] He wrote:

> Many such boys have come my way; and I have generally found that, with a little prudent handling, they have become staunch and most valuable members of the sodality. Indeed, it may be taken as a general rule that boys, who get into trouble and get the name of being 'juvenile delinquents', have in them the stuff of which leaders are made. A boy, for instance, who has the initiative and courage to break and enter a house, has in him the natural qualities of leadership; and these qualities, when properly directed and supernaturalised, will make him a great apostle. Time and time again in our experience, some of these 'gang-leaders' (many of them with formidable criminal records) have succeeded in bringing the whole gang into the sodality.[15]

Now if that is not a good example of lateral thinking in 1953, it would be difficult to imagine what is! It begs the question, should the church or Irish society be trying to revive the sodalities? In fact, the entire article is a triumph of the kind of psychological approach both to take, and definitely not to take, if one wants to attract boys into the sodality, to cultivate their loyalty and an *esprit de corps*, and keep them involved. He goes on to point out the ultimate aim, that if the boys 'can be brought to look upon themselves as members of a "movement", their interest and loyalty will be intensified and will influence their whole life'.[16] Because the sodality was formed as a juvenile branch of the very successful confraternity of the Sacred Passion, they adopted a secondary title – 'Crusade of the Cross', to emphasise the idea of the boys being active participators with

---

[13] Ibid., p. 29.

[14] Paul Madden, C.P., 'Organizing and working a boy's sodality' in *Irish Theological Quarterly*, xx (1953), p. 304. Interview with Fr Paul Madden, Mount Argus, Dublin.

[15] Ibid.

[16] Ibid., p. 312.

Christ in his passion, and went on to have first and second line Crusaders, the latter being obliged to go to mass on one day of each week and the former to attend daily mass.[17]

But the influence of the confraternity went far beyond the spiritual and also involved itself in the boys' material welfare. Because many of the members were extremely poor, and were unable to attend meetings or Sunday mass for want of proper clothing, the idea of a 'Crusade wardrobe' was born, to distribute clothing and footwear to needy members.[18] Also, hundreds of members left school annually and joined the ranks of the unemployed and this suggested to them the establishment of the 'Crusade labour centre', which, he pointed out, 'proved successful beyond our most sanguine expectations'.[19] By circularising city firms, aided by the services of a part-time agent, he described how they had been able to secure worthwhile positions for most of the boys and that the labour centre also involved itself in fixing up difficulties that might arise in their employment, and in securing improved working conditions for boy-workers.[20] He stated that before the labour centre had begun to function successfully, many members had been forced to emigrate. However, they had kept in touch with them, and formed them in the course of time 'into a guild of their own under the patronage of "Our Lady, Queen of Ireland", so that they still belong, in the full sense of the word, to our Crusade'.[21]

Another example of the kind of influence that the confraternity could exercise on behalf of its members is captured in some hand-written notes attached loosely to a directory, compiled by the Limerick Holy Family confraternity director in 1942, 'with a view to helping future directors who may be called upon to take up office on very short notice'.[22] The Redemptorist archconfraternity, first established in Limerick in 1868, was one of the best-known, and influential confraternities, affiliated to it,

---

[17] Ibid., pp 313–14.

[18] Ibid., p. 314.

[19] Ibid.

[20] Ibid.

[21] Ibid., pp 314–15.

[22] Directory compiled by the Limerick Holy Family confraternity director, 1942 (Foreword), Redemptorist archives, Mount St Alphonsus, Limerick.

spread throughout the country. The directory of typed notes relates to traditional procedures 'for various ceremonies and also all useful information for the efficient management of the confraternity'.[23]

What is of equal interest, however, is the hand-written section with the heading 'useful men in the city',[24] which indicates the extent to which the confraternity reached into every corner of city life in terms of its influence. It provides a comprehensive list of the names of people in key influential positions in the city, whom the director of the confraternity can contact to assist him in resolving issues. For instance in the event of 'labour problems' the president of the Trades Council was named, who 'will give every help and get director in touch with right men'. For matters of crime in the city two detective sergeants are named, who 'will assist'. A sergeant in John Street is named, who is 'good also'. The notes further record that the chief superintendent is 'in Conf.' and that the 'super is ex Maynooth man'. For matters to do with the Great Southern Railway and the Electricity Supply Board, two names are given for each institution. In all cases, those cited are 'secretaries', presumably in the confraternity. The mayor's name is given – he is 'not in confraternity' but is regarded as 'very kind and helpful'. The names of a Labour, Fine Gael and Fianna Fáil T.D. are given, all of whom are 'in Conf'. For matters to do with the Corporation or the City Hall, the names of three men 'all secretaries of Conf. and working in City Hall' are given. In St Mary's parish the name of the sacristan, who is 'trustworthy and helpful', is cited. In St Munchin's parish the names of three individuals who are 'all secretaries' and live in the parish and 'can help' are cited. The city manager is recorded as 'not in Conf. but will help'. Under the heading 'Soldiers in b[arrac]ks' a commandant's name is given. He is 'an old member of confraternity and helpful'. Under the same heading the name of another gentleman is recorded, who 'will be able to direct to right man in most difficulties. His knowledge of city is invaluable'.[25] These informally

---

[23] Ibid.

[24] Handwritten notes attached loosely to directory.

[25] Ibid.

written notes provide a unique insight into the confraternity's ability to mobilise influence on behalf of its members. While religious associational culture was primarily concerned with the spiritual and devotional life of its members, the fraternities could also promote the idea of social solidarity and provide informal access to power and certain types of social capital in the temporal sphere.

In 1968, the Limerick Confraternity celebrated its centenary with a jubilee publication entitled *'One hundred years young!': Archconfraternity of the Holy Family, 1868–1968*.[26] The year 1968 was a watershed year in more ways than one in the life of the Catholic church in Ireland and abroad. To place the centenary year in context – it was three years after the close of the Second Vatican Council and Irish television was still in its early honeymoon period, already exercising a powerful influence on Irish society. Profound policy-driven changes were transforming education. Pope Paul VI promulgated *Humanae vitae*, his long-awaited encyclical on artificial birth-control in that year, the censorship laws were being relaxed and the women's movement was about to take off. Irish life had changed enormously by 1968, and this was only the beginning. In 1969 the Northern troubles broke out. In 1971 the lobbying for relaxation of the laws on contraception began. In the same year the constitutional clause which upheld the 'special position' of the Catholic church in the 1937 Constitution was removed on the basis of a referendum vote, and in the following year Archbishop John Charles McQuaid, very much the symbol of the church of confraternities, sodalities and traditional Catholic devotion, retired from office.[27]

The author of an article, 'Confraternities in the post-conciliar church' in the Limerick jubilee publication was keenly aware of the challenges facing the confraternity movement in the new Ireland, when he pointed out that 'confraternities are sometimes decried nowadays, as though their day in the Church were done'.[28] He went on to point to the importance of not rejecting

---

[26] *'One hundred years young!' Archconfraternity of the Holy Family, 1868–1968* (Limerick, 1968).

[27] Fuller, *Irish Catholicism since 1950*.

[28] 'Confraternities in the post conciliar church' in *One hundred years young*, p. 25.

confraternities out of hand, and of ensuring that 'they keep up their true spirit and render practical service to the church in accordance with changing conditions of life and changing needs in the church and in the world', continuing that 'a confraternity must be lively, enterprising, adaptable. Otherwise it will stagnate and cease to fulfil its spiritual and apostolic function'.[29] Given the context in which he was speaking, and on the basis of evidence from the Limerick confraternity itself, it is undoubtedly the case that these comments were reflecting what was already happening, as opposed to what was on the horizon. The writing was well and truly on the wall for the confraternity movement by the late 1960s. This was despite the fact that the confraternity had adapted to the times by setting up a very successful credit union,[30] a teenage dance club[31] and a social centre to cater for the needs of confraternity men and their families – which numbered 'in all, a total of approximately 25,000 people'[32] at that time. It was noticeable that the confraternity of Our Lady of Perpetual Succour junior division attendance book, 1954–72 was well kept until 1961, less well kept in 1969–70 and then poorly kept.[33]

Judging by observations made in another article in the Limerick jubilee publication, *One hundred years young*, it was also clear that the author was well aware of the challenges posed by a new era. Referring to 'the young men who wear the bright green ribbons today', the writer pointed out that 'he expects the church to speak to him in a way that takes into account modern conditions and problems … he is a young man of the sixties, and he expects his confraternity to be in the sixties also.'[34] But despite the confraternity's awareness of the 'urgent need to up-date itself', and the fact that it '[looked] forward with confidence to its second exciting century',[35] this was not to be.

---

[29] Ibid.

[30] Ibid., pp 25–9.

[31] Ibid.

[32] Ibid.

[33] Redemptorist archives, Mount St Alphonsus, Limerick.

[34] See article 'One hundred years young' in publication of the same name, *One hundred years young*, p. 31.

[35] Ibid., pp 31–2.

It begs the question as to whether all that could be realistically done was to accept that confraternities had had their day. The author of the article in the Jubilee publication rightly refers to economic affluence and education, and the influence it exerted from the 1960s. In this respect, the reports of the deans of residence or chaplains of the universities, which were sourced in the Galway diocesan archives made interesting reading. The dean of residence report for University College Galway for 1964–5 notes that the sodality was disappointing.[36] In 1966–7 he states that it can only be described as poor;[37] in 1967–8 he points out that 'my best efforts to improve attendance have met with no success'.[38] In 1968–9 there is no comment[39] and by 1969–70 the sodality listing is gone![40] Similarly, the University College Cork report for 1965 gives an indication of the situation there. There is mention of a sodality of Our Lady meeting weekly on Tuesday afternoon and devotions held on Sunday at 7 p.m. It was noted that 'the attendance, both on Tuesday and Sunday, could not be termed satisfactory'.[41] Given that the late 1960s was a revolutionary time in the Catholic church and society in general, it is not surprising that ways of thinking and institutions that had served the church and society well heretofore would begin to falter. Whereas the confraternity and sodality movement typified Irish Catholic culture in the 1950s, by the early 1970s movements like Charismatic Renewal and Women's Liberation bespoke a profoundly altered cultural landscape in Ireland.

In Gorey, County Wexford, the confraternity of the Most Blessed Sacrament which began in 1914 and the confraternity of the Sacred Heart, which pre-dated it, were strong until the 1960s. In 1989, a publication to commemorate the sesquicentenary of the church in Gorey, *St Michael's, Gorey, 1839–1989*, evidenced the confraternity as 'the most obvious feature of the

---

[36] Dean of residence report for University College Galway, 1964–5 (Galway diocesan archives, Cathedral, Galway).

[37] Ibid., 1966–7.

[38] Ibid., 1967–8.

[39] Ibid., 1968–9.

[40] Ibid., 1969–70.

[41] Dean of residence report for University College Cork, 1964–5 (Galway diocesan archives).

parish for decades before the renewal of Vatican II'.[42] It pointed out that:

> The confraternities continued to thrive until the Second Vatican Council when the devotional side of the church changed. The advent of evening mass saw the end, or very near the end, of evening devotions and in May 1968, Bishop Herlihy gave permission to have evening mass on the occasion of the confraternity meeting. By the late 1970s, the confraternity mass had become no different to any other evening mass. There were no shields, no prefects and very often more women than men at the men's confraternity mass. Eventually, the confraternity masses disappeared altogether.[43]

This short paragraph (unwittingly) holds the key to the demise of the confraternity, which has to be understood in the broader context of the fundamental ground-shift that took place in the Catholic church, in both theory and practice at the time of the Second Vatican Council. This was set to revolutionise Catholic life and culture. Ironically in Ireland, neither bishops nor clergy on the whole saw any need for far-reaching changes – because Catholic life and practice were working very well, to their mind, at that time. Churches were full, Catholic devotional life revolved around mass, confraternities, sodalities, pilgrimages, processions, benediction, novenas, holy hours and May and evening devotions.[44] Indeed, the fact that Bishop Herlihy gave permission to have evening mass in the slot occupied by the confraternity meeting, which would have been an institution at that time, whether he did so deliberately, or by default, is revealing. And this is the tragedy of the confraternal movement – while there are those who might now lament its demise, if for no other reason than that an enormous reservoir of energy was allowed seep away – it was allowed to happen, and it appears that nobody thought to channel or re-direct it. It was simply lost. So it is understandable that reference to confraternities might elicit mixed emotions from clergy.

---

[42] *St Michael's Church, Gorey 1839–1989*, p. 109.
[43] Ibid.
[44] Fuller, *Irish Catholicism since 1950*, pp 19–36.

A similar pattern was observable in the confraternity of the Holy Family, established in Ennis, County Clare in 1876 and affiliated to the archconfraternity of the Holy Family in Limerick.[45] Ennis was one of the more successful visitations of parish archives – there was a full complement of banners of the various guilds, a full register of members compiled in 1955, and updated to include members who joined in 1964. There were two ledgers recording meetings from 1957 to 1963 and from 1963 to 1968, as well as ledgers relating to accounts and several other items such as guild attendance books, enrolment cards, membership cards, and reminder cards for members' monthly communion. A handwritten note (on loose leaves), relating to a meeting of prefects and sub-prefects held on Monday night 3 December 1962, gives a flavour of the standing of the confraternity in the parish in the early 1960s:

> Rev. Fr Carroll introduced himself to those present and exhorted them to do their utmost to make the confraternity worthy of the cathedral town of the diocese … Mr Kelly suggested that boys about to leave school be contacted beforehand and invited to join section of their choice. It was also suggested that prefects in the different areas of the town be requested to interview non-members in their own locality and endeavour to get them to join. Fr Carroll also agreed to interview with prefect and sub-prefect lapsed and irregular members in the different sections. To avoid a clash between members of confraternity and third order on holy communion Sundays it was agreed to seek a transfer of children's holy communion day to second Sunday of month instead of first Sunday as heretofore. Prefects were requested to ascertain reason for absence of members from weekly meetings and monthly holy communion, and to report same to spiritual director.[46]

---

45 See summary notes on history of confraternity in register of Holy Family Confraternity, compiled in 1955 and updated to 1964, in the Cathedral, Ennis, Co. Clare. In a loose page in the register mention is made that a general enrolment was made of all adult members present in Feb. 1960. However, on perusal of the diary, it was noted that a number of members had joined in 1964, hence the reference to the fact that it was updated in 1964.

46 Handwritten note recording meeting of prefects and sub-prefects held in sacristy on Monday night 3 Dec. 1962, included in ledger recording minutes of meetings of prefects and sub-prefects and confraternity council, men's confraternity, Ennis, as from Monday 8 Apr. 1963. In addition to these two meetings a further meeting is recorded on 23 Nov. 1964 (Archives, Cathedral, Ennis, Co. Clare).

The last meeting recorded in the ledgers examined was the meeting of Monday, 29 January 1968.[47] While one hesitates to draw definitive conclusions from any one such piece of evidence, all the findings as well as anecdotal evidence and interview sources again allow for the conclusion that confraternal activity was drawing to a close by this time. In fact, in many cases, it had disappeared altogether. An interesting finding in Ennis was, that while all the minute books sourced relate to the men's confraternity, many of the guild attendance books which have survived actually relate to the women's confraternity, and it would appear that the latter had a very healthy membership listing, and such records exist for the 1970s and 1980s.[48]

A very popular sodality until the 1960s was the Children of Mary, particularly in schools. Often confused with the sodality of Our Lady, it was in fact a separate entity, but affiliated to the sodality.[49] It was recorded as perhaps, the oldest of all sodalities in Gorey parish, 'introduced to the senior pupils of the Loreto Abbey in 1856'.[50] From small beginnings it increased yearly until 13 June 1965, when '20 pupils of the pre-leaving certificate class became the last girls to be enrolled in the sodality'.[51] On feast days such as Corpus Christi and the Immaculate Conception, 'the members, wearing the blue cloaks of the sodality, walked in procession or formed a guard of honour when the Blessed Sacrament was being honoured in a special way'.[52] The Gorey publication recorded that 'after 1965, as no new members were being enrolled in the secondary schools, the sodality of Our Lady membership became more and more depleted with the result that meetings and processions became less frequent until finally they ceased completely'.[53]

This is borne out in a register and minute book combined, sourced in the Sisters of Mercy archives, Charleville. It belonged

---

[47] Ledger commencing Monday 30 Sept. 1963 ending with meeting of Monday 29 Jan. 1968 (Cathedral, Ennis, Co. Clare).

[48] Section attendance books, 1960s, 1970s, 1980s for women; 1960s, 1970s for men (Cathedral, Ennis, Co. Clare).

[49] *The Little Companion of the Child of Mary*, 23rd ed. (Cork, 1957), p. 1.

[50] *St. Michael's Church, Gorey*, p. 110.

[51] Ibid.

[52] Ibid., p. 111.

[53] Ibid.

to the boarders of the convent of Mercy, Carrick-on-Suir, was dated February 1958 and runs from the school year 1958–9 through to 1967–8.[54] In 1965–6 meetings were summed up in one line: 'held in September, October, November, December'. This took a half page, the rest of the page was blank and none were recorded after that. For 1967–8, only two meetings were record-ed, the first on 6 October 1967, which went as follows: 'Said the Litany. Discussed how we boarders could be active members of the sodality and so prepare for later life. Decided to hold weekly meetings on Fridays'.[55] The second meeting was on 23 October and recorded: 'Read part of document on Vatican Council II. Discussed Apostleship of Prayer and Crusaders of the Blessed Sacrament.'[56] The rest of the page was blank, as was the rest of the ledger! So it would appear that the discussion about how to be active members, a significant entry in itself, and the resolu-tion to hold weekly meetings came to nought, if one can judge by this ledger. It seems significant also that the final meeting recorded here made reference to the Vatican Council, given that so many references have been made to the effect that the Vatican Council spelt the death knell of aspects of Catholic devotional life, which appeared set in stone.

Confraternities and sodalities were part of the complex devo-tional life built up by the church in response to the Reformation challenge to Mary and the saints. Reflecting on this and on the demise of popular devotions in the post-Vatican II church, Donal Flanagan, writing in the *Furrow* in 1990, pointed out that while 'these devotions added colour and imagination to reli-gion',[57] they had become problematic. He wrote that 'some popular devotions had grown out of proportion and had, perhaps, assumed an importance in people's lives that belied their basically secondary role in the prayer life of the church'.[58]

---

54 Children of Mary sodality, register and minutes ledger, boarders' section, Convent of Mercy, Carrick-on-Suir, Feb. 1958. Register begins in 1958–9. Last group recorded, 1967–8. Minutes of meetings from 9 Feb. 1958 to 23 Oct. 1967 (last meeting recorded) (Sisters of Mercy archives, Charleville, Co. Cork).
55 Ibid.
56 Ibid.
57 Donal Flanagan, 'A people in search of devotions' in *The Furrow*, 41, no. 9 (Sept. 1990), p. 495.
58 Ibid., p. 491.

One of the main aims of the Vatican Council was to re-centre devotion in the liturgy. Because it 'concentrated on the liturgy' and 'did not concern itself with popular devotions, apart from some general admonitions', he pointed out that 'this may have seemed to some a signal for their demise'.[59] Whether this was because they were seen as old-fashioned, or no longer suited to the times, or whether it was for ecumenical reasons, the result was, he stated, that 'it damaged the traditional framework within which most Roman Catholics had been reared. It generated a profound vacuum in the devotional lives of many ordinary people'.[60]

In attempting to explain the demise of confraternities and sodalities, another factor may also have been operating. One of the most important developments in continental Catholicism at the close of the nineteenth century and in the first quarter of the twentieth century was the growth of the Catholic social movement. Catholic action, along continental lines, as inspired by *Rerum novarum* 1891,[61] was slow to develop in Ireland. It was a model of church that would be developed and refined right through the twentieth century by means of encyclicals like *Quadragesimo anno*,[62] *Mater et magistra*,[63] *Populorum progressio*,[64] and *Gaudium et spes*, the Vatican II document, *The church in the modern world*.[65] The main object of pious associations such as confraternities and sodalities as defined by the *Catholic Encyclopaedia* of 1912 was 'the practice of piety and works of charity'.[66] In the *New Catholic Encyclopaedia* of 1967, quoting from the code of canon law, it was pointed out that the specific purpose and distinguishing element of the confraternity was the promotion of public worship. 'Whereas a sodality may be founded for any religious purpose', it stressed that 'a confraternity is

---

[59] Ibid.

[60] Ibid.

[61] *Encyclical letter of Pope Leo XIII on the condition of the working classes*, 1891.

[62] *Encyclical letter of Pope Pius XI on reconstruction of the social order*, 1931.

[63] *Encyclical letter of Pope John XXIII concerning a re-evaluation of the social question in the light of Christian teaching*, 1961.

[64] *Encyclical letter of Pope Paul VI on the development of peoples*, 1967.

[65] *Pastoral constitution on the church in the modern world* in Walter M. Abbott, S.J. (ed.), *The documents of Vatican II* (London, Dublin, 1966).

[66] *Catholic Encyclopaedia*, xiv (New York, 1912), p. 121.

established for the promotion of public worship', such as assistance at mass, nocturnal adoration, processions, public recitation of the rosary.[67] Allowing for the fact that the lines between confraternities and sodalities were always blurred, the main aim of the confraternity as defined was to attain piety, while that of the sodality was 'chiefly to promote the spiritual and corporal works of mercy'.[68]

As time went by, however, it would appear that the ethos of both confraternities and sodalities was, on balance, chiefly concerned with the practice of piety and the attainment of personal holiness. In the case of the sodality movement, two booklets, one written in the 1930s and the other in the late 1970s, evidence this. A booklet of the *Irish Messenger* series, published in 1934, *The sodality of Our Lady in action*, impressed on the readers that the aims of the sodality of Our Lady were two-fold, as defined in the sodality manual: 'personal holiness and Catholic action',[69] reminding them that 'sodalities in former years were not merely pious gatherings to recite the office of Mary'.[70] Giving an overview of the historical development of the four-hundred-year-old lay movement, Francis K. Drolet writing in 1978, pointed out that 'many groups had become totally pietistic and devotional, unrelated to the apostolate; and yet the age was that of Catholic action!'[71] This may have spelt the undoing of sodalities and confraternities alike. Notwithstanding distinctions which have been made in theory, in practice the lines between sodalities and confraternities were blurred and the terms were used interchangeably. Interestingly, in the reports of the deans of residence for Galway, cited above, alongside the reference to the dean's failed efforts 'to improve attendance' at the sodality in the 1967–8 report, in the margin alongside there was a reference to 'Social action',[72] which seemed pertinent. Bearing social

---

[67] *New Catholic Encyclopaedia*, iv (Washington, 1967), p. 154.

[68] *Catholic Encyclopaedia*, xiv, 1912, p. 121.

[69] D. W. Rourke, S.J., *The sodality of Our Lady in action. Irish Messenger* series (Dublin, 1934), p. 4.

[70] Ibid., p. 3.

[71] Francis K. Drolet, S.J., *Christian communities from sodalities of Our Lady. Irish Messenger* series (Dublin, 1978), p. 14.

[72] Dean of residence report, University College Galway, 1967–8, Galway diocesan archives, Cathedral, Galway.

witness to the gospel very much epitomised the mood of the Irish church from the late 1960s and this was in keeping with the social and political mood of Irish society.[73]

That said, the sodalities of Our Lady did, in fact, attempt to adapt and renew according to the spirit of the times. Originally founded in the Jesuits' Roman College, the sodality was canonically established as the Prima Primaria by Pope Gregory XIII in 1584.[74] The period after the restoration of the Jesuits witnessed a time of vast expansion in their numbers – women's sodalities under the guidance of religious sisters and parish sodalities under groups of priests began to be affiliated to the Prima Primaria.[75] Their renewal was in progress even before Vatican II, as early as 1948, when Pope Pius XII issued an apostolic constitution, *Bis saeculari*,[76] which amended church law regarding sodalities. Essentially its message was that the new and urgent demands of a changing world called for a refined and renewed sodality instrument, so that its members might be in the vanguard of the church's lay apostles.[77] The fact that the Children of Mary sodality of Carrick-on-Suir was aware of these developments is borne out in the minutes of their meetings in 1958, which recorded that they 'read part of *Bis saeculari*' and in several meetings they 'discussed Catholic action works'.[78]

Drolet points out that the predominant image of the church for almost four centuries was the institutional image. It was strong in central authority and law, defending itself against attacks of heretics. It over-identified with clergy leadership, largely had an obedient, pious laity, often generous in good works, but mostly untouched by responsibility for the church's development.[79] The importance of lay involvement was emphasised at the Second Vatican Council,[80] and in keeping with this, there was a sense that sodalities should broaden their

---

[73] Fuller, *Irish Catholicism since 1950*, pp 133–4, pp 213–20.

[74] Drolet, *Christian communities from sodalities of Our Lady*, p. 11.

[75] Ibid., p. 13.

[76] Ibid., p. 14.

[77] Ibid.

[78] Children of Mary register and minutes ledger, Carrick-on-Suir, 1958, pp 1–2 of minutes.

[79] Drolet, *Christian communities from sodalities of Our Lady*, p. 18.

[80] Ibid., p. 19.

philosophy as to what Christian living and responsibility entailed. Their new general principles were approved by Pope Paul VI on 25 March 1968, the traditional feast of the sodalities, to replace the common rules of 1910.[81] The changed terminology of course was highly significant. As Drolet points out, the term 'principles' allows for some flexibility and freedoms while operating within general Christian ideals.[82] Rules, so much a feature of Catholic life in the past, were very much out of keeping with the *Zeitgeist*. This was the theory – but how did it translate into practice on the ground? Essentially the Christian Life communities never established themselves in the way that the sodalities had done. The evidence from Gorey and Carrick-on-Suir suggests that the sodalities simply fizzled out before they could evolve in the manner which was planned for them. This is not hard to understand for a variety of reasons. It is important to remember that church 'renewal' was top down, was, so to speak, imposed. In Ireland even the bishops and clergy for the most part saw no necessity for it. When one reflects on Catholic devotional life pre-Vatican II at this remove some forty odd years later, it is not difficult to understand how the revolutionary new thinking might have been a bridge too far for many devout Catholics.

Suddenly a whole way of thinking and practising religion, it seemed, was no longer valid. So many absolutes of Catholic life and practice were literally turned on their head, or simply left hanging in mid-air. An example of this was the cult of indulgences, which had been very much a part of the confraternity and sodality tradition. Membership combined with certain prayers, or devotions, carried indulgences – spiritual benefits remitting penance, or time in purgatory, calculated in days or years and granted by the pope. The way that the system could be misconstrued, is captured in the following descriptive passage by Gene Kerrigan in his book, in which he reflects back on growing up in Ireland in the 1950s. Notwithstanding the cynical tone, the remarks have an authentic ring. He wrote:

> The system of indulgences presupposed some kind of heavenly accountancy department which kept track of every verbal

---

[81] Ibid., p. 23.
[82] Ibid., p. 22.

ejaculation or silent prayer, identifying the person gaining the
indulgence, and updating the file which specified the appropriate amount of parole to be allowed against the purgatorial
sentence ... You could bank the indulgences against the day
you might find yourself in purgatory, or you could use them
to reduce the amount of time a loved one had to burn in the
purgatorial fires. As a means of getting lots of people to engage
in endless, repetitive recitation of one prayerful formula after
another, it was inspired.[83]

In an article on indulgences in the post-Vatican II church in the
Irish Theological Quarterly in 1966, Denis O'Callaghan wrote:

Today's emphasis on personal holiness, on the individual's
need to work out his salvation by use of the resources available
to him in his own particular nature and situation makes people
suspicious of anything which promises salvation by proxy.[84]

He went on to say that 'when false emphases and exaggerations
are cleared away it is seen that indulgences have a place in the
programme of salvation',[85] while on the other hand admitting
that 'one feels that most theologians would be quite happy to
ignore this embarrassing growth on the fringes of theology'.[86]
And he points out that at both the Council of Trent (despite the
fact that it had been the immediate occasion of Luther's revolt),
and Vatican II, the question of indulgences was, as he put it,
'left hanging fire'.[87] Given that indulgences were an essential
component of the culture of confraternities and sodalities, the
fact that Vatican II, for practical purposes, side-stepped an
awkward question, again, did not inspire confidence in the laity.

In reflecting on the profound changes in *mentalité* that Irish
Catholics had to accommodate to, in the context of a church in

---

[83] See Gene Kerrigan, *Another country: growing up in '50s Ireland* (Dublin, 1998),
p. 112.
[84] Denis O'Callaghan, 'Indulgences' in *Irish Theological Quarterly*, 33, no. 4 (Oct.
1966), p. 291.
[85] Ibid., p. 308.
[86] Ibid., p. 291.
[87] Ibid., p. 292.

which laws were previously seen as immutable – changes in liturgy, change in fasting laws, Marian and other paraliturgical devotion de-emphasised, limbo and purgatory virtually forgotten about – it is easy to see why clergy and laity alike might have lost confidence and enthusiasm for aspects of Catholicism, which had formerly been taken for granted, as a way of life. It is also the case that individual piety, primarily geared to securing personal sanctification and salvation, which typified the Irish Catholic way of life in the pre-conciliar era and was exemplified *par excellence* in the ethos of the confraternity and sodality movement, was displaced by the theological renewal inspired by Vatican II, which emphasised the participative, communitarian, social dimensions of Catholicism and action to promote social justice. It might be pointed out that these dimensions were essential aspects of the confraternity movement, and (ironically) indeed they were – but it was essential that they be re-cast in keeping with the signs of the times, and the updating required by Vatican II. Creative renewal was called for, but by the time this was realised, it was already far too late for any reversal of the decline.

9

Charity, church and the Society of St Vincent de Paul

Máire Ní Chearbhaill

As a lay Catholic organisation, the Society of St Vincent de Paul shared many characteristics of the confraternities and charitable associations that emerged in response to social or spiritual need in nineteenth-century Dublin.[1] When members of the Society held their first meeting in 1844 in premises near the Four Courts, the confraternity in the nearby parish of St Paul on Arran Quay was already well established as a large body of laymen, whose varied activities included raising funds for the new church tower, preparing children for first communion, and acting as stewards at devotional gatherings in the parish.[2]

Bartholomew Woodlock, vice-rector of All Hallows missionary college and a priest of the Dublin diocese, is acknowledged as the principal founder of the Society of St Vincent de Paul in Ireland.[3] He had expressed concern at the lack of religious zeal among young gentlemen in Dublin,[4] which suggests that his attraction to this new lay French association stemmed from the opportunities it offered for strengthening laymen in their faith while engaging in charitable deeds. Archbishop Daniel Murray was pleased to grant permission for the establishment of the Society in the diocese:

> ... a source of consolation springs up within me when I find that according to one of those beneficent plans which that

---

[1] T.P. O'Neill, 'The Catholic church and the relief of the poor 1815–45' in *Archiv. Hib.*, xxxi (1973), pp 132–45.

[2] *Freeman's Journal*, 28 Nov. 1839.

[3] Kevin Condon, *The missionary college of All Hallows, 1842–1891* (Dublin, 1986), p. 195.

[4] *Memoir of the Most Rev. Dr Woodlock* (Dublin, 1903), p. 5. See also *All Hallows Annual, 1903–1904*, pp 12–14.

great servant of God, your glorious patron, St Vincent de Paul,
pointed out for the alleviation of human misery, you have been
moved by divine grace to form yourselves into a society ... I
approve most warmly of your holy project.[5]

For Frédéric Ozanam, principal founder of the Society in
Paris in 1833, the Society benefited both the givers and the
receivers, bringing about 'the reconciliation of those who have
not enough with those who have too much, by charitable
works'.[6] Ozanam believed in practical responses to poverty.
'The knowledge of social well-being and of reform is to be
learned, not from books, nor from the public platform, but in
climbing the stairs of the poor man's garret ...'[7] Although a
proclaimed republican, he had little faith in the ability of political or legislative institutions to answer social ills and preferred
to rely on charity based on religious principles.[8]

After their first meeting in Dublin in December 1844, the
members set about establishing the work that would become
principally associated with the Society: the bringing of relief to
poor families in their homes. Within a week of their foundation,
they were negotiating with local purveyors to procure food
tickets that could be exchanged for groceries.[9] Twenty-four
branches, known as conferences, had been established in Ireland
by end of 1850, seven of these within the Dublin city area.[10] The
Dublin-based leadership was asked to take on an additional
duty in 1855 when the Society's council-general in Paris
requested that it take responsibility for translating its monthly
journal, the *Bulletin*, and distributing it to members in the

---

5 Daniel Murray to members of White Cross conference, 1 Feb. 1845, transcribed
in White Cross minutes, 3 Feb. 1845 (Dublin, St Vincent de Paul archives [here-
after SVPA]).

6 Ainslie Coates, *Letters of Ozanam*, translated from the French (London, 1886),
p. 81.

7 Louis Baunard, *Ozanam in his correspondence*, translated from the French by
SVP, Council of Ireland (Dublin, 1925), p. 279.

8 Austin Fagan, 'The political and social ideas of Antoine-Frédéric Ozanam
(1813–53) and their relation to the movement of ideas in his time', M.Litt. thesis,
University of Newcastle Upon Tyne, 1971, pp 16–18.

9 White Cross minutes, 23 Dec. 1844 (SVPA).

10 *Manual of the Society of St Vincent de Paul* (Paris, 1850), p. 366.

English-speaking world.[11] It was an arrangement that was to endure until the late twentieth century.

As an organisation, the Society of St Vincent de Paul developed well-defined objectives and structures. The local conference was linked through parish, diocesan and national levels to its overseeing body, the council-general, in Paris. A young man joining the Society at any time from the 1840s until the mid-twentieth century would have been reminded that the primary purpose of membership was his own sanctification, achieved by service to the poor.[12] The society's *Manual* with the Rule, first published in 1835 and to remain essentially un-changed for a hundred and twenty years, was his guide. The new recruit would be assured that more experienced brothers were there to provide support and to introduce him to the works of the conference. The prayers and publications of the Society would motivate and sustain him spiritually. Cordiality and a sense of unity among members would be reinforced by attendance at the quarterly general meetings. As a voluntary member who freely gave his time and services to the Society, the authority of the various higher councils would be based entirely on 'acceptance, good example and persuasion'.[13]

While sharing similarities with other lay associations, the Society of St Vincent de Paul had its own distinguishing emphases and rules. Humility in the performance of good deeds was a virtue particularly to be valued.[14] Should members participate in public events, they were cautioned not to wear identifying badges of any kind.[15] Confraternity members were apparently not constrained by such self-effacement. At the procession in the streets of the capital in 1875 to celebrate the centenary of the birth of Daniel O'Connell, the *Irish Times* described how the members of the confraternity of St Francis, distinguished by 'the variety and richness of their banners', marched between the Dublin Saw Machinists and the Hackney Car Owners' Association. Further along the procession, two

[11] Council of Ireland minutes, 28 Dec. 1855 (SVPA).

[12] *Manual*, Rule, article 1 (Dublin, 1958).

[13] *Manual*, article 5 and commentary (Dublin, 1929).

[14] *Manual*, 1958 ed., Introduction, pp xvi–xvii.

[15] Council of Ireland minutes, 4 Apr. 1864 (SVPA).

stewards from the confraternity of St Augustine, mounted on horseback, marshalled their members.[16] Three years later, the funeral of Paul Cullen, archbishop of Dublin, provided another occasion for a show of lay Catholic associational strength. The identity of St Vincent de Paul members may not have been obvious from external insignia, but the *Irish Times* was able to report that five hundred of them marched with confraternities, sodalities and temperance societies, 'including many of the leading citizens of Dublin, among whom were several members of the learned professions and leading merchants'.[17]

Although the visitation of poor families in their homes was the main work of the Society of St Vincent de Paul, and essential for all active members, no work of charity was deemed foreign to the Society.[18] In 1855, St Vincent's orphanage and school had been founded in Glasnevin, as 'a male orphanage for the destitute children of Dublin'.[19] Fears of the threat to Catholic orphans from zealous mission groups influenced the decision but an immediate need was also generated by the number of Irish boys who had lost fathers in the Crimean war and in the Indian mutiny.[20] Another early initiative, the penny banks, was established to encourage modest savings among people of little means, and had several branches in Dublin by 1865.[21]

Confraternities and sodalities traditionally confined their activities to church-based devotional practices, although some also had an apostolic dimension. The children of Mary sodality for past pupils of Sacred Heart schools met regularly in Dublin from the 1860s for prayer and spiritual exercises, but also made outfits for poor families, provided first communion dresses for poor children, and gathered materials to make vestments for workhouse chapels.[22] Fr James Cullen, founder of the Pioneer Total Abstinence Movement and of several sodalities

---

16 *Irish Times*, 7 Aug. 1875.

17 *Irish Times*, 28 Oct. 1878.

18 *Manual*, 1958 ed., art. 2, p. 2.

19 Council of Ireland minutes, 13 Dec. 1855 (SVPA).

20 *St Vincent's, Glasnevin, Centenary Record*, 1856-1956 (Dublin, *c*.1957), pp 10–11.

21 Ibid.

22 Minutes of Child of Mary, Sacred Heart, Glasnevin, later Mount Anville and Harcourt Street branches, 1860s (Mount Anville Archives).

throughout Ireland, expected the laity to engage not only in prayer-related activities but in promoting temperance and in charitable works.[23]

By the later decades of the nineteenth century, all the main Christian churches in Dublin were engaged in a wide range of initiatives for those in need. Many similar works would come to be undertaken by the Society of St Vincent de Paul as it expanded in the early twentieth century.[24] The Church of Ireland had opened a night shelter for men in Poolbeg Street in 1894 that was catering for 47,000 annual admissions thirty years later.[25] Its Fishamble Street Mission was engaged in 'evangelistic and temperance work' and had a coal club, a savings bank and a clothing section.[26] The sick poor were visited in their homes by the Methodist-run Strangers' Friend Society.[27] The Country Air Association had been organising a rest and a change of environment for Dublin's Protestant poor in farmhouses and rural districts since 1886.[28]

Given that the Society of St Vincent de Paul had both a temporal and a spiritual dimension, it was often felt necessary to clarify the precise nature of this dual identity. Writing from Paris in 1915, the president-general explained that the aim of the Society was to:

> do a great deal of spiritual good to its members through the exercise of charity, and to do a little spiritual and temporal good to a few poor families in the name of Jesus Christ ... If it were to seek only the sanctification of its members through pious exercises, there is no lack of confraternities and third orders to meet that need. If, on the other hand, it were to seek only the relief of the temporal miseries of the poor, it would only add one more to the list of public and private institutions founded for that purpose.[29]

---

[23] Lambert McKenna, *Fr James A. Cullen, S.J.* (London, 1924), p. 189.

[24] See Máire Ní Chearbhaill, 'The Society of St Vincent de Paul in Dublin, 1926–1975', PhD thesis, NUI Maynooth, 2008, chapter 8, pp 169–95.

[25] *Thom's Directory, 1927*, p. 341.

[26] Association of Charities, *Dublin charities* (Dublin, 1902 ed.), p. 182.

[27] *Thom's Directory, 1903*, p. 279.

[28] Association of Charities, *Dublin charities*, p. 27.

[29] Cited in *Manual*, 1958 ed., p. 95.

By the early twentieth century, the Society of St Vincent de Paul had become the largest charity in Ireland, with the most varied range of works. The Mansion House Coal Fund annual report for 1931 gives some indication of the scale of the work undertaken by the Society compared to other charities. Fuel vouchers in that year to the value of twenty-five tons of coal were issued to the Sick and Indigent Roomkeepers' Society for its clients, and several other charities received a combined total of sixty-five tons, but the Society of St Vincent de Paul alone received vouchers to the value of 150 tons.[30]

On a national level, the Society had shown a steady growth from 120 conferences in 1880, to 280 by 1925.[31] Social legislation like the Workmen's Compensation Action, 1897, the Old Age Pension Act, 1908, and the National Insurance Act, 1911, provided some measure of protection from extreme hardship but had little impact on the overall levels of poverty and need. Under the leadership of Matt Lalor, president of the Dublin council, the Society grew, both in conference numbers and in the diversity of its special works, in the early decades of the twentieth century.[32]

One such work was the night shelter in Back Lane, established in 1915, and described in the 1930s as a place where 'many respectable men who for one reason or another have not the means to procure a shelter and a bed without which health and life are endangered'; men were accommodated and supplied with food, clothes and boots.[33] Other new ventures that would follow included the visitation of hospitals and institutions, a centre for seamen on Sir John Rogerson's Quay, advice bureaux, a service for juvenile offenders, as well as numerous boys' clubs, and a holiday home for children at Balbriggan.

Despite its many undertakings, visitation work continued to be its core activity. Families relied on the Society to provide food, cash, clothing, footwear and bedding. The conditions in poor homes could prove daunting for new recruits, and retention of members was an ongoing concern. Young civil servants, newly arrived in Dublin, were often persuaded to take up

---

30 *Irish Independent*, 1 Jan. 1932.
31 *Thom's Directory*, various, 1880 to 1925.
32 *Catholic Standard*, Matt Lalor obituary, 26 Feb. 1937.
33 *Bulletin*, lxxxiv, no. 4 (1939), Apr. Supp., p. 11.

voluntary work in the evenings, but soon found they were unable to cope with the reality of extreme poverty. A spiritual director of the Society wryly commented in 1928 that when young men, reared in a 'hot-house environment', get the 'first cold blasts whistling down the tenement stairs, they die'.[34]

Over the years, conferences expanded their aid beyond simply handing out food vouchers or cash. Special grants were given to help clients become self-supporting, or to further their chances of finding work through training or education. A Rathmines conference in 1927 paid for motor driving lessons for a man and persuaded him to dispose of his horse and cab.[35] In 1928, a cabinetmaker was supplied with wood and tools, and a coal hawker with weights and scales. The same year, twelve poor girls had their technical school fees paid to allow them attend a course in needlework and domestic economy.[36] Social work as a separate profession did not begin to emerge in Ireland until the 1960s,[37] which meant that voluntary groups like the Society of St Vincent de Paul often had to provide an informal service. In the 1940s, visiting brothers were asked to familiarise themselves with the section in the *Catholic social workers' handbook* that covered current social legislation so that they could keep families informed of their entitlements.[38]

While the Society of St Vincent de Paul entered an expansionary period in its range of charitable initiatives from the early twentieth century, accounts in the *Bulletin* and in its annual reports indicate that its members also shared enthusiastically in the devotional activities that played such a central part in Catholic life at the time and crossed all social groups. That the laity were devout and had close ties with the church and clergy has been well documented.[39] In his visit to Ireland for the Eucharistic Congress in 1932, the papal legate, Cardinal Lorenzo

---

[34] *Bulletin*, lxxiii, no. 6 (1928), June Supp., p. 9–10.

[35] *Annual Report*, 1927, p. 37.

[36] *Bulletin*, lxxiii, no. 4 (1928), Apr. Supp., p. 9.

[37] Caroline Skehill, *The nature of social work in Ireland* (Lewiston, c.1999), pp 99, 156.

[38] *Catholic social workers' handbook* (Dublin c.1942 ed.).

[39] See J.H. Whyte, *Church and state in modern Ireland* (Dublin, 1971); Maurice Hartigan, 'Catholic laity of Dublin, 1920–1940' in James Kelly and Dáire Keogh (eds), *History of the Catholic diocese of Dublin* (Dublin, 2000), pp 81–125.

Lauri, expressed his great pleasure at the enthusiasm shown by the people of Ireland, and 'in particular by the poor classes living in the small streets of Dublin'.[40]

Society members participated in a range of liturgical and devotional activities themselves, and also encouraged zeal in their clients. An annual six-day retreat for members was introduced in the 1920s, and enclosed retreats at the Jesuit-run houses at Rathfarnham and Milltown Park were earnestly recommended 'as a sure means of achieving the objects of our membership of the Society'.[41] Reading material was provided when visiting the homes – the *Sacred Heart Messenger, the Irish Catholic, Our Boys, the Catholic Standard* – both to inspire devotion and to help combat the inroads of evil literature.[42] Families were recommended to attend sodalities, and to have their homes consecrated to the Sacred Heart.[43] Conferences assisted their local parish in practical ways by providing first communion outfits or helping with funeral expenses. Clubs either had their own sodality, or the boys were encouraged to join sodalities locally.[44] Over four weekends in the summer of 1942, Westland Row parish conferences took 750 pilgrims to Lough Derg, an achievement that was considered 'highly satisfactory' in view of the war-time restrictions on trains.[45]

Material and spiritual services blended. Although men of all creeds were free to avail of the facilities of its Seamen's Institute, the members had a particular mission to those who were Catholic, pointing out the location of the numerous churches in the vicinity of the quays.[46] On Sunday mornings, the conference attached to St Patrick's Training College in Drumcondra visited men who lived alone in drab lodging houses, bringing them 'clothes and boots, holy-water fonts and other small necessities'.[47]

---

[40] Dermot Keogh, *Ireland and the Vatican: the politics and diplomacy of church–state relations, 1922–1939* (Cork, 1995), p. 99.

[41] *Annual Report, 1928*, p. 5.

[42] *Annual Report, 1932*, p. 37.

[43] Éamonn Dunne, 'Action and reaction: Catholic lay organisations in Dublin' in *Archiv. Hib.*, xlviii (1994), pp 107–18, at p. 113.

[44] *Annual Report, 1942*, p. 127.

[45] *Annual Report, 1942*, p. 145.

[46] *Annual Report, 1926*, p. 123.

[47] *Annual Report, 1950*, p. 67.

The Society operated the Labour Yard in Vicar Street from 1915, where men with physical disabilities could earn some money from chopping wood while maintaining their self-respect 'which even the most prudent charity tends to sap'.[48] All the men joined in the daily recital of the Angelus at noon.[49]

Yet, despite the prevailing high levels of religious observance, the members were expected to be aware that there might be lost sheep in their midst, or that there were those who needed a little encouragement. When dealing with such sensitive matters, they were urged to exercise charity, and a cautious, tactful approach was recommended:

> The visitor may use his own discretion as to the best means of introducing into the poor family the love of religion and the practice of their duties.[50]

Allowing for a certain over-exuberance in reporting in the *Bulletin*, the impression given is one of willing participation by the laity in general, and by the members of the Society of St Vincent de Paul and their clients, in a wide range of devotional activities, especially during the 1920s and 1930s. If there were signs of deviation from this pattern they were rarely recorded. The Rathgar conference did admit in 1948 that its efforts to interest adults in membership of the local sodality 'did not meet with the desired effect',[51] and in 1957 there were difficulties in promoting the display of the Sacred Heart image in the homes, because, 'like the family rosary crusade, members tend to blow hot and cold'.[52] The size and content of the *Bulletin* was greatly reduced in the 1950s and detailed accounts of traditional devotional activities such as retreats, sodalities, Society masses and gatherings, no longer feature. Cost was cited as the reason for the journal's curtailment, but it may also suggest that some weakening of the Society's links with such activities was already becoming evident at this time.

---

[48] *Bulletin*, lxxvii, no. 6 (1932), June Supp., pp 7–8.
[49] *Annual Report, 1955*, p. 25.
[50] *Visiting the poor in their homes* (Dublin, 1932 ed.), p. 15.
[51] *Annual Report, 1948*, p. 70.
[52] *Bulletin*, cii, no. 11 (Nov. 1957), p. 269.

From the 1940s, there are indications of change within the Society of St Vincent de Paul in Ireland, often in small ways, and the beginnings of a quiet process of re-evaluation of its traditional ways. A number of key factors in the coming years, including the emergence of imaginative and energetic leaders at home and abroad, converged to introduce fresh thinking, overhaul traditional methods and attitudes and promote greater engagement with the international dimensions of the Society. In 1947, members travelled from all over the world to Paris to discuss how best to help the European countries in the aftermath of the war. The Society in Ireland sent large amounts of tinned foodstuffs and condensed milk via the Irish Red Cross to France, Germany and Austria.[53] Attending the meeting in Paris was Lonan Murphy, president of the council of Ireland. As well as participating in discussions on more serious issues, he was surprised to learn that conferences in Europe were running dances to raise funds, a practice frowned upon in early editions of the *Manual*. He also noted that many women were now associated with the Society.

Charles Kavanagh Murphy, Cork president, and one of the few commentators on social issues within the Society at the time, rejected the old notion of almsgiving as an adequate response to charity in the 1950s and called for a more professional approach to addressing the causes of poverty in the future:

> Unquestionably it brought comfort to the poor. But it was not sufficiently effectual against the causes of their sufferings ... the members of the Society of St Vincent de Paul in the future will have to give careful attention to these things and to take the initiative in intellectual charity ... in devising means to meet the evils of society.[54]

In 1959, the new pope, John XXIII, urged the Society's president-general to address the issue of the spiritual formation of its members.[55] Later that year, it was to be the theme at the annual meeting of presidents in Dublin. If the organisers expected to

---

[53] Council of Ireland minutes, 1 Jan. and 18 Mar. 1948 (SVPA); *Bulletin*, vol. xciii, no. 6 (1948), Ir. Supp., p. ix.

[54] *Bulletin*, xcix no. 12 (Dec. 1954), p. 268.

[55] *Bulletin*, civ, no. 4 (Apr. 1959), p. 122.

hear an open discussion on the delegates' personal spiritual experience, they were to be disappointed. It was deemed to be 'an intimate matter about which men do not care to speak in public'.[56] However, some interesting new attitudes were recorded in the discussions. Presidents of conferences were urged not to 'spend all their lives worrying about the state of the souls of their brothers'; greater emphasis should be given to scripture readings at the meetings, and, it was suggested, that all the activity of a conference – the meeting itself, routine discussions, the visitation work – were forms of 'prayer'.[57] It would appear that, even ahead of the new theology about to be ushered in by the Second Vatican Council, members of the Society in Ireland were being liberated from over-concern with the spiritual welfare of others.

Another significant development at the time was the election of Bill Cashman as president of the Council of Ireland. An energetic and enthusiastic disciple of the emerging developments in the church before and during the Second Vatican Council, with his brother, Bob, who succeeded him as president, they would steer the Society through a period of rapid change. In 1960, Bill Cashman attended an international meeting of the Society in Paris, where there were calls for the adoption of conferences in developing lands for the purposes of mutual exchange.[58] Within two years, Irish conferences had been twinned with over eighty conferences in Africa and Asia.[59]

The 1950s and 1960s produced some visionary thinkers within the Society, at home and abroad. Pierre Chouard, elected president-general of the Society of St Vincent de Paul in 1954, was one of a group of leading scientists and intellectuals that had assembled in the post-war years to explore international concerns, including the problem of world food shortages.[60] In attempting to understand the role of the Society in the future, Choard suggested that its rule be presented in the

[56] *Bulletin*, cv, no. 1 (Jan. 1960), p. 19.
[57] *Bulletin*, cv, no 1, (Jan. 1960), p. 20.
[58] *Bulletin*, cvi, no. 9 (Sept. 1961), pp 204–5.
[59] *Bulletin*, cviii, no. 10 (Oct. 1963), p. 237.
[60] http://www.worldacademy.org/?q=node/18 (viewed 28 Apr. 2008).

'language appropriate to our changing times'.[61] Bill Cashman, the president of the Council of Ireland allowed himself, in 1966, to look into the future:

> I see the Society advancing along particular paths, not alone but in company with others, retaining its own rule, spirit, traditions and autonomy but not too concerned about its own independence ... I see the Society working in the closest association and contact with other organisations operating in the field of charity, whether Catholic, Protestant or non-denominational, doing our best to get rid of suspicion and mistrust, both our own and others.[62]

Many of Cashman's predictions quickly came to pass. In 1969, the Society provided offices at Ozanam House for the newly-established Free Legal Advice Centre (FLAC).[63] It began cooper-ating with the Salvation Army to provide meals-on-wheels for elderly people.[64] At a meeting of the Council Ireland in the 1970s, one of the delegates spoke of his admiration for the work of the Simon Community:

> Even though ... we have a finger in most pies, we recognise that there are certain areas where the job can better be tackled by those who have a specialist flair ... the Simon Community... are working for alcoholics, drug addicts and drop-outs.[65]

Attitudes to publicity within the Society also took a radical change at this time. The old approach, inherited from the experi-ence of church–state tensions in nineteenth-century Paris, when the founding members feared that all newspapers were organs of government, gave way to a new openness. When a member enquired in 1966 whether it was in order for councils and confer-ences to give accounts of their activities and expenditure to their local newspapers, he was told: 'Not only is it permissible, but it is most desirable. It is the best possible way of rendering an account of how we use the money given to us by the charitable

---

[61] *Bulletin*, cv, no. 11 (Nov. 1960), p. 254.
[62] *Bulletin*, cxi, no. 9 (Sept. 1966), p. 219.
[63] Pádraig, Ó Moráin, *Access to justice for all: the history of free legal advice centres, 1969–2003* (Dublin, 2004), pp 7–8.
[64] *Bulletin*, 117, no. 5 (May 1972), p. 103.
[65] *Bulletin*, 116, no. 11 (Nov. 1971), p. 236.

public.'[66] In an effort to engage the members more fully in the debates of the time, the editor of the *Bulletin* introduced a correspondence page and invited contributions – provided that letters were interesting and contained constructive criticism.[67]

Nevertheless, despite extensive coverage and debate in the *Bulletin* on the documents of the Vatican Council and on the new understanding of the role of the lay church in the world, no clarity was emerging as to what form the Society's own spiritual identity should take. Commenting on the deliberations at an international meeting in Paris, Bill Cashman had to admit that the debate on the spirit of the Society was 'rather skimpy', with no effort being made to define its nature.[68] The *New Rule*, published in 1968, did attempt to apply the insights of the Council to reinterpreting its traditional practices. Many of the prayers, printed in Latin and English and running to seven pages in the 1958 edition of the *Manual* were shortened or dropped; a prayer for Christian unity was added.[69] The spiritual director was renamed 'spiritual adviser'.[70] The range of indulgences, long presented as the ultimate reward for perseverance and zeal, were curtailed and simplified.[71] The spiritual director of the council of Ireland in the 1960s, was irritated at the 'narrow and self-centred air' that had in the past stressed personal sanctification as a reward for charitable deeds.[72] The *New Rule* used a different language to explain the motivation of members from a spiritual perspective:

> The Society of St Vincent de Paul is composed of Christian lay persons seeking to develop in themselves a life of charity and to manifest it by fraternal participation in works bearing witness to the love of Christ.[73]

---

[66] *Bulletin*, vol. cxi, no. 5 (May 1966), p. 135.

[67] *Bulletin*, cxi, no. 1 (Jan. 1970), n.p.

[68] *Bulletin*, cxiii, no. 1 (Jan. 1968), p. 8.

[69] *The Rule of the Society of St Vincent de Paul, 1968-1973*, article 20 (Dublin, c.1968).

[70] Ibid., article 8.

[71] *Bulletin*, cxiii, no. 9 (Sept. 1968), pp 212–13.

[72] *Bulletin*, cxi, no. 10 (Oct. 1966), p. 248.

[73] *Rule of the Society*, article 1.

As church-related groups struggled to redefine their identity in the aftermath of the Second Vatican Council, the Society of St Vincent de Paul was fortunate in that many of its traditional works for socially-disadvantaged people fitted comfortably with the new emphasis on social justice. Most of its existing undertakings simply required a new language and focus. Its work with Traveller families had been defined in the 1920s as 'primarily of a spiritual nature' whereas by the 1960s it was seen from a justice perspective. The government-appointed Commission on Itinerancy had urged voluntary organisations such as the Society of St Vincent de Paul and the Legion of Mary to interest themselves in settlement programmes.[74] An account of the Society's activities in 1969, sent to the archbishop of Dublin, John Charles McQuaid, illustrates what this closer involvement in the sensitive issue of resettlement entailed for the Society:

> In a number of areas, Itinerant settlement committees were entirely composed of our members and in most places the Society was strongly represented on these committees. Our members bore the brunt of local opposition to settlement proposals and suffered vilification and threats. It was encouraging to learn that they stood up and were counted in the cause of justice for a suffering and unpopular group of people.[75]

From the 1960s, the leadership of the Society of St Vincent de Paul was more likely to engage with the social sciences in addressing the causes of poverty in Ireland than in seeking guidance from its *Manual*. Closer liaison with statutory bodies and pre-budget submissions to government on social welfare matters became standard practice. The Legion of Mary, on the other hand, continued to define its role as spiritual. Both the Legion and the Society of St Vincent de Paul had close ties through the years because of the shared nature of many of their activities. The Legion members visited homes, distributed Catholic literature, organised retreats, ran hostels for homeless people and girls' clubs, and engaged in prison and hospital

---

74 *Report of the Commission on Itinerancy* (Dublin, 1963), pp 64, 75, 107.
75 'Review of 1969', typewritten report to John Charles McQuaid (DDA, McQuaid Laity file, AB8/b/xxi).

visitation work.[76] The committee in Sunshine House, the holiday centre for children in Balbriggan, relied heavily on the women members of the Legion to act as stewards during the holiday week for girls.[77] Nevertheless, the Legion of Mary saw itself as having a fundamentally different objective:

> To give to the poor is a good work. Done with a supernatural motive, it is a sublime one. The systems of many great societies rest upon this principle; notably that of the Society of St Vincent de Paul ... But to the Legion is assigned a different field of duty. Its system is built upon the principle of bringing spiritual good.[78]

Despite its many efforts at renewal from within, it is evident that in the mood of the time, the Society of St Vincent de Paul was suffering from an image problem as a lay Catholic body and was having difficulty attracting young people. A survey on religious practice found that 22 per cent of women aged between eighteen and thirty were no longer attending weekly mass by the 1970s, and nearly 50 per cent of young people had difficulty with the Catholic church's teaching on doctrinal, moral or disciplinary matters.[79] A journalist writing in *Bulletin* on the difficulties associated with retaining young members in the Society, commented:

> Many young people don't want to be involved in an overtly religious activity, although they may have very active social consciences. As a journalist, reporting the activities of the Simon Community, I have always been struck by the number of former Vincent de Paul members among Simon's ranks.[80]

Although women's conferences were introduced in Ireland in the early 1960s, many potential volunteers were evidently looking elsewhere. When one member was asked to explain why she transferred to Simon, she replied: 'I wanted to help

---

[76] *Catholic social workers' handbook*, c.1942 ed., p. 19.

[77] *Bulletin*, cv, no. 9 (Sept. 1960), p. 210.

[78] Legion of Mary Concilium, *The official handbook of the Legion of Mary* (Dublin, 1953), p. 271.

[79] Máire Nic Ghiolla Phádraig, 'Religious practice and belief in Ireland' in *Ten years of research and development, 1971–1980* (Maynooth, 1981), pp 34, 36.

[80] *Bulletin*, 118, no. 3 (Mar. 1973), p. 59.

people, fine, but I was beginning to question my old, traditional Catholicism in a way which made me unwilling to help them in the name of some saint. I just wanted to help them for their own sakes, as fellow human beings.'[81] Thus was Vincent de Paul, seventeenth-century religious founder, champion of the poor, and patron of the international charity that bore his name, dismissed as 'some saint'.

Not only were the young opting for secular voluntary groups rather than for church-based organisations, some members themselves were also re-evaluating their traditional identity. A Society member who carried out a survey among voluntary organisations at University College Dublin in 1974 sent questionnaires to 120 conferences of the Society of St Vincent de Paul throughout the county. When asked to cat-egorise the Society according to its activities, the vast majority of conferences opted for the 'charitable' classification rather than the 'religious/denominational' label.[82]

However, although the Society may have been perceived as less attractive than the modern, secular voluntary bodies, in a small survey of 1,000 members of the public, when asked in 1975 to give their views on the organisation and its work, 76 per cent stated that they did 'a great deal of good work in Ireland'.[83]

Change advocated by the Second Vatican Council and the Society's commitment to renewal within the organisation was bewildering for some long-serving members accustomed to traditional ways. A meeting of presidents in 1970 expressed regret that many members appeared reluctant to make adjust-ments in outlook in order to 'progress significantly towards the achievement of justice for those in need'.[84] The following year, a member wrote to the Bulletin in 1971 lamenting the fact that the Rule, revered from the foundation of the Society, had been 'abruptly cast out the window'.[85] Active concern for the spiritu-al welfare of others, lauded in earlier years, was now deemed to be intrusive; charitable deeds were considered to be the only

---

[81] Bulletin, 118, no. 3 (Mar. 1973), p. 59.

[82] Cited in Bulletin, 119, no. 12 (Dec. 1974), p. 12.

[83] Cited in Bulletin, vol. 121, no. 1 (Jan. 1976), p. 5.

[84] Bulletin, 115, no. 1 (Jan. 1970), p. 16.

[85] Bulletin, 117, nos 7–8 (July–Aug. 1973), p 170.

acceptable form of christian witness.[86] Bob Cashman, at an international meeting of the Society in Dublin in the 1970s said that the admission of people of other faiths into the Society was then being considered but acknowledged that there were dangers when leaders of an organisation 'went too far ahead of its members'.[87]

In the years when confraternities, sodalities and other devotional practices were rapidly losing popular support and disappearing completely in the last quarter of the twentieth century, the Society of St Vincent de Paul was working on a number of fronts to re-evaluate its own philosophy and activities. Through an enthusiastic leadership at a critical time in its history, it reviewed its methods and language, its stance on social justice issues, its understanding of the causes of poverty, its relationships with community bodies, with other churches and state institutions, while still trying to keep its focus as a gospel-inspired body within the Catholic church. In time, its ecumenical and inclusive approach would make it a more accessible organisation to members of other faiths or none.

Confraternities and sodalities, on the other hand, scattered throughout the dioceses and parishes of Ireland, did not have the structures to record or to debate the general decline as it was unfolding. They did not succeed in introducing new liturgical forms that had wide appeal, and were unable to redirect their energies to worthy social causes that might have provided fresh impetus as church-based devotions faded away. If the new understanding of the Society of St Vincent de Paul as a lay organisation was debated mainly by a few, its general members through their local conferences continued to answer the day-to-day demands for assistance. Whether they or their clients adhered to old religious practices, or embraced the new ways mattered little. The hugely practical response to pressing social need ensured the Society's continuing relevance.

---

[86] See *Bulletin*, 116, no. 12 (Dec. 1971), p. 268.
[87] *Irish Times*, 11 Sept. 1973.

10

Afterword: Confraternities, social capital and civil society: comparisons, contexts and questions

Nicholas Terpstra

… enter gladly into the Confraternity or Sodality that is established where you live. These sodalities and confraternities are so many Noah's Arks which will save you, who live in the world, from the deluge of sin and temptation that everywhere surrounds you …[1]

I wanted to help people fine, but I was beginning to question my old, traditional Catholicism in a way which made me unwilling to help them in the name of some saint. I just wanted to help them for their own sakes, as fellow human beings.[2]

These two statements, barely fifteen years apart, mark two different worlds which converged in Ireland in the mid-twentieth century. The first was written by a priest of the Congregation of the Most Holy Redeemer in a prayer book for laymen, and speaks both to the fear that a flood tide of immoral popular culture was inundating Ireland and to the conviction that confraternities represented the best defence against drowning. The second was written by a laywoman who had left the Society of St Vincent de Paul in order to join the Simon Community so that she could more directly live in a helping relationship with the poor. It speaks by contrast to a determination to jump out of the Ark and enter directly into a different rising tide, a tide of poverty, in order to help those people most immediately threatened by drowning.

---

[1] Leo O'Halloran, CSsR, *Prayer book for men* (Dublin, 1957) p. 49, cited in Louise Fuller, 'Confraternities, their decline and the problem of sources: background, analysis and review', in this volume.

[2] *Bulletin*, 118, no. 3 (Mar. 1973), p. 59, cited in Máire Ní Chearbhaill, 'Charity, church and the Society of St Vincent de Paul', in this volume.

The essays in this collection speak to the central role that confraternities played in Irish society from the fifteenth through the
twentieth centuries. A series of authors who have contributed to
this ambitious research project on religion and social identity in
Ireland offer views on distinct aspects of confraternal sociability, educational work, material culture and devotional life. This
valuable work joins a steadily broadening literature on confraternities in various times, places, and religious cultures. As we
conduct our research into confraternities and parish associations, how do we best demonstrate that confraternal studies are
not simply some minor niche pursuit? Do fraternities offer some
distinctive way of understanding early modern and modern
social organisation and historical developments, such that
historians outside the fields of church or religious history can
learn from them? A key question which many historians aim to
address is the collapse of religious culture in the middle of the
twentieth century, and confraternities are certainly a critical part
of that larger social history. How was it that confraternities
could be so central and public a part of Irish religious culture for
four hundred years before largely disappearing in the space of a
few decades? The question has particular force in Ireland,
though it resonates across many parts of the Catholic world
where similar scenarios played out. The speed of their demise
seems to undermine any arguments we may aim to make about
their importance for civil and social life.

Comparative research on confraternities elsewhere can shed
some light on this paradox. Beyond these brotherhoods, work
being done into the broader phenomenon of social kinship and
its operation across the early modern world – from Italy to the
Americas and Asia – may reveal parallels or trigger ideas. The
historiography of confraternities has shifted dramatically over
the past few decades, with different interpretive models being
applied to explore more fully how social kinship groups functioned in cities, rural areas and global empires. Their functions
extended far beyond religious duties and worship and into the
very dynamics of class relations, social programmes, political
activity, and the ways that authority was both exercised and
resisted. We move from religious history into larger questions
of social organisation and political society. Navigating these

questions may help us understand why so many Irish confraternity members abandoned the very image of Noah's Ark and why
that ark then sank so quickly below the waves.

HISTORIOGRAPHICAL BACKGROUND AND SOME
THEORETICAL MODELS

There has been a long history of research into European
confraternities, and from the eighteenth into the twentieth
centuries many of the books produced were largely descriptive, institutional, parochial, and celebrative. Most were
written by members of the brotherhoods themselves as an
outgrowth of extensive catalogues of spiritual benefits that
their group had received over the centuries. Their histories
were rich in lists of indulgences, descriptions of buildings and
artworks, and transcriptions of burial plaques, and a bit thin
on context and analysis. Critique was considered somehow
disloyal and hence beyond the pale. The result was often the
History of Good Intentions, presented in antiquarian institutional studies that seldom probed the contexts of how the
brotherhoods had risen out of particular social conditions, or
had interacted with other groups or individuals, or had
shaped their societies. What comparative work developed in
this period tended to be under the umbrella of larger institutional histories, usually the histories of religious orders. These
suffered their own distinctive myopia. The standard histories,
like Moorman's history of the Franciscan order or Hinnebusch's
of the Dominicans, came from the pen of clerical insiders, and
tended to treat confraternities as a bit of an afterthought.[3]
For all their value and interest, confraternities were really
the laity's sideshow to the main narrative, which remained
resolutely – and unsurprisingly – clerical. Authorised histories
of these kinds frequently contained nuggets of pure archival
gold, but to the extent that they asked no questions, triggered
no discussions, and couldn't peer outside and beyond the
niche, they were often narrow, institutional, and not a little
tedious.

---

[3] John Moorman, *A history of the Franciscan Order from its origins to the year 1517*
(Oxford, 1968); W. A. Hinnebusch, *The history of the Dominican Order, vol. II:
Intellectual and cultural life to 1500* (New York, 1973).

From the 1940s and 1950s, the sociologist Gerard Le Bras and French *annaliste* historians demonstrated different possibilities. Le Bras posited the confraternity as a voluntary parish, that is, a lay-directed form of the local church. The *annalistes* were more strictly functionalist, treating confraternities largely as burial societies whose rituals could be used to test theories on attitudes towards death in medieval and renaissance culture, and whose notarial records could be used to chart the rise and fall of belief in purgatory, heaven and hell.[4] These authors dug into the archives with a vengeance and turned up wills, legacies, rituals, rites and statistics. Their work was more often comparative and cumulative, and always analytical and critical. What was sometimes missing was a sense of the confraternities as multi-faceted vehicles of spirituality and sociability that had organised not just their members' deaths, but also their lives. The one-dimensional functionalist approach was a far step beyond the old institutional histories, but sometimes it simply substituted one niche for another.

By the 1970s, American authors were experimenting with far more speculative and theoretical studies, particularly in connection with Italian confraternities. Social scientific models were drafted into the job of making sense of a phenomenon, traditionally seen as being outside the range, if not beneath the contempt, of serious social historians. Richard Trexler's *Public life in Renaissance Florence* (1980) and to a lesser extent Edward Muir's *Civic ritual in Renaissance Venice* (1980) applied the anthropological theories of Arnold van Gennep, Victor Turner and Clifford Geertz, drawn from site research in Africa, Bali, Mexico, and elsewhere, to the role of ritual in organising social life and personal community in these leading Renaissance cities.[5] The assumption here was that site work into pre-modern societies in different parts of the globe could offer methodological tools for understanding social dynamics in pre-modern European society. In a slightly different vein, Ronald Weissman's *Ritual*

---

[4] Gerard Le Bras, *Études de sociologie religieuse* (Paris, 1955–6); Jacques Chiffoleau, *La comptabilité de l'au-delà. Les hommes, la mort et la religion dans la région de l'Avignon à la fin de moyen-age, vers 1320–vers 1480* (Rome, 1980).

[5] Richard Trexler, *Public life in Renaissance Florence* (New York, 1979); Edward Muir, *Civic ritual in Renaissance Venice* (Princeton, 1981).

brotherhood in Renaissance Florence (1982) took the model of
the Chicago school of interactionist sociology to explore how
confraternities mediated antagonistic social relations – he
memorably began by asserting that Florence was a city of
anxiety and betrayal where you could trust neither family nor
neighbour, and then aimed to show how Florentines used
the constructed brotherhood of confraternal kinship to create
for themselves a warmer psychological home.[6] Reaching just
outside of Italy, Andrew Barnes in *The social dimension of piety*
(1994) drew on social psychology and physiology to explore
what might have animated the flagellants of Marseilles through
the early modern period. In one fascinating article, Barnes
explored how flagellation might have affected bodily states and
mental processes, and to reconstruct from that an understanding of the spiritual pull of the flagellants' cords.[7]

These were fascinating, stimulating and provocative studies.
They often followed the common format of a first chapter laying
out the theoretical model followed by chapters that applied that
model to materials drawn out of confraternal and other
archives. That, by the way, is the model of the North American
dissertation, and many of these were indeed revised disserta-
tions. The approach was promising, but in many cases was not
sustained or broadened into further studies. Moreover, the
method itself was challenged as an approach – too many
anachronisms, too many procrustean beds, too many flawed
assumptions. It's possible to underestimate the distance from a
tribe on Bali to a brotherhood in Bergamo or Balbriggan, and
some of these studies showed the strains of attempting to span
that distance of space, time, and mentality.

The problem was in some ways the inverse of that found in
the earlier institutional histories. If those had been too loyally
pious, then these were perhaps too aggressively secular. Many
assumed that religion was little more than a social construction,
part of society's superstructure in the Marxist sense, and hence

---

[6] R.F.E. Weissman, *Ritual brotherhood in Renaissance Florence* (New York, 1982).

[7] Andrew Barnes, *The social dimension of piety: Associative life and devotional change
in the penitent confraternities of Marseilles, 1499–1792* (New York, 1994). Other important studies of French confraternities include: P. T. Hoffman, *Church and community in the diocese of Lyon, 1500–1789* (New Haven, 1984); K. P. Luria, *Territories
of grace: cultural change in the seventeenth century diocese of Grenoble* (Berkeley, 1991).

fundamentally a fraud. As a result, most made little effort to understand spirituality. I think that this is one of the reasons why – for all their indisputable value in putting confraternities in social and political context – they so often failed to rise beyond functionalism to capture the deeper pull of fraternalism or social kinship.

Much current work is less aggressive and experimental, and generally less theoretical. Yet the social studies of the 1970s and 1980s still sit astride the field and populate its bibliographies, fortunately preventing any return to the earlier narrow pious institutionalism. Even the current work that avoids theory cannot avoid putting confraternities into their social and political contexts, and cannot avoid asking questions of how confraternities shaped and were shaped by these contexts. Almost all current work demonstrates a far greater determination to understand confraternities as fundamentally spiritual–pious bodies that gave a framework and purpose to individual's lives and that as a result had legitimacy and influence in deeply Christian societies.[8]

One more recent author who has encouraged historians to focus on the longer-term sociological contexts and political outcomes of confraternal kinship is not a historian, let alone a

---

[8] Recent work can best be surveyed through a few recent essay collections, including: Christopher Black and Pamela Gravestock (eds), *Early modern confraternities in Europe and the Americas: International and interdisciplinary perspectives* (Aldershot, 2006); Bernard Dompnier and Paola Vismara, (eds), *Confréries et dévotions dans la catholicité moderne, mi-XVe – début XIXe siècle* (Rome, 2008); J. P. Donnelly and M. W. Maher, (eds), *Confraternities and Catholic reform in Italy, France, and Spain* (Kirksville, 1998); Enrico Fasana, (ed.), *Le confraternite cristiane e musulmane: storia, devozione, politica* (Trieste, 2001); Albert Meyers and Diane Hopkins (eds), *Manipulating the saints: religious brotherhoods and social integration in post-conquest Latin America* (Hamburg, 1988); Nicholas Terpstra, (ed.), *The politics of ritual kinship: confraternities and social order in early modern Italy* (Cambridge, 2000).

See also the following field surveys: Bram van den Hoeven van Genderen and Paul Trio, 'Old stories and new themes: an overview of the historiography of confraternities in the Low Countries from the thirteenth to the sixteenth centuries' in Emila Jamroziak and Janet E. Burton (eds), *Religious and laity in Western Europe, 1000–1400* (Turnhout, 2006), pp 357–84; Nicholas Terpstra, 'De-institutionalizing confraternity studies: fraternalism and social capital in cross-cultural contexts' in Black and Gravestock (eds), *Early modern confraternities in Europe and the Americas*, pp 264–83; S.V. Webster, 'Research on confraternities in the colonial Americas' in *Confraternitas* 9 (1998), pp 15–21; Nicholas Terpstra (ed.), *Faith's boundaries: laity and clergy in early modern confraternities* (Turnhout, forthcoming).

student of confraternities. The American political sociologist, Robert Putnam, balances functionalism with an appreciation of the inner character of kinship groups in a way that is both controversial and suggestive. In *Making democracy work* (1993), Putnam conveyed the results of a two-decade effort to determine why some parts of Italy were successful, prosperous, and responsive societies, while others were not. He focused on those social institutions which accustomed Italians to compromise, trust, and negotiation, particularly when it came to exercising power outside the family unit. Among these he included guilds and confraternities above all.[9] Putnam's Italian case study has raised issues of broader applicability, and despite significant methodological flaws, has offered a theoretical language which scholars of Netherlandic, English, Italian, and Irish confraternities have found fruitful – even if only as creative irritants.

Putnam is among the key modern commentators on concepts of civil society and social capital. By 'civil society', Putnam means a civic community marked by an active and public spirited citizenry, egalitarian political relations, a social fabric of trust and co-operation, and a range of vibrant institutions and associations breeding habits of co-operation. 'Social capital' includes features of social organisation, such as trust, norms, and networks that can improve the efficiency of society by facilitating coordinated actions between individuals and groups. It represents an internalised discipline or orientation that people exercise freely, and not under legal compulsion. To the extent that it facilitates collaboration and co-operation, it reduces the need for other capital investments, and so is more efficient and productive. In Putnam's work social capital and civil society are pretty clearly dependent on each other and almost constitute a circular form of reasoning. No civil society can function without a large store of social capital, and the primary gauge of the available reserves of social capital is a functioning civil society.

Putnam articulates these concepts through a series of subsidiary terms. '*Trust*' is an essential component which lubricates co-operation, while the '*reciprocity*' is the implicit understanding that you help me as I help you. Both constitute '*moral resources*'

---

[9] R. D. Putnam, *Making democracy work: civic traditions in modern Italy* (Princeton, 1993).

and are critical to generating social capital – they increase with use and decrease without use. Hence the exercise and experience of trust, collaboration, and mutual aid generates more of the same. '*Networks of civic engagement*' are either vertical or horizontal, formal or informal. '*Vertical networks*' represent classic patron/client relations. They do not naturally foster trust and co-operation, and their authoritarian element often undermines horizontal networks (often deliberately so, since the patron wants to ensure that the client relies on him or her rather than on peers). '*Horizontal networks*', by contrast, connect peers in voluntary ties of mutual obligation. '*Formal networks*' are built around legal obligations and blood kinship; they may fill in the gap where free or internalised discipline doesn't exist. But '*informal networks*' (weak ties of acquaintance like shared membership in an organisation or friendship) suggest a greater pool of social capital. When measuring social capital, the '*weak ties*' of acquaintance are a more important gauge than the '*strong ties*' of blood. Finally, social capital can be either '*bonding*' if it focuses largely on strengthening the inner ties of a closed social group, or '*bridging*' if it extends connections to other groups and so enlarges the social circle.

Putnam is above all a social scientist, and he developed his views by studying Italian society of the 1970s and 1980s, a period when Italy redrew internal regional political boundaries and redistributed political powers, with the new regions gaining responsibility for a wide and growing range of services including urban affairs, health, housing, agriculture, public works, economic development, and vocational education. Putnam wanted to test what conditions created strong, responsive, effective representative institutions, and for two decades carried out nationwide surveys, extensive studies of institutional politics, regional planning, and legislative records, detailed statistical measures of performance (economic, demographic, educational), and numerous personal interviews with councillors and regional leaders.

Putnam's analysis confirmed a familiar distinction between a progressive north and backward south. His chief causal argument was a historical one which reached back into the medieval period: northern Italian cities like Florence, Venice, and Bologna had developed vaguely republican civil societies where power and authority were diffused horizontally through a host of groups like guilds, confraternities, and councils. Citizens here had many overlapping ties of voluntary mutual obligation. By contrast, southern regions had weaker cities and stronger nobilities who exercised power vertically. Here family and patron were paramount. Social kinship was the key in northern societies, and blood kinship in the south. Northerners used groups like confraternities to organise social life and so expanded their links of trust, their experience of governance, their expectations of accountability. Avoiding these social institutions, Southerners instead prayed for miracles and trusted only family. As Putnam saw it, this historic distinction made northerners expect and demand better government, made them participate in it, and made their politicians deliver it. Southerners expected less of government, frequently circumvented it through clientage, and got weak institutions and poor performance as a result. Northern Italians made democracy work, while Southern Italians got the Mafia.

Putnam made explicit connections to confraternities, and how they worked within society: 'It would hardly be an exaggeration to suggest that the lay confraternities provided the single most important lesson about cooperation of any Italian civic institution.' Why? They built trust, habituated members to the norms of reciprocity, and were the nodes around which networks of civic engagement operated. Members of confraternities built wide ranging informal networks whose weak ties of social kinship built up more social capital than blood kinship could. This capital could be bridging or bonding, depending on how engaged or exclusive the groups were.

Putnam's work presents us with a different kind of theory and a different kind of functionalism than characterised by the sometimes wooden social theories of the 1970s and early 1980s. It respects the core identity of confraternities and tries to understand how they shaped social attitudes and traditions and how that shaping resonated through the centuries. It focuses above all on social kinship, which is critical to both social capital and civil society. That said, it should be noted that few historians have found Putnam's work to be entirely persuasive. Whether dealing with Netherlandic, Italian, or Irish brotherhoods, many agree that social capital was generated in medieval and renaissance kinship groups, while nonetheless rejecting the idea that this capital kept growing uninterruptedly through the religious, social, and political changes of the early modern period and was ready for investment in nineteenth and twentieth century societies. Moreover, most have found it perplexing that despite his ambitious methodology, Putnam reverts in his causality to traditional north–south stereotypes which are rooted more deeply in nineteenth-century liberal historiography than in his own social scientific research.[10]

While there may be problems in Putnam's application of the concepts of social capital and civil society, some historians have found the idea of social kinship useful as a means of exploring the historical impact of fraternities. They have also been more successful in bridging the gap between the pre-modern and modern periods. Historians like Maurice Agulhon, Richard Grew and Katherine Lynch have noted kinship groups active in the expanding civil society of the eighteenth century, and have based their analysis more clearly on the material conditions of medieval and early modern society.[11] Lynch roots her study in urban demographic and economic conditions – high urban death rates meant that growth came primarily through migration, but since migrants had left their families behind, they relied on other voluntary kin groups like guilds and confraternities for survival. Christianity's validation of the kin community made virtues of these necessities. It set kin-based charity into a theological context that embraced eternity and into an institutional context that embraced politics and economics. With kin

---

[10] Key critiques and adaptations of Putnam's work may be found in two essay collections: R. I. Rotberg (ed.), *Patterns of social capital: stability and change in historical perspective* (Cambridge, 2001). See particularly the essays by Gene Brucker and Edward Muir; Nicholas Eckstein and Nicholas Terpstra (eds), *Sociability and its discontents: civil society, social capital, and their alternatives in late medieval and early modern Europe* (Turnhout, 2009). See particularly the essays by Abulafia, Marino, Hanlon, and Black.

[11] Maurice Agulhon, *Pénitents de Francs-Macon de l'ancienne Provence* (Paris, 1968); Raymond Grew, 'Finding social capital: the French Revolution in Italy' in Rotberg (ed.), *Patterns of social capital*, pp 69–96; K.A. Lynch, *Individuals, families, and communities in Europe, 1200–1800: the urban foundations of Western society* (Cambridge, 2003).

groups active across society, Europeans exercised the disciplines and opportunities of civil society and tested that society's boundaries: your community was those you were obligated to help, and if you were a member of a society, you were entitled to assistance. The link of social kinship, civil society and entitlement of assistance was a critical feature of European social and political development from the medieval communal period through the Reformation and on to the French Revolution. It played a critical role in late eighteenth-century movements for political and economic reform, and can be found underlying concepts of the 'national community' that spread across Europe with the French Revolution and its cry of 'liberty, equality, fraternity'.

Those making that revolutionary cry could count on their hearers having some ingrained notion of what 'fraternity' represented. There were recognised sets of rituals, norms, and myths that provided frames of reference for action and that interpreted experience and constructed reality for members. These had evolved through communal, guild, and ecclesiastical templates, and could take rather different forms over time as they evolved with local traditions and conditions. Fraternalism also built up networks of horizontal and vertical ties which gave occupations and identity to members, communicated ideas, and activated members. A common sociological vocabulary can be traced from medieval guilds and confraternities on to nineteenth-century fraternal organisations, unions, and political movements. Behind the language of kinship lay commitments to merging professional activity and general (and often exclusively male) sociability, mutual assistance, and collective identity. Fraternalism was clearly a powerful tool for mobilising solidarity in industrial society. Both proponents and opponents of that society used its cultural forms and social resources to express their ideology and organise their actions.

SOCIAL CAPITAL, CIVIL SOCIETY, AND CONFRATERNITIES IN
THE EARLY MODERN WORLD

Yet fraternalism has discontinuities as well as continuities. Recent studies of early modern confraternities in Europe and particularly in other parts of the world highlight these differences, and show how changes of the Catholic and Counter-Reformation reinforced some of the traditional features which built social capital and civil society while undermining others. This work may offer some comparative research that can help us understand both the growing strength of confraternities in Ireland from the eighteenth into the twentieth centuries, and then their sudden collapse.

The Jesuits were perhaps the most determined early modern proponents of confraternities, yet also the group which most changed medieval fraternalism's horizontal orientation. Ignatius Loyola certainly embraced fraternalism as a cultural form and social resource, and he built the Society of Jesus on fraternalism. It began *as* a confraternity, and *all* of its extensive missionary and charitable outreach was structured around and funded by confraternities and by the Marian congregations. This was neither coincidental nor purely pragmatic. Loyola believed that the reform of the church universal had to begin by rebuilding individual piety and collective action around the spiritual discipline of fraternalism (thinking here in Putnam's terms, of both the networks of engagement and also of the moral resources of trust and reciprocity by which members both assisted each other and called each other to account). In this programme of 'christianisation', he followed the thirteenth-century mendicants, who employed confraternities extensively in their own urban missions.[12]

The disciplined fraternalism of Jesuit confraternities aimed to remind members and Catholic laity at large of their spiritual and charitable obligations, to expand the means of exercising these obligations, and to habituate Catholics into this deeper and more activist practice of the faith. We can see all of this as an

---

[12] Scholars increasingly are working out the details of the Jesuit programme of christianisation, because Jesuit activity defines so much of the broader Catholic reform. Among early modernists, Mark Lewis has examined Jesuit efforts to expand catechetical training and cultic worship while Lance Lazar traces the rapid spread of Jesuit charity to prostitutes, converts, orphans, and prisoners, all of it organised, delivered, and funded by new model confraternities. Mark Lewis, 'The development of Jesuit confraternal activity in the kingdom of Naples in the sixteenth and seventeenth centuries' in Terpstra (ed.), *The politics of ritual kinship*, pp 210–27; Lance Lazar, *Working in the vineyard of the Lord: Jesuit confraternities in early modern Italy* (Toronto, 2005). For further context, see also: J. W. O'Malley, *The first Jesuits* (Cambridge, 1993).

acculturation into Catholic reform, active in urban and rural settings both in Europe and in American and Asian missions. But Jesuit fraternalism also departed from medieval and renaissance models on two critical points. It was unapologetically hierarchical, with distinct groups for artisans, professionals, and elites in deliberate rejection of the medieval ideology of cross-class brotherhood; Loyola in this way favoured bonding over bridging social capital. The Jesuit fraternities were also deliberately clerical, an unambiguous sign that the laity was valued for its auxiliary and supportive role, but that this should never be confused with trust in lay ability to maintain orthodoxy without firm clerical direction. What had been defined idealistically around horizontal relations of mutuality was being reshaped around vertical lines of authority. Loyola unapologetically believed that only with these changes could fraternalism respond effectively to the Protestant threat, be central to Europe's missionary drive overseas, and draw marginals and deviants into the Catholic mainstream.

Tridentine reformers generally shared this conviction and reshaped the institutional forms of fraternalism as a result. Their efforts were not immediately or entirely successful, but they did achieve what we might call, adapting John Bossy, the 'translation' of confraternal kinship around more fixed and hierarchical lines, at least in Europe.[13] If we shift our focus to the Americas and Asia, we find that recent studies have highlighted examples where local dynamics and power structures generated further adaptations and uses of fraternalism that moved beyond anything that missionaries or the clerical hierarchy may have desired. These muddle the picture significantly, and they underscore how confraternities could act to undermine imperial authority, organise resistance, and grant some agency to subordinated groups in colonial settings – actions that we also see in contemporary Ireland under the penal laws.

A rapidly expanding literature highlights the value of seeing fraternalism in the Americas as a cultural form and social resource to understand the dynamics of acculturation and resistance in colonial society. The Franciscans established the

---

[13] John Bossy, *Christianity in the West, 1400–1700* (Oxford, 1985).

first confraternity in Mexico City in 1527, and by the end of the century there were approximately 300 groups in that city alone. Confraternities were the 'primary didactic mechanism for the dissemination of Christian doctrine and ritual' across the Americas, and they built most of the churches as well. While some mendicant promoters aimed initially to establish groups that extended bridges across racial groups as a way of underscoring the universality of the Catholic church, recent studies in Brazil, Peru, and the Yucatan peninsula show that distinct fraternities soon emerged to separate and bond together African slaves, indigenous believers, Spanish and Portuguese settlers, and mestizo or creole populations. The black African and indigenous American groups frequently preserved indigenous cultural identity in a context where almost all other pre-Hispanic cultural institutions were suppressed or persecuted because lay members had more authority within them.[14] These informal networks generated significant stores of social capital which members used to improve their lives individually, and through which they developed forms of a communal civil society operating parallel to colonial institutions.

In Asia, the dynamics varied depending on how the confraternities fit into the colonising agendas of European powers. Missionary numbers were small at best, and lay confraternities could be a critical means of making Catholicism indigenous and allowing it to expand. Yet they could also be agencies of those same colonizing powers, in which case they seldom managed to extend far beyond the European elite. The Portuguese Misericórdias were perhaps the best examples of the latter. Multi-faceted brotherhoods directly tied to the Portuguese

---

14 Nancy Farriss, *Mayan society under colonial rule: the collective enterprise of survival* (Princeton, 1984); Patricia A. Mulvey, 'Black brothers and sisters: membership in the black lay brotherhoods of colonial Brazil' in *Luso-Brazilian Review* 17 (1980), pp 253–79; idem, 'Slave confraternities in Brazil: their role in colonial society' in *The Americas* 39 (1982), pp 39–44; Emma Sordo, 'Our Lady of Copacabana and her legacy in colonial Potosí' in Black and Gravestock (eds), *Early modern confraternities in Europe and the Americas*, pp 187–203; Susan Verdi Webster, 'Confraternities as patrons of architecture in colonial Quito, Ecuador' in Black and Gravestock (eds), *Early modern confraternities in Europe and the Americas*, pp 204–25; Nicole von Germeten, *Black blood brothers: confraternities and social mobility for Afro-Mexicans* (Gainesville, 2006).

government, they were closely identified with its colonising efforts in the Azores, the Madeiras, Macao, Brazil, and North Africa, and eventually spread to Spanish colonies as well.[15] They were centralized, political, and powerful, with royal privileges, monopolies, and tax concessions that gave the Misericórdia confraternities protection from ecclesiastical authorities, the power to absorb competing lay charitable brotherhoods and hospitals, and the resources to build churches, patronise the arts, and stage impressive rituals. The Misericórdias attracted many patrician members and exercised considerable political, social, and even judicial authority, making them paradigmatic examples of formal networks that generated bonding social capital among members. They were also critical elements of colonial administration and cultural cohesion in Portugal's far-flung empire of fortified entrepots. Early converts in Japan and Vietnam initially adopted the Misericórdias, but soon abandoned these in favour of fraternities that were not so thoroughly identified with a colonising mission.

The Jesuit missions in Japan and China aimed initially to promote indigenous confraternities. Through the mid-sixteenth century the groups initiated by a handful of missionaries in Japan had gathered 215,000 converts. Japanese confraternities organised festivals, charity, and mutual assistance, and their informal networks became the core of an underground church once persecution began in 1587.[16] In China, a parallel situation developed some decades later. Jesuit missionaries like Matteo Ricci initially focused their efforts on court and intellectual circles, and when their successors adopted a more overtly missionary approach oriented to conversion, Chinese authorities became suspicious that the secretive cells were potentially seditious. Accelerating persecution from 1616 to 1620 led high-born

---

[15] Isabella dos Guimarães Sá, 'Assistance to the poor on a royal model: the example of the Misericórdias in the Portuguese empire from the sixteenth to the eighteenth century' in *Confraternitas* 13 (2002), pp 3–14; Juan Mesquida, 'Negotiating charity, politics, and religion in the colonial Philippines: the brotherhood of the Misericórdia of Manila (1594–1780s)' in Terpstra (ed.), *Faith's boundaries: laity and clergy in early modern confraternities*, forthcoming.

[16] Jaoa Paulo Oliviera Costa, 'The brotherhoods (*cofrarias*) and lay support for the early christian church in Japan' in *Japanese Journal for Religious Studies* 34 (2007), pp 67–84.

and educated members to drop away and the Jesuits then concentrated on planting confraternities among merchants and peasants, using the statutes, rituals, and spiritual disciplines that defined their sodalities and congregations in Europe.[17]

In Vietnam, French missionaries revived some Misericórdia groups that had emerged out of Portuguese missionary movements but that had gone dormant. From 1646, they recast these in the form of indigenous communities of 'Amantes de la Croix', secret communities that gave shelter, subsistence, and education to female believers. Women made up the majority of Catholic converts in Vietnam, and the social resource of the confraternity allowed them to 'survive the dual pressures of subsistence agricultural life and the expectations of seventeenth century Vietnamese gender norms'. It also kept distant the restrictions of the cloister and so preserved some forms of mobility. The Amantes were not the extension or adaptation of any existing European sodality or order, but arose as part of a missionary effort to legitimate and channel the women's practice of living communally for mutual protection and survival. Their hybrid of cloistered and confraternal life was growing more common in France itself through the seventeenth century and, in the form of groups like the Daughters of Charity, allowed unmarried French women to play a more active role in schools and hospitals.[18] The Vietnamese Amantes constituted informal horizontal networks built around relations of trust and reciprocity, supporting themselves by means of farms and market stalls, and focusing their charitable activity on getting women out of organised prostitution, often by inviting them to join the community.[19]

One characteristic of this recent work is that it aims explicitly to recover the voices and experiences of confraternity members, rather than depending primarily on the records left by their

---

[17] Liam Brockey, *Journey to the East: the Jesuit mission to China, 1579–1724* (Cambridge, 2007).

[18] Susan Dinan, 'Confraternities as a venue for female activism during the Catholic Reformation' in Donnelly and Maher (eds), *Confraternities and Catholic reform in Italy, France, and Spain*, pp 191–213.

[19] Nhung Tuyet Tran, 'Les Amantes de la Croix: an early modern Vietnamese lay sisterhood' in Gisèle Bousquet and Nora Taylor (eds), *Le Vietnam au Feminin* (Paris, 2004).

clerical supervisors. This is far harder for older groups than it is for those active into the twentieth century, though in both cases the drive to access that experience sometimes necessitates more reading between the lines of official documentation. Adapting Putnam's framework draws out some sociological distinctions between confraternities for the colonisers and for the colonised, and facilitates comparisons between groups in very distinct global contexts. We can see from this work that confraternities remained critical forms of voluntary sociability that built social capital within marginalised groups, and that allowed members to develop the forms of civil society through informal networks where they demonstrated trust and exercised reciprocity. They often exercised quasi-judicial or political roles, and this allowed members to preserve their distinction from the cultures around them. Their roles shifted radically in response to social context: as an informal vehicle of social organisation, fraternalism could organise resistance, opposition, and underground activities in contexts of social and political oppression. Yet it could just as easily become the means by which a dominant group would extend the formal networks that consolidated its privileged position. The records of privileged groups which constitute part of a governing group are often abundant, accessible, and easier to read. Yet they are a greater challenge to interpret – they are dominated so thoroughly by officials and their pronouncements that the viewpoints they record and promote have to be taken with an extra grain of salt before we can get a taste of the social reality underneath.

SOCIAL CAPITAL, CIVIL SOCIETY, AND CONFRATERNITIES IN IRELAND

The earliest histories of confraternities demonstrate the limits of a celebrative and uncritical antiquarianism, while some of the work of the 1970s and 1980s demonstrates how some theories can impose a determinism which reduces confraternities to simply one group among many in a fundamentally secular social order. More recent work shows that concepts like civil society, social capital, cultural form and social resource can have a heuristic value that fosters critique, directs our analytical gaze beyond the group itself, and opens up social and religious realities. If we resist the urge to absolutise them, these concepts can provide us with the kind of theoretical framework and critical language that helps us insert confraternities into broader historical discussions where critical comparative analysis will underscore the formative role they played in society.

As we look at the negotiations and adaptations of social kinship across the past centuries, we come to a better understanding of its powerful pull and how it can be a critical tool of historical analysis. Europeans employed fraternalism very deliberately to negotiate the challenges of overseas expansion, religious schism, and the relations between mainstream and marginal groups. Within and beyond Europe, early moderns turned to it as a means of providing individual security and community when death or migration put them beyond the help of their natural families. The metamorphoses of fraternal groups paralleled social change such that they retained relevance while changing shape: where medieval guilds and confraternities had trained members in the disciplines and accommodations of communal government, their early modern counterparts trained members in the manners and hierarchies of societies with more demanding authority structures. Older fraternities that had resources, traditions, and a history of active civic engagement tended to recruit upper class members, while merchants and artisans gravitated towards the newer parochial confraternities. The common threads included identity, mutual accountability, and a broader public purpose.[20]

The research project on religion and social identity in Ireland aimed at precisely this nuanced and probing examination of how fraternalism functioned in Irish society over a four-hundred-year period. A large team of researchers drawn from key universities and including professors, post-doctoral fellows, and students worked together with local historians across

---

[20] David Garrioch, 'Lay religious associations, urban identities, and urban space in eighteenth century Milan' in *Journal of Religious History* 28 (2004), pp 35–49; Idem, '"Such a despotic rule": confraternities and the parish in eighteenth-century Paris and Milan' in Terpstra (ed.), *Faith's boundaries: Laity and clergy in early modern confraternities*, forthcoming; Stefano Simiz, *Confréries urbaines et dévotion en Champagne, 1450–1830* (Villeneuve-d'Ascq, 2002); Gervase Rosser, 'Going to the fraternity feast: commensality and social relations in late medieval England' in *Journal of British Studies* 33 (1994), pp 430–46.

Ireland in order to explore precisely these questions and generated a massive body of research. The essays gathered in this collection represent only the tip of the iceberg. What they demonstrate above all is how confraternities functioned in distinct ways at different periods and within different communities. Colm Lennon's 'Long view' surveys these changes and identifies three key stages of survival, revival, and decline, marked in part by distinctions in their organisation, their culture and their engagement with secular and ecclesiastical authorities. It also demonstrates that the theoretical models seen above underscore parallels between the histories of confraternities in Ireland, Europe, Asia, and the Americas.

Confraternities came to Ireland with the mendicant orders, but up through the fifteenth century, social realities made confraternal life in Ireland distinct in some ways from what it was on the continent.[21] Family networks and civic priorities dominated fraternities in the Pale, while mendicant models, and particularly those of the Observants and the Tertiaries, had greater influence in Gaelic areas. In both, the strong ties of family outweighed the weak ties of social kinship. Since the Tudor settlement of religion did not directly eliminate them, confraternities developed into an informal underground support network for missionaries and Catholic laity built largely around trust and reciprocity. Limits on Catholic clerical activity strengthened horizontal relations, allowed the laity to expand their role within the church, and turned the confraternities into de facto alternative parishes where masses were celebrated, the sacraments were available, and charity was distributed. Stuart political changes challenged the privileges of corporate bodies, and Protestant and Catholic elites converged to defend the traditional rights of these agencies of civil society. At the same time, Tridentine devotional changes filtering in from the continent promoted new pious sodalities that were less socially-engaged or lay-driven than the traditional fraternities. Clerics took a larger role in setting the direction for sodalities that

---

21 Colm Lennon, 'The survival of the confraternities in post-Reformation Dublin' in *Confraternitas* 6 (1995), pp 5–12; Idem, 'The confraternities and cultural duality in Ireland, 1450–1550' in Black and Gravestock (eds), *Early modern confraternities in Europe and the Americas*, pp 34–52.

recruited from select social groups and aimed above all to strengthen their internal bonds and their relations of dependence on the Catholic hierarchy. While regular and secular clergy aimed to foster more passive and internal devotions, they did not hesitate to recruit confraternity members into their internecine disputes, even as the penal laws were lowering the boom on all Catholic organisation and worship.

The eighteenth-century revival of Catholic institutions took place in the twin contexts of ecclesiastical demands for a more thoroughly devotional piety and political demands for educational, social, and moral reform. While these did not run at cross purposes, they tended to generate different confraternal forms. As Cormac Begadon shows, groups dedicated to Christian Doctrine, to the Rosary, and to the Sacred Heart pointed to a higher level of vertical organisation within a Catholic church that was determined to assert its universality through standardised devotions and archconfraternities, and that prized lay engagement in the work of promoting missions and devotions. Church and state authorities both looked for help in their campaigns to fight poverty and to advance literacy, temperance, and moral reform, and saw more formal networks of confraternities as convenient vehicles to organise, fund, and deliver these goals. Dáire Keogh shows that among the currents animating educational efforts was a determination to fight parallel Protestant efforts which were advancing either directly through church missions or indirectly through state schools, and which easily capitalised on widespread disaffection with church institutions among poorer Catholics in urban areas.

Confraternities expanded rapidly in numbers and membership in the nineteenth and twentieth centuries, and they became central to parish life in many communities, as Colm Lennon and Robin Kavanagh show when sketching the 'flowering' of confraternities from 1860 to 1960. Confraternities multiplied and memberships exploded by the tens of thousands, initially among men but increasingly among women until by the end of the period women comprised the bulk of memberships. Priests, regular clergy, and even bishops were the driving force behind most groups which, though administered by lay committees, remained under close episcopal control. While some charitable groups like St Vincent de Paul societies described by Máire Ní Chearbhaill did emerge, the real expansion in this period was among the more quietist and devout confraternities where, as Lisa Godson shows, membership could be marked, rewarded, and disciplined by the use of medals. Their role as broad genera-tors of social capital narrowed steadily as they became lay auxiliaries to clerical activity, and particularly as clergy took the leading positions and set the agendas. The rapid expansion of the cultural form of the fraternity – whether as inward-looking pious sodalities or as more activist, social and charitable groups – masked a shift from the horizontal to the vertical in power dynamics, and limited reciprocity. The laity looked for the sociability of meetings, excursions, music, and sporting activities and the mutuality of savings banks. The clergy looked for disciplined attention to meetings, devotions, processions, and the sacraments. In traditional society these two goals could co-exist and even support each other: lay members pursued friends, entertainment, and job prospects through their fraterni-ties, and the clergy pursued even more vigorously the goal of a holy society that resisted secular temptations.

The tectonic social shifts of the 1950s and 1960s broke the im-plicit pact between laity and clergy as the former simply drifted away to pursue their goals elsewhere. Perhaps the only thing more poignant than the rapid demise of the confraternities is the perplexed response of the clerics, many of them quoted in the essays gathered here. Dublin archbishop John Charles McQuaid saw youth confraternities as vital tools to counter popular culture and maintain spirituality and morality among teenagers, but Carole Holohan shows how the clergy generally worked towards these goals tirelessly though with ever diminishing success. Louise Fuller paints the same dismal picture in Catholic sodalities and confraternities across Ireland, although she notes that a closer look at the records shows steadily eroding attendance and ever scantier record-keeping from at least the 1940s. The purely devotional focus of many traditional confra-ternities seemed insular, dated, and unappealing to many youth and adults more attracted to the social thrust of Catholic Action and to forms of sociability which they themselves controlled and directed. Vatican II then revised and implicitly discredited the old disciplines of fasting, Marian piety, and indulgences. In the rapidly shifting ecclesiastical and national landscapes of the 1960s, Irish confraternities lost their past and couldn't find a future.

As Lennon points out, this dramatic collapse was not simply a result of broad social forces undermining traditional ecclesiastical forms. It was a problem which arose in part out of the clergy's own determination to control fraternities, and the consistent subordination of horizontal networks to vertical ones. The Irish church hierarchy had re-organised and institutionalised a cultural form without paying sufficient attention to how that form had generated valuable social capital at a critical period in Ireland's own past, and how it might best do so in the future. Fears of secularisation and immorality made them see only threats around them, and even those who didn't adopt the image of Noah's Ark thought of the confraternity as primarily a protective refuge that would guard pious Catholics from the world. Many laity, like the young woman who joined the Simon Community, aimed for a more activist engagement of faith in the world and greater agency in realising it. They wanted neither the ark, nor its clerical skipper, yet this was what the very form of the confraternity had been reduced to. When laity like this realised that they could find other cultural forms outside the fraternity that would be more active and fulfilling, they walked away from the fraternities altogether, taking their social capital with them. They could join groups that would allow them to be more active agents in the production of social capital, rather than being the passive agents of others' initiatives. Some confirmation of this dynamic may be found in Martin Maguire's study of parochial institutions within the Church of Ireland. Founded and run by laypeople, they were actually closer to the medieval model of the confraternity than contemporary Catholic models and on the whole they seem to have succeeded in engaging and retaining a broad membership.

Of course, it is problematic – delusional to the point of being comic – to argue that we might understand the success or failure of modern Catholic confraternities by gauging the degree to which they abandoned or preserved medieval modes of organisation. One way of moving beyond hypotheses to test these theories is to simply ask former confraternity sisters and brothers their views. Confraternities may have disappeared but they left more than their official records. The modern researcher has a critical resource that a medievalist or early modernist can only dream of, and that is the large number of former members still living who can be interviewed for their views on what initially held them in and eventually held them back. The move from archival to oral history can add breadth and depth to the research around religion and social identity, and certainly brings a direct human dimension to this particular question that no medievalist or early modernist could match. It may in turn also shed light on dynamics within those earlier confraternities.

The broader subject of the research project on religion and social identity is not simply a sub-field of religious studies. It is sociological, anthropological, political, and historical. Studies of confraternities have sometimes been at the margins of historical work, reflecting perhaps the marginalisation of religious concerns in the modern academy. Yet regardless of a historian's own religious convictions, or lack of same, if she aims to understand the deeply religious societies of the past, she must engage with those institutions through which lay believers adapted, exercised, projected, and implemented their beliefs in the day-to-day world. And she must engage not just with quaint parochial institutions, but with the powerful and constantly mutating force that is social kinship, or fraternalism. This collection of essays moves that research forward and points to further fields and forms of inquiry.

Index